THE AMERICAN POET

Weedpatch Gazette

For 1990-1991

Samuel D. G. Heath, Ph. D.

iUniverse, Inc.
New York Bloomington

The American Poet
Weedpatch Gazette For 1990-1991

iUniverse books may be ordered through booksellers or by contacting:

iUniverse
1663 Liberty Drive
Bloomington, IN 47403
www.iuniverse.com
1-800-Authors (1-800-288-4677)

ISBN: 978-1-4401-6017-2 (sc)
ISBN: 978-1-4401-6018-9 (ebook)

Printed in the United States of America

iUniverse rev. date: 07/13/2009

Contents

CHAPTER ONE

CHRISTIAN PERSPECTIVE

SEPTEMBER, 1990

ROMANS 8:28

It is beautiful here in the mountains that I have come to love. The air is clear and at night you can still see the Milky Way, a profusion of stars that boggles the mind. A major distraction is the number of satellites passing overhead. Last night I counted six of them. I love seeing "shooting stars," but somehow these machines of men leave me somewhat unsettled in my mind.

When I was eleven years old, my grandparents, with whom I lived, moved from Bakersfield to Kernville. Actually, we moved to a mining claim my grandfather had acquired in return for a loan a country singer named O'Dell Johnson couldn't pay back. The only song I remember of Mr. Johnson's was "Kernville, California U.S.A." I don't think it made the "Top Ten." The only line of the song I remember is: "Snow capped mountains, ripplin' streams, it's not heaven though it seems, in Kernville California U.S.A." A real toe-tapper.

The claim consisted of two, one room tarpaper wrapped shacks, a hand-dug well with an iron pump and an open ditch called a "placer" which justified the name "mine." Kernville was a thriving metropolis of 115 souls and four miles south was the little burg of Isabella, pop. 36. But Isabella had its very own "mad scientist," complete with live-in housekeeper who had a boy named Larry. Larry and I became good friends and this gave me enviable access to the peculiar "goings on" in the home.

The one decided detraction of the living conditions on the claim was the fact that electricity was non-existent (as was in-door plumbing). This meant that all heating and cooking was done on a wood stove and fireplace. My grandfather actually added the fireplace at a latter date.

Under such conditions, the Saturday night bath (whether you needed it or not) was no joke, particularly in the winter. Imagine a washtub (clothes) and heating water on a wood stove. Yes, the washtub and scrub board were grim realities.

My grandfather was the hero of my life. But he had the preposterous notion that an eleven year old boy should have the sole responsibility for all the wood needed to cook and heat. While other children dreamed of bicycles, I dreamed of a chain saw. I never got one. If any of you have ever had to fell trees, saw them up and split the logs by hand with a maul and wedge, you will readily sympathize with my plight. I learned that a "two- man saw" worked just fine with just one boy and how to keep the tree resin cleaned off with a rag stuck in a bottle of coal oil (we never called it kerosene). Coal oil was always handy since oil lamps were all we had for lighting. I also had the responsibility for cleaning the chimneys, trimming the wicks and keeping the lamps filled.

Sam Clemens had the Mississippi; I had thousands of acres of the Sequoia National Forest as my private playground. Having been raised without the mind-stultifying effects of television and having the benefit of a background of Zane Gray, Swiss Family Robinson, The Last of the Mohicans, Robinson Crusoe, Saturday Evening Post and Colliers (1940's editions), National Geographic, and a great-grandmother that still remembered covered wagons and how the West was won, my imagination found fertile soil in the wilderness of those days.

Such was life in my forest fastness that every summer I slept outdoors under the pines. There is still no greater music than the wind sighing softly through pine needles. I would go to sleep looking up through the branches at the stars and lulled by my own, private, heavenly choir. Nor was there ever a need or thought of locked doors or "crazies" roaming about.

While guns were a natural part of life in the country, they were for hunting and predators, not for "protection." I had my first re-loading outfit at age 14. I bought it from Guy Shultz, the local, elementary school bus driver, custodian and "Dollar a year man (Fish and Game). Mr. Wallace was then the elementary principal/junior high teacher. When I became a freshman, Mr. Wallace and Guy gave me the job as the very first "junior custodian" for the school. I was a mean man with a broom and did my best to justify their faith in me.

I have always wished I could have provided such a "Tom Sawyer and Huck Finn" environment for my own children. The Kern River with its glorious wildness, unfettered by a dam, traced its way through the valley. Sloughs were home to abundant wildlife including Bullfrogs (best eating in the world), catfish, birds of every description and even deer.

It was a wondrous thing to come across undisturbed, Indian camp and burial grounds, to imagine yourself the first white man to set foot on ancestral paths. Such was childish imagination; but how real it could be to a boy in such an environment.

But the point of my reminiscences begins, properly, in Weedpatch, CA. Not many people can say (or would want to) that they were born in Weedpatch but I have a birth certificate to prove it; my one claim to fame.

I was born on a farm (Cotton patch), in a society of Dust Bowl immigrants known as "Okies." Actually, my grandad was the qualified Okie and my grandmother (maternal), was a "Blue-bellied Yankee." My grandfather's mother disowned him for this moral lapse and did not speak to him to her dying day.

Sometime after my third birthday, my brother was two, our father left us and we never saw him again. It was years later that I came to know my mother well enough to stop blaming him. Don't misunderstand me, I loved my mother but she went through several men before she found one that could stick it out with her. She was beautiful but had a violent temper. But to this day I have no use for a parent that can simply leave their children and show no concern for their welfare.

Shortly thereafter, we moved to the corner of Cottonwood and Padre in Southeast Bakersfield, an area that carried the designation of "Little Oklahoma," peopled by (according to my grandparents) "White trash and every Okie and Arkie on the lam." Dirt roads and tarpaper shacks. Just across the railroad tracks (really) and north of us was the community of "Nigger Town." My grandad was one of the very few Caucasians ever accepted in that area. This because it was recognized that he was not prejudiced, even though he always said "Nigger" as a cultural expression and he was a Pentecostal preacher and jack-of-all-trades. My grandad's religion was "color-blind" unlike many of his heritage.

Of course grandad had proven his own lack of cultural discernment and pride in the South by marrying a Northerner. It was not too surprising that he should carry his fault over to a distinct lack of any real prejudice or bigotry. He was not the stuff of a "good Klansman."

Another fatal flaw in my grandad's character religiously was his and my grandmother's peculiar idea that they should never "take up a collection" in the church. When asked about this decidedly irreligious heresy, grandad made the preposterous statement that "God never made a beggar out of any man or His church." Since he built the church himself on his own property and was the sole arbiter of its function, he could pretty well "call the shots." Grandad had a box at the front of the pulpit and donations could be placed in that for the poor. He worked regularly and took nothing for himself; altogether peculiar for a preacher.

Grandmother's piano playing and grandad's thunderous, hellfire and damnation preaching made them a "dynamic duo." It should be pointed out that in such a culture and environment, the church was the only "game in town" when it came to social function. Few people had cars; the war was on, there was no television or movie house. Greater Bakersfield with all its "cultural amenities" was far away by foot.

It was fortunate for my brother and me that we were blessed with a mother and grandparents that were literate and intelligent. Schooling and reading were made important to us.

Those of us old enough to remember the war years (WWII) as children, will remember how thoroughly propagandized we were through the comic books and movies. With Superman, Captains Marvel and America, Humphrey Bogart and George Raft teaching us about the "rotten Japs and "stinking Knocksies'" (no child my age called them Nazi's), our games were as apt to be killing the enemies of Democracy as playing cowboys and Indians.

A real drawback of the war for us boys was the fact that you could not get cap guns. Even inner tubes went to the war effort and "rubber guns" were hard to come by. Slingshots (in Little Oklahoma sling shots were called by a racial ethnic epithet) were in very short supply.

It is the license of advancing age to think of the past as better than the present, to say "The old days were better," but it cannot be gainsaid that we older ones had a simpler time of it. There is also a very basic wisdom in the command that "Thou shalt not remove the ancient landmarks!" It is also the purview of age to "skip around," to ramble in reverie and "forget" with convenient memory, a blessing of time passing, how very harsh life could be without many of the blessings of technology mixed as they are.

I would not willingly give up the wonder of flipping a switch for light and heat, nor would I trade my tap for a well handle or bucket. Certainly, none of my age misses the stench of the old "privy." But I do admit to wishing there were more of the people that seemed to be around in time gone by; people to whom a good name was important and a handshake was a bona fide contract. I miss the simple verities of being able to tell who the "bad guys" were and the black and white issues that stealing was wrong and liars were going to hell.

It seems that heroes were easier to come by and identify with in that time not long past. They helped the down and out; they came to the rescue of the weak and helpless (Who was that masked man?). Right was right and wrong was wrong. Preachers, teachers and policemen were our friends. The president was our trusted leader and our country was the ideal for an oppressed society anywhere else in the world. The Statue of Liberty stood tall and George Washington was not a liar.

I admit to being an embarrassment to my learned colleagues, those like myself with the alphabet after their names. But like a great, old man, Vance Havner, I prefer "Plain Vanilla." Maybe Weedpatch, Little Oklahoma and Sequoia Forest will forever prejudice me.

No amount of quoting the ancient Greek philosophers will make this generation the same as those gone by. There is a difference in the "music" our young people dance to. There is a difference in the amount and complexity of evil that threatens them. There is a clear warning of that "generation without natural affection" that presages the end, an end that carries the unmistakable hallmark of hopelessness.

The rugged mountains, the desert's sere vastness, and a clear, swift trout stream with a star-spangled canopy overhead are still my main attractions. These marvels continue to keep the best part of the miracle of childhood alive in me, to keep things in their proper perspective and priority.

Perhaps the cities, while exciting in their own right, are in such chaos because city-dwellers lose sight of these things. Many children, sadly, have never experienced a smogless day or night; have never seen a live trout stream. I will never forget one young man I had taken camping putting his finger in a small stream and asking me; "Is this real water?"

No matter the number of museums and ballets attended, a ghetto or barrio child will never know the magic that properly belongs to them until they see a shooting star or are able to read Swiss Family Robinson for themselves. It is farcical to pretend that education can ever be achieved without hope. And there is no hope in the present system for the millions of children confined in meaningless and irrelevant institutions that plainly declare that the children themselves are unwanted; as one teacher so truly and succinctly put it: "It would be a great job if it weren't for the kids!"

In California, our "Silver-spoon" State Superintendent, good and well intentioned though he is, can never grasp the need of 85% of the children of whom he is in charge. He is eminently well equipped for the needs of the 15% that are not educationally, emotionally and culturally deprived. Perhaps our "Conspirators" are at work in this.

I entered my career in education as a high school teacher. Although majoring in English Literature with minors in German and History, I discovered the L.A. City Schools were more interested in my background in Aerospace. Agreeing to pursue Vocational credentials, I was soon a "shop" teacher at Jordan High School in the Watts District of L.A.

Thereafter, my primary assignments in the districts I served in were primarily shop and math classes. I quickly discovered that young people readily learned to read, write and compute when they saw these were necessary skills to properly understand blueprints, run a lath and mill, construct projects or fix a car.

It was my sad experience to witness the sixty's disasters of the "New Math," disposal of phonics and other travesties of the so-called "Innovative

Learning" methodologies introduced with such fanfare by the "experts," primarily those with worthless doctorates in education.

Those of us with "Real World" skills could see that the "Ivory Tower" idiots were undermining the entire educational program. But no one in the hierarchy, those that had never had to punch a clock for a living, was about to listen to a bunch of "unwashed" shop teachers. That was part of my motivation for earning a Ph. D. But they still wouldn't listen. It took a while to learn how paranoid school administration is when faced with people who have a legitimate education and practical skills.

The travesty of orienting schools to prepare all students for college is now abundantly clear. National Alliance of Business president, William Kolberg, puts it rather neatly: "We have abandoned the millions of kids who don't plan to attend college, somewhere along the way (I could certainly tell him where) we lost respect for the skills we now so desperately need in our factories and on the front lines of our service industries." Kolberg adds: "We are on a collision course with the reality that America is developing a second-class work force whose best feature in the future compared with other nations will be low pay." And to think that some people have dared to call me pessimistic.

Good people like Rousas J. Rushdoony (Intellectual Schizophrenia), professor Damerell (Education's Smoking Gun), The Holmes Group and so many others sounded the warnings of failed education, some in the fifties. We knew then that the bottom fifteen percent of college graduates were becoming teachers, administrators and counselors. It didn't take much to make a flowchart where this would lead, just where we are now.

It is well known among the educated that the schools of education are an embarrassment and a laughing stock on university campuses. No wonder. Since the educational establishment is typically made up of people (Like Superintendent Honig) who have no practical knowledge of real world skills or the needs of Industry, they do what they do best; engage in "fairy-land" curriculum.

This all reminds me of the time the skunk "went off" in our cabin one night. Probably the only time I had neglected to put our old hound, Tippy, out before going to bed. I never forgot again. It was winter time. We had added a room to one of the old shacks that served as kitchen, living room and my bedroom. This was nice since the fireplace and wood cook stove were in this room; a reward for my labors as supplier of fuel.

One night I heard a noise and discovered a skunk had gained entrance and was looking for food scraps. As any child, I was entranced by the idea of having my very own pet skunk. Thereafter, I purposely left scraps out for my secret (why should I tell my grandparents? Somehow I sensed they might disapprove), nocturnal visitor. Now, the night I forgot to put Tippy out!

While we didn't see the skunk right away, it didn't take imagination to know what had happened. The smell was horrendous and a smoky, blue haze hung in the air. The point is that both the skunk and the dog had done what was natural to both. And when you mix them the outcome can easily be predicted.

My grandfather was not happy about my secret visitor. He, in fact, exhibited a very uncharitable attitude toward skunks in general and my skunk in particular. So prejudicial was he, in fact, that he set about immediately planning my pet's demise.

His nefarious plan was to set out cyanide-laced sardines for the skunk. But, the skunk, probably miffed by the dog's unwillingness to be friendly, did not return. But grandad's plan did bear fruit. A few days later I discovered our pet cat stretched out stiffer than a board. I missed the cat.

There are several applications of the story to education. Our young people, parents and industry are paying the price for the skunk. The innocent, the cat, only saw a good meal. All I wanted was a pet skunk. But in befriending the skunk, I was directly to blame for an odor that lasted for weeks and, indirectly, the untimely decease of a good cat.

By apathy, greed, egotism, selfishness, too-busyness, naiveté, we have allowed the educational establishment to have its own way and that way has led to destruction for our society. Certainly our civil leadership from the President on down share in the abysmal state of education but we get the kind of leadership we actively support.

It is not a skunk's nature to cooperate with our best interests. And if you forget to put the dog out, you precipitate a crisis of your own making, good intentions notwithstanding. And the cat dies.

By continuing to ask the same people for solutions who created the problems, we can only expect disaster. Will Rogers was right, we need "dirtier fingernails and cleaner minds!" But is it too late? It is after the skunk goes off.

Now we are forced to live with the smell all around us; not only in education but also in every institution of our society. Who does not smell the skunk in the sudden price rise at the gas pump? Whether legitimate or not, we cannot be blamed for thinking we smell something. My particular bias is that we would be astounded if we knew who all was cooperating with the latest "madman," Hussein. And if I can figure this out, I am sure there are many others that can do so as well.

I've had the, mostly unhappy, experience of being a landlord. I've also built houses. There is a definite "skunk" in the works when we talk about the "homeless."

Our inimitable (and, I fear, ineluctable) leaders in Sacramento think the following would be a good idea based on another "study:" Developers should be given incentives to build government subsidized housing that includes large family sized units. City planners should encourage homeowners to jointly develop backyard space into park areas and childcare centers. The state should strengthen rules that prohibit housing discrimination to protect new immigrants with large families and other racial minorities who must confront barriers to housing.

The "criminals" who are thwarting the plan for your backyard being turned into "open space" are builders who still think that they can get away with building homes for families that can afford them. They are accused of the "Ozzie and Harriet" mentality. God forbid that such families should intrude their wants over the greater need for "large immigrant, mostly illegal, families!" Who says Assemblyman Tom Bates and Senator Diane Watson don't have their fingers on the pulse of the electorate?

And now we go to Washington (Foggy Bottom). "The income gap between the rich and the rest of America grew so fast during the past decade that the wealthiest fifth of households will receive as much after-tax revenue as everyone else combined this year!" You really have to stop a moment and think about that one to have a grasp of its significance. Simply stated, the rich got (get) richer and the poor, poorer; but at an alarmingly, accelerated rate.

Some headlines the past month: "Executives Find Workers Ill- prepared! Labor Studies Show Expanding Range In Wages! Study Says Wasted Work Time Totals 3 ½ Months During Year!" Each of these is worthy of a book of their own. How about: "Despite Landmark Legislation, America's Saving And Loan Debacle Is Deeper, Broader Than Ever!" The litany of woes goes on. "Boost Taxes To Aid Kids!" Who would dare argue with that one?

It is most unfortunate that church leaders have been responsible for making Hell a much more interesting place than Heaven. But who in their right mind wants to float on a cloud plucking a harp for eternity? At least Hell sounds like where the "action" is. Who is so foolish as to deny the "glory" of evil? And what are we told about the "glory" of Heaven to compare; foolish generation to forget the hard-won lessons of Phillip Wylie and Sinclair Lewis. Better to revel in the "purity" of C.S. Lewis and the seeming spirituality of Watchman Nee.

As is becoming increasingly clear to even the most obtuse, young people are becoming ever more illiterate. A sense of purpose and hope are needed to exercise self-discipline and achieve goals. All the so-called educational reforms in the world will not change what young people see about them as grim realities.

They have taken up the cause of the devil because there is no percentage in doing good. Young people are not stupid. I just received a wonderful letter from my daughter, Karen. Now you parents know that a letter from one of your children is as rare as a blizzard in July, something precious unless they are asking for money, something Karen never does.

I mention her letter because she is only twenty years old and represents the thinking of most young people. She has dreams and aspirations and worries about conditions and circumstances that may prevent her from achieving her dreams. I would give anything to prevent trouble and sorrow in her life, to shield her from all the ugliness about her. But I cannot. The best I can do is let her know at all times that I love her and will always do all I can for her. She is more precious than life to me.

I wish I could make it clear to her and so many others that only by doing right themselves, no matter what society at large may dictate can they have any hope of success. Education has fallen on desperately hard times but real education is still the best hope young people have. The tragic thing is that it must be gotten in spite of a system that is anti-learning and a culture that too often seems to reward the "short-cut" artists.

People need a reason for doing good, for doing what is right and "Because" doesn't cut it. In all my years as a high school teacher I never met a young person that could relate to doing what was right without a reason for doing so. Most of them knew that "not everyone talking about Heaven is going there."

In the words of Douglas MacArthur: "The problem is theological." By kicking God out of the home, the school, and government, and the churches making Him look like a ridiculous beggar or benevolent but somewhat doddering and absent minded and tolerant, old graybeard, we have reaped the whirl wind. As He says for Himself, He will not be mocked and what a person or a nation sows, they will reap. The churches bear the brunt of the blame for the spinelessness of "hirelings" in the pulpits. Men who should have known better but kept silent at best or lent their voices in approval at worst, to the moral holocaust that now consumes us.

And at the bottom of all our woes is the lack of morality. We no longer face choices between good and bad but bad or "badder." My list of "Insoluble" problems is the direct result of the failure of moral leadership from the churches. When the power of righteousness is gone from the pulpits and the pews, just who is supposed to take up the cause?

If theologians were more interested in people than making a name for themselves they might have the mind of God. As it is, they are mere caricatures of religion. Why; because God's main concern is for people, not whether someone is Pre-mill or Supralapsarian. God's business is a people business.

But, sadly, the cause of God languishes because ignorance and selfishness is rampant in The Lord's Camp. Who have you met that can make a case for Him and make serving Him exciting and worth the price?

We were just a bunch of dumb "Okies" in those simple days of "Little Oklahoma." We took it for granted that our country would always stand, like Superman, for truth and justice. Church was a "fun" place and, as children, we felt secure in the simple lessons of David and Goliath, of Moses in the bulrushes. The Sermon on the Mount had a comforting relevance to our everyday lives and the Golden Rule was not sneered at.

The old claim is now Boulder Gulch campground. But some of the huge, old boulders and a few of the great, old pines that used to sing me to sleep are still there. I go there sometimes when the camp is empty and reflect on those golden, magic times so long gone.

My grandmother and great-grandmother both died in the old cabin. Grandad passed away a few years ago. So much gone that made for love and security that helped me believe in doing right no matter what others might do. How I wish I could have given all that was mine to my own children and the thousands of young people I have dealt with over the years. How I wish they had the security and love to dream and imagine a bright future for themselves.

CHAPTER TWO

CHRISTIAN PERSPECTIVE

OCTOBER, 1990

HEBREWS 5:14

It was a great day for fishing. Charlie and I were at the old bridge just South of Kernville. Trout and catfish liked to laze in the shadows and if you didn't spook them, you had a chance at some good ones. J.L. had gotten a five-pound trout just the other day not far from where the aqueduct went South of Erskine creek.

Fishing season had just officially opened for the "tourists" and "flat-landers." They came, primarily, from the "Big" city: Bakersfield. Occasionally, we got some real foreigners from L.A.

We arrived at the bridge too late to try any serious fishing and, being bored, tried to think of something to do while drowning our worms to no effect. Once in a while a car full of "out-landers" would disturb our reverie.

Charlie was twelve and I had just turned thirteen, a "teenager" at last. Big time! So I suppose it naturally fell to me as the "mature" member of the duo to find something to do.

I had noticed an old can on the bank and in desperation thought it might be fun to hang it on my hook and let it drift downstream. Then, I thought, I could play it like a fish. At least I could enjoy the tug of something on the end of my line.

The scheme worked well. As the can filled with water and sank, drifting downstream, there was a very satisfactory, weighty pull on the end of the line, just as if I had hooked a big cat. I would let it drift out a distance and begin to "horse" the giant in, rod arched in a good, honest, bamboo bow.

Charlie and I were having our usual, innocent fun when a car full of tourists stopped at the end of the bridge. There were four men in the car, obvious fishermen, who, upon seeing me holding nicely arched rod in hand, naturally assumed they had come upon a real Norman Rockwell bit of *Americana* in progress; a country boy hooked onto a real lunker.

11

Immediately the men started shouting encouragement and advice: "Don't lose him boy! Play him! Atta boy! Be careful; he's a big one! Give him line! Don't horse him so much!"

Now, my gentle readers, you must not think that cruelty to innocent people was a part of the early child-hood training of the youth in the old Kern Valley. We were civilized and took off our caps indoors and always said "Thank you, Yes mam or sir," etc., but an angel could not be blamed if he succumbed to the ensuing lapse of morality that followed this golden opportunity.

It occurred to Charlie and I that we might have a good thing going here. With an audience of out-land adults shouting encouragement, Charlie naturally joining in now, I redoubled my efforts not to allow this leviathan of the deep (the can) to outwit me and escape. And then another car pulled up behind the first.

No actors on any stage could have been our equals in the life and death struggle unfolding before our most noisy and appreciative audience. And a third car stopped at the other end of the bridge.

A niggling twinge of doubt began to intrude itself on me as to the wisdom of our little joke. Then a fourth car stopped. We now had about fourteen, enthusiastically screaming adults cutting us off at both ends of the bridge. It occurred to Charlie and me that there might be some expression of disappointment on the part of all these people once the "game was up" and I hauled in the can. Besides, my arms were getting tired. Fortunately, I don't to this day know why, no one had left their car to come onto the bridge to personally inspect the "action." I attribute this to a profound belief in children's guardian angels.

I told Charlie to get ready to make a run for it. Our only chance was to jump the bridge and run along the bank until we were where no one could follow. Why, in our childish innocence, we thought anyone would take offense at our little prank, I don't know. It just seemed like a wise precaution to assume the worst.

On the signal, I hauled in the can. As it came into view, there was a hush over our audience. This, of course, was momentary. As Charlie and I cleared the railing of the bridge, we were hastened on our way by some of the most colorful and imaginative language we had ever been privileged to hear. Some of the words and phrases were decidedly new to us and threatened most unusual acts on our various anatomical parts. It gave us new insights and made us popular among our peers in the retelling. No one had ever heard the term "Twats" before for example. I won't bore the reader with the many other examples of our newly learned vocabulary.

I hope this provides the reader some insight into my own concerns for the education our young people are decidedly not getting. No, I don't worry that their slang and profane vocabulary is lacking; would that it were. But it does lack imagination. The Arabs have it all over us in imaginative cursing. This is not to say that our "victims" were entirely lacking in their knowledge of expletives and epithets that, hurled in our direction, hastened Charlie's and my departure, but, American cursing just does not compare with: "May the fleas of a thousand camels nest in your nose!"

There are many moral lessons to be derived from my little joke on the fishermen. But the truth is that in today's society, the threats might just be actually carried out. Today, someone might pull a gun and shoot us. Of course they don't need the excuse of being made fools of today. They might shoot just for the "fun" of it. Such is the world our young people face today.

I wonder if others my age recall the vocabulary of those old comic books. It was actually quite elevated and challenging to us as youngsters. They presumed a literacy that would baffle today's youth.

During the war (WWII) my mother married, at various times, a Sailor (Brown), a soldier (Mahoney), another Sailor (Pospieszynski), and a guy in the Army Air Corps (Blain). Brown I was too young to know and, besides, he was stationed in Pearl Harbor when it was attacked. My mother had the "good fortune" to be there as well and a shell landed and exploded in her kitchen. My grandparents always maintained this affected her mental processes. These came into question on a number of occasions as my brother and I were growing. One such was the morning we decided to wash all the electrical appliances in the bathtub.

Mahoney was all right. He was into hunting and fishing and had some great "souvenirs," such as flags, guns, knives and Jap cigarettes. Lots of "war stories."

But Pospieszynski (how we struggled with learning to spell that one) was a machinist by trade and taught me to build model airplanes. Some of you will remember the old balsa and tissue models, stringer and former construction that required such patience and ability to construct. You learned to read blueprints, understand instructions, handle tools and delicate materials and when you were finished, you had something of value far beyond the individual product. You had an education in craftsmanship and something that generated self-discipline, patience and self-esteem.

After the war, the "plastic" models hit the market. I well remember my first encounter with these monstrosities. The "kits" consisted of a few, perfectly formed pieces that any imbecile could glue together. The molds had each little rivet perfectly embossed. The only thing I found of interest in these "pre-fabricated" toys was the way they burned with such a wondrous black smoke and the acrid smell.

I was only a child but I still sensed that there was something sinister about these things that were being foisted off as "better" than the old model kits. There was nothing to learn and no challenge to your ability to "do," and, hence, nothing of yourself in the things. I felt cheated by adults that tried to pass these travesties off as anything of real value. To you marble players; you know how you felt when someone tried to cheat you with a "doughie" instead of a real marble or a "purie" for a plain old marble? That's how I felt with these "better, adult" toys: thoroughly cheated and betrayed: "Better living through chemistry." Over the years I have often wondered at the loss that this one example of cheating children out of learning represents.

I last worked in state education as a "Resource Specialist." I was responsible for the "special education" programs for five, rural school districts. In all my years in education I have never witnessed such a damning indictment of the schools as in this area called *Special Education*. I took the job out of curiosity as much as anything else. I made a few enemies, not the least of which was the "leader of the pack" at the county office.

If I were to tell all I experienced in that short year, few would believe it. In no other area of education is the public and legislators as thoroughly hood-winked as in this boondoggle. It is bureaucratic empire building at its worst. The trouble is that the so-called "experts," mostly the benighted Ed. D.'s including Honig, administrators and "psychologists" are committed to this scheme to put kids in ever increasing numbers into these worthless, even detrimental, classes.

These "programs" are another fruitless attempt to make up for the lack of discipline, values etc. that children must have in order to learn. But, by obfuscating the system with the usual rhetoric of "Educationese" and utilizing the mounting number of "specialist" personnel and bearing the imprimatur of the "arch dioceses" of universities, the scam is turning out to be the envy of professional cons everywhere. This is education's version of the S&L gravy train.

In no other area of education have our "conspirators" been so successful, with the cooperation of legislators, in bilking the public and hurting the children. Imagine earning $40,000 a year for "teaching" five children at a time! I have seen "classes" of ONE!

The Bakersfield Californian recently ran a series of articles on education. As usual, the "experts" consulted suggested a variety of approaches as the paper headlined: "Public Wants Sweeping Changes In Education!" The Roundtable, an organization of 90 chief executive officers of the state's major corporations, made the statement: "The problem is the system itself, not a lack of money or an absence of dedicated and competent teachers."

While everyone might agree on the comment concerning the system and we know that enormous amounts of money are being wasted in education, I would certainly take exception to the part about "dedicated" and "competent" teachers. It is appalling to find how many "teachers" in math and science are without majors and credentials in these areas. I know personally of too many Home Ec. and P.E. teachers "plugged" into these spots simply because the system needs a warm body to fill the slot.

Further, no one who has not served directly in the system really understands or can know how bad it really is. When a person goes directly out of high school to college and then into the classroom to teach, how are they to understand the demands and needs of the real world; hence the expression; "Those that can, do; those that can't, teach," a too often deserved opprobrium. But, let's not lose sight of the fact, as I used to tell parents, "Don't expect teachers to do the job that you, as a parent, can't or won't do!"

The failure of education is a societal one. Failed homes and a failed value system are ultimately to blame. The educational system is a true reflection of national priorities and values. Just as we get the kind of elected leadership we actively support, we get the kind of schools that answer to, and mirror a society. As to the system itself, one has to ask why, when we know that asking the same people who created the problems for solutions is lunacy, we continue doing so? It is simply because it is not recognized as such.

If universities crank out and authorize such people as "experts," who is to confront such idiocy? Perhaps, to paraphrase Shakespeare's excellent advice; "First we kill all the lawyers," and hearken to Damerell's; "Abolish all the schools of education on university campuses," we might have an approach to a solution; but not without a national revival of ethics and "old world" values. And what think ye of that, oh unwashen masses? For discipline in the home you first need a home. And, one in which the children can't have the parents jailed for enforcing discipline. Of course, most of you are aware that there is a national movement afoot to make it a Federal crime to physically punish a child. As if we weren't raising little devils fast enough as it is. This, like our inability to administer justice to criminals, can only hasten our national demise.

Not so many years ago, I wrote a curriculum for a Negro leader, Stanley Long, of Oakland. Stanley is an educated and sincere man who recognizes the need to teach young people saleable skills. Unfortunately, he could never generate the support the program required. It was simple. It was probably too simple. Had it contained the Kaplan Matrix and a few other niceties, five-step lesson plans etc., it might have flown. But no one understood an educational plan that simply emphasized practical skills and the realities of a structured, learning environment.

There is material enough here for a cosmic joke, not unlike God's sense of humor in telling Adam he was to rule over his wife. Some sober brows have missed the humor here; but consider it in the light of God's intention of passing judgment on Adam's sin. One cannot, thereby, fail to appreciate the irony and justice.

Most people are amused by practical jokes as long as they are not malicious and no one is hurt. I still enjoy Abbott and Costello and their pratfall routines. Unfortunately, most of today's so-called "comedy" is so thoroughly imbued with sex, violence, and prejudice that it does nothing more than makes bad situations worse in our society. And, look at what the public is asked, even supported by our government, to accept as "Art!"

We are the laughing stock of the world on a number of counts, not the least of which is our utter lack of being able to determine what is of cultural value and what is just plain filth. It is a disgrace to our nation that a supposedly mature, educated and enlightened body, i.e. our Supreme Court, cannot tell whether flagrant homosexuality and pornography are good or bad.

But, in an age when employers cannot choose the best workers on merit alone, when "minority rights" take precedence over productivity and quality, when the victims of crime are legally prevented from protecting themselves and cannot even get legislators to act for them, when honest, hardworking people pay the insurance for deadbeats to drive, one cannot help but wonder how much longer such a system can or should survive.

Along with my long list of insolvable problems I am compiling a list of idiotic, bureaucratic "Bumbles." To begin, if one should wonder why "Foggy Bottom" has so much trouble operating with any degree of efficiency, simply visit our capitol offices and look at the personnel manning the "switch." They are, largely, the illiterate ignorant (as opposed to the educated ignorant; these have a corner on the market in state education). Civil service is a joy to those that claim a "right" to employment based on their skin color and gender alone.

But, human nature being what it is, can anyone blame those that take advantage of the situation for employment? No more than we can blame the people that saw a gold mine in the S&L fiasco.

I thought I had such a chance once when I was a boy. My grandad said he thought he had found a job for me with the Army Corps of Engineers. This was the agency responsible for Lake Isabella. The dam was nearly completed and grandad said I could get a job patting frogs and get them to pee thereby filling the lake; great kidder, my grandad.

But, seriously folks, a lot of the jobs the government seems to hand out seem to fall into the category of "patting frogs" and to just as qualified applicants as I represented as an ignorant country boy. If they had offered to pay me enough, I would have been rounding up frogs whether it made sense or not.

It seems that some states are voting to limit the terms that their elected "representatives" can "serve." It is well argued that this will result in the loss of some good, experienced people but, realistically, how much worse can it be? My grandad had a simple voting formula: "If they're in, get em out!" I suspect he was right more times than not. After all, the Founding Fathers never intended entrenched, "professional" politicians to represent the people. How can we in California do any worse than "Willie" Brown for example?

My dear, old friend, Gary North, has suggested I might write a handbook entitled: "Lessons From Grandad." Might not be a bad idea. My grandfather represented a time of simple honesty and hard work that is far removed from the society we have inherited. Even though he only had a third grade education, he was an exceptionally intelligent, ambitious and entrepreneurial man. Further, he had more than his share of a rare commodity, common sense (a misnomer if there ever was one). I have always maintained that with a university education, he would have been downright dangerous particularly to politicians and religious charlatans.

"Cracker barrel" politics aside, Negro leadership has fallen on desperately, hard times. The lunatic fringe is taking over and, as I've often said, these people like Farrakhan, will lead their own to destruction. In a large, metropolitan, inner-city high school recently, it was found that of 71 Negro seniors only four even bothered to take the S.A.T. in order to enter college. Of this same class, 21 were sent to prison. This is not an exceptional statistic for Negro people. In California, a Negro male has a three times greater chance of being murdered (invariably by another Negro male) than being admitted to a university. The end of such a culture in a high tech society is easily predictable.

Illiteracy is not confined to young people, Caucasian or Negro, but to "educated" adults as well. I know this from the fact that many people that should be writing to me have lost the ability to write. I'm sure this comes from lack of practice because "what you don't use, you lose!" This sad condition even exists among some of my Ph. D. "Brethren."

Seriously, I know that time constraints are bogging down people. There just doesn't seem to be enough time anymore. All the supposed timesaving gimmicks we live with seem to take more time to keep functioning than they save us. And if we add up the time it takes to earn the money to pay for them and their repairs? One wonders?

We have just experienced a marvelous thunderstorm here in the Valley. The air is clean and fresh and the mountains are beautiful. How grateful I am to be here in this country and have time to enjoy it.

I just got back from a trip to my "silver mine" with one of my old students, George Taylor. A beautiful trout stream runs through the claim and in spite of drought, the stream was running nicely and we caught trout. I cooked them on the blade of my machete and ate them right beside the stream. Now how can you beat that for quality living! The country is so rough that it keeps the riff raff out and only other noble souls (fishermen) frequent the spot.

The first time I ever visited the place (in 1948) was at the invitation of an old man (probably my age now). He was the stereotypical "prospector," grizzled, gray beard, gnarled hands, stooped back, Levis, flannel shirt, slouch hat, etc. He happened by our cabin one day and was invited to lunch. While eating, he learned of my passion for fishing. He described where he was living and how to get there. He said there was a great trout stream with waterfalls and deep pools and plenty of large trout begging to be caught.

The old fellow lived in a tin shack on the claim by the stream. He made enough panning the creek to supply his few needs and came down to town (Kernville) only when absolutely necessary. He recognized in me a kindred spirit and the first chance I got I took the rough map he had drawn for me and, with tackle in hand, went calling.

The stream was everything he said it was. A few other tales might have been embellished though. He showed me a dent in the shack at the side of the doorway that he said he made chunking a rock at a bear. According to him, the mine was last worked about 1928. It was a Lode claim and every winter the stream would flood it out. There were some old model T or A engines and an old straight eight that they had used to try to keep the shaft (a stope) pumped out. He said they quit when they couldn't keep up with the water.

I filed on the claim, naming it the Laura Jean, some years later. Only then did I discover that the old boys that had worked the mine had never bothered with this nicety. They simply took the silver and didn't bother notifying Uncle Sam of their enterprise.

As a high school teacher, I have taken many of my students back to this pristine, wilderness site and given them the chance to share the wondrous joy of an unspoiled, mountain stream and the wildlife. So many magic hours with young people, my own children especially, in this truly magnificent setting.

It has seemed a sacred trust to maintain this spot. Its very ruggedness has, thus far, kept it so. Only the hardiest can make the hike in and these are, invariably, kindred souls. It is in such settings that we clean out our minds and souls and get our priorities right. There is no other counsel or medicine its equal. But that might be my Cherokee blood (on my grandad's side) speaking; strong prejudice for the land and "critters" there.

It must be admitted that we live in perilous times. Even as we gear (fear?) up for war so the oil can keep flowing, we long in our hearts for the simple verities of an age seemingly (though not truly) long past. The complexities of everyday living seem to overwhelm us. George Will and Pat Buchanan constantly remind us of disasters made or in the making (Academia's trajectory is down. Protecting Israel, actually our own interests, will lead us to war, etc.). And there is always Schuller, Robertson, "Oral and son" et al. to tell (fortune-tell) the future for us for a price.

It all leads me to more and more relish the kind of story I read recently. It seems a truck driver was recommended to the service of an especially talented woman in a bordello. It turned out to be his wife; homemaker by day and call girl by night. Imagine their surprise at meeting under such circumstances. She has filed charges against him for hitting her.

Anthony Lewis, syndicated columnist, relates this story. William Weld, former U.S. attorney, a Yankee moderate, makes the statement that: "Only in Massachusetts would a convicted felon be able to ... tell us who's fit to be a judge." You have to read the story to believe it. In short, a reputed organized crime figure, the convicted felon, Joseph Langone, sits on the Governor's Council whose function is to confirm judges.

Edwin O'Connor's "Last Hurrah" still lives. But when you consider judges to fall somewhere between used car and real estate salesmen, maybe experienced criminals are better able to determine a judge's fitness for office? I can't help wondering how grandad would react to that bit of philosophy? As much as I miss him, how he would agonize in frustration at such madness.

How I agonize for the children and young people trying to make any sense of their world. War, in spite of it being the most unreasonable act of man, may make sense in a world gone mad enough. But, when a situation becomes desperate enough, solutions that would never be given serious credence come readily to mind in a world gone mad. Beware the "Hitlerian" solutions that will so obviously become attractive in such desperate circumstances!

Benson's recent political cartoon: "We the people of the Middle East, in order to form a more perfect OPEC, establish prices, insure continued Western dependency on foreign oil, provide American lives for the common defense, promote the monarchical Welfare, and secure the Blessings of Billions to ourselves and our Families, do ordain and establish this Operation Desert Shield for the United Sheiks of Arabia." That's pretty blunt, political honesty. The oil must flow no matter the means.

George Will has some interesting comments on John Silber's recent Democratic nomination to be Massachusetts' governor. Seems Silber's use of

Shakespeare's "Ripeness is all.' When you've had a long life and you're ripe, then it's time to go." Silber is accused of advocating genocide for his call for the elderly to get on with the business of dying so government can get on with the budget. He also stands accused of calling the state a "Welfare magnet." Imagine accusing a politician of being so blatant about the things I have been warning of! Of course, as with the rejection of Robert Bork and the confirmation hearings of Judge Souter, the pols have the idea that they can do business as usual in a world gone mad; the media, often blind to the pulse of the people as well, give a black eye to any who are contrary to their own agenda.

The cities grow increasingly hostile to their human inhabitants, particularly children, and commuters are resorting to flying to work in L.A. and going "home" to Phoenix. And, as travel becomes so expensive that people are increasingly trapped in crime-ridden, "beehive" slums, the "desperate solutions" I have been outlining become ever more plausible, even attractive; worst of all, they become necessary as more and more politicians will begin to recognize and start advocating.

The automobile will fast become a luxury item and the same conditions will prevail that fostered budding labor movements 150 years ago. I wish this were extremist ranting. It isn't. God continues to judge nations and people. Jerry Falwell is now discovering the truth of what he should have believed.

I am so very grateful to have been raised in a loving environment and with all the "Old-world" values such as believing God and His Word. But I know The Lord believes education is important. I think He is learning as well. He made men in His image and the very nature of God must, therefore, be susceptible to some of our own, seeming, vagaries. Maybe, as the Scriptures declare, He has changed His mind on occasion. But it would clearly be a mistake on His part if Heaven does not have a trout stream.

CHAPTER THREE

NOVEMBER, 1990

Psalm 119

Ghost stories are fun. There is a man (Larry) out there somewhere still telling, no doubt, about the night a huge beast almost "got him" in the Piute Mountains. I am ashamed to admit that I am responsible for this lurid, dread tale that may have falsely captured the imaginations of countless folks. Thanks to me, the "Piute "Bigfoot" began his legendary career.

Back in the late forties, my grandad managed to acquire a "mineral light." Tungsten is a very valuable mineral, essential to making steel. Tungsten and uranium prospecting was popular in our hills and the light would allow us to look for tungsten "traces" at night. This material fluoresces a strikingly, beautiful blue under ultraviolet. My first experience using the light was startling. I discovered scorpions are fluorescent. I was also amazed at how many of the varmints were out and about our place of a summer's eve. In further nocturnal forays, I was more careful about being barefoot. One night I came across a large, rose quartz boulder one side of which lit up like the starry heavens. Nearby, I found a nugget about two inches long. I knew I had "struck it rich!" Unhappily, try as I might, I could find no other traces of these magnificent specimens. For those of you that are interested in treasure maps, I'm open to offers. Time, and sore, old joints permitting, I may even take up the search myself someday. At least I know where to start.

But enough of mundane, everyday wealth to be found in the ground; back to the serious matter at hand. Harold and Ruby (remember the mad scientist of Isabella?) and Ruby's boy, Larry, invited me to go tungsten prospecting in the Piutes. We camped at Saddle Springs and began our search. The days were beautiful in these high mountains and we scarcely ever saw another soul. The nights were glorious. We spent part of our day looking for promising spots to check out at night. We thought we had really found "It" once but the material turned out to be something used in manufacturing fireworks. We also discovered that while it had some value, it was cheaper to ship the stuff from China than to mine it here; an early lesson in foreign trade economics.

One day while in camp trying to amuse myself, a couple of tin can lids caught my attention (I still think kids are better off using cans and boxes than most of the trash that passes as "toys" today). Harold, Ruby and Larry had gone to "town" to get supplies and "the idle mind is the devil's playground." A plan, unbidden mind you, to "destroy" Larry began to invade my dark side. It was a sheer stroke of genius worthy of de Sade, an inspiration to a future Stephen King.

Now I want to make it clear at the outset that I have never been a particularly mean or malicious person, not even as a child. But some "opportunities" present themselves that one, in all responsibility, cannot avoid. This was one such. I am also constrained to point out, in my defense, that Harold did not care much for Larry and children are quick to recognize good "professional victim" material when they see it. I was really fond of old Harold and he and I had a good relationship.

Unfortunately, this militated against the "victim." Grownups should be more cautious in making their likes and dislikes clear to children, particularly about other children. I knew, as a result, that I would have a willing ally in my diabolical plot against the hapless victim, Larry. It was sheer genius in its simplicity. Taking two can lids, I folded them in half. Next, I found a suitable length of firewood about two feet long and nailed the lids to it about a foot apart and slanted them slightly. I placed my "eyes" up the side of the mountain from our campsite where I knew they would easily be "caught" in the beam of a flashlight. Genius.

That evening, when the folks returned, I took Harold aside and unfolded my sadistic plot. He was genuinely proud to take part in such an imaginative undertaking whose end, we hoped, would not only strike total terror in Larry and Ruby. As usual, that evening, we stoked up the campfire and once it was blazing nicely, according to our plan, Harold "suggested" we tell ghost stories for the "fun" of it. I had "primed the pump" by telling how I had discovered strange tracks of some large animal around the camp that day. The night was pitch black, no moon, and the heavily forested mountains, in the firelight, provided all the shadowy backdrop a Vincent Price or Bela Lugosi might well envy.

In the middle of an especially lurid tale of a little boy entering a haunted house on a dare (Harold doing the telling at this point), I suddenly whispered, "What was that!" indicating by my manner that I had heard something on the mountainside. Now everyone was listening, Harold and I pretending, for the suspicious sound. Harold: "Yes, I hear it now!" Me: "I'll get the flashlight." Of course there are natural, night sounds in the forest but Larry and Ruby were sure they also heard something strange now. Switching on the light, I began to "play" it around the side of the mountain until, suddenly, my "eyes" lit up in its beam. The reaction was most gratifying. Larry and Ruby's eyes suddenly plumbed new dimensions of growth and the stifled screech of Ruby was accompanied by a satisfactory burrowing of Larry's whimpering head into her lap. I used the light in such a way as to make it appear that the "creature" had moved out of the way into the trees. Grabbing my rifle, I said to Harold, "Let's go see if we can spot it!" Bravery to the nth degree.

Harold and I proceeded up the mountain where I then picked up the *eyes* and moved them to another spot. Coming back down to the camp and finding Ruby and Larry clutching each other in abject terror was most gratifying. We explained that while we were unable to see the creature, we had found very large "tracks" that looked like a cross between human, Grizzly bear and mountain lion. Hunkering down to the fire, Harold and I repeated the scene of "hearing something" and, using the flashlight I was able to pick up the "eyes" in their new location. Three times this experiment in terrorism was repeated. By now our victims were reduced to the satisfactory level of hysteria and, crawling into our sleeping bags, Harold and I could sleep the sleep of self-righteous terrorists. Ruby and Larry kept a large fire stoked all night.

It has occurred to me over the years that the great Tehachapi earthquake that took place a couple of days later might be, in some measure, due to The Lord's attitude toward my little joke. It literally pounded us out of our sleeping bags. You could actually see the ground heaving up and down, throwing gravel into the air. At any rate, while I repented of my wickedness, neither Harold nor I ever disabused Ruby or Larry of the notion that somewhere in the Piutes there lurked a phenomenal beast of terrifying proportions and features. Between the beast and the ensuing earthquake, our prospecting was soon halted and we returned to civilization. Larry and Ruby did acquire some little renown in describing their close encounter with the creature and Harold and I enjoyed the status of brave and intrepid men who fearlessly faced certain death at its jaws and claws. Hence, the "Piute Bigfoot" still lurks in the forest and only now is the truth, ashamedly, told. Confession is good for the soul and perhaps I am seeking absolution by laying bare, to all, this sordid act.

But, if there is a moral to be derived from this story it has successfully eluded me. I enjoyed frightening the wits out of Larry and, apart from the earthquake that may not have been directed at me at all, and the fact of starting a local legend, I got away with it. My grandad gave it four stars. But, then, he didn't particularly care for Larry either. No morality there. And you might guess who contributed the "quirky" gene for my own sense of humor. But that is another story which belongs in the category of waking to a river running through our cabin,, Herb "rolling" his drunken uncle and then running over his legs at Jack's place in old Garfield (the competing "cuttin' 'n' shootin' joint to Pappy Hall's in Isabella) and other mundane, workaday trivia of which I'm sure the average reader has similar experiences enough.

Of course, according to my old friend, a story has to have a moral, so, scratching my sensitive conscience, I conclude that frightening people is fun. But it isn't fun to have to contend with the real horror all about us. The tigers "...burning bright, in the shadows of the night" as with the Devil, that "...roaring Lion, seeking whom he may devour," seem to be getting the upper hand. They have many unwitting, and even willing, accomplices. It hardly makes The Lord's answers appear sensible when He has "helpers" that make Him look foolish.

A Texas "evangelist" has raised an "army" to wage war against the Adversary, even going to the length of supplying "dog tags" to his followers. This man, Larry Lea plans an attack on Satan's seat of San Francisco on Halloween. Leave it to Pentecostals to have all the fun. Lea and his followers will exorcise demons; confront sins like free sex, homosexuality, acid rock music, etc. Some wet blankets are accusing this "righteous soldier of the cross" of conducting a religious sideshow. Count me as one of the detractors. It isn't that homosexuality isn't an abomination to God and his people, it is. It isn't that immorality and licentiousness, covetousness, greed, adultery, selfishness are things that God has ever changed His mind about; He hasn't. I believe the first chapters of Romans makes that clear.

But God has never asked for, or deserved, the kind of bad press this fruitcake and his cohorts are constantly forcing on Him. The "world" rightly sees these kinds of shenanigans for exactly what they are; fools acting out their queer egos. I would ask my professional friends in this area of expertise, those with the theological credentials, erudition and forums, why aren't you answering these idiots with plausible, Scriptural, exegetical and hermeneutical proofs that will take the wind out of their sails? Are we left to the mercy of Hal Lindsey and Billy Graham to explain all? Now I like these men and don't want to appear mean but where are God's "scholars?" I imagine that most are, as I have experienced in this "modern" age, "stomping ants while the elephants are rampaging through the village." Some others that surely know better are cozying up to the charismatics because that is where the "action" is; i.e., the money, the media and the audiences. No matter the convoluted nonsense that passes for "healing, visions, prophecies and tongues," Shakespeare has your number: "What damnable error but some sober brow will approve it and bless it with a text."

If, as I believe, Jesus "... appeared to destroy the works of the devil," 1 John 3:8, He certainly doesn't want people like Popov et al. helping the Devil rebuild behind Him. Wishing as I do, that my learned colleagues would take up the gauntlet, I will act the "gadfly" and try to get them to take a sensible position against all the charlatans that are passing themselves off as "God's men and women." And speaking of women preachers (in spite of what God has to say about it), I am reminded of Spurgeon's comment when asked his opinion. "Frankly," said the great preacher, "I am reminded of a dog that has been taught to walk on his back legs. I am not surprised by the fact that he does it badly, I am surprised that he does it at all!"

I am grateful for the fact that The Lord has a sense of humor. He has, of course, the finest sense of humor of all. In spite of the fact that He must be the best parent, thereby seeming to "spoil" all the fun while we are growing up, He does bear with a lot. My grandparent's church in "Little Oklahoma" was a happy place. I am an "honorary Okie" myself by virtue of my birth in Weedpatch and early "raisin" in Southeast Bakersfield.

The little tarpaper "temple" had an actual steeple and bell. One of life's little pleasures was ringing that bell on Sunday mornings. Cottonwood and Padre: dirt roads and living but proud people. No one stole from friends or relatives. "Tooking" wasn't stealing and considerable "tooking" took place from the local rail yard and packing plant. The aroma of the plant together with the oil fields gave Bakersfield an early start on air pollution. But, as with the outhouses, there is a perverted kind of nostalgia I associate with these fumes. Blue and Austin Hall were my closest, childhood friends. Their mother was the literal spitting image (thanks to the ubiquitous snuff and chewing tobacco) of "Mammy Yokum." Being honest pagans, Blue and Austin's parents didn't often attend church but sent the kids.

The war was on and here and there you saw the small flags in the windows with blue, and, tragically, occasionally, gold stars. We children bought "war stamps" at school (Mt. Vernon) and turned in toys for metal drives. I helped grandad flatten tin cans for this purpose. My mother dutifully "painted" stockings on her legs and my brother and I helped her peel the foil from cigarette packages and roll it in a ball for the war effort. Meat was rationed and we raised rabbits. My grandparents had the largest rabbitry in Kern County at this time. We saved grease and lard and listened to Gabriel Heatter and the Lone Ranger. We watched from the schoolyard as planes from Minter Field engaged in mock combat overhead. Teachers warned about finding any strange items on the school grounds, as they might be explosive devices cleverly left by saboteurs. Israeli children know this drill too well.

The war was made very real to us as children and we were thoroughly "propagandized." The media from comic books to movies taught us to hate the "rotten Japs and Knocksies." I can imagine how children in other countries are taught to hate us. But we were simple folks, believing in the righteousness of our cause and our leaders, even, I'm sure, as do the simple folks in other lands now. There were few "social services" and we didn't think of ourselves as poor or underprivileged because there was no TV or bureaucrats coming around telling us we were poor and underprivileged.

The "uniform deguere" for children was bare feet and bib overalls for summer (sans shirts) and, if you had them, shoes and overalls for winter (with shirts). Socks and underwear were "sometime" things. While Bakersfield winters could be cruel, the summers were glorious. We could swim in the weir or the irrigation canals, shoot marbles, catch frogs and catfish, pick cotton (my brother and I were forbidden this noble occupation, I suspect from the exalted position my grandparents held in the community) catch lizards and other local reptiles and, in sum, enjoy being children. Shoes, if you had them, were the first things to go in summer. And not just among the children. Most of the womenfolk went barefoot as well. The warm, alkali dust felt marvelous to our feet, particularly if you had spent the winter shod. At night, if you chanced around an electric light (they were scarce in Little Oklahoma) you could find June bugs and mammoth moths; worlds of fun with these critters.

I wonder how many of you "real" Kern Countyians recall a song of the time that went: "Dear Okie, if you see Arkie, tell him Tex has got a job for him in California, picking up prunes; they're all out of oranges." How about you, Willie?

You shouldn't get the impression that we children were perfectly innocent of "worldly" things just because we lacked the preeminent teacher, TV, in that area. There were "certain" ones that exhibited a certain "savoir faire" and knowledge of things illegitimate and carnal beyond their tender years (many of "that old gang of mine" went to the 'pen' or got a permanent crease cooked into their trousers from some state's special seating arrangement).

Fortunately, any trouble my brother and I got into in this regard was easily attributable to wicked companions, not our own proclivity for evil. Or so our grandparents believed to our good fortune. When memory turns back to that simple church and time, the old songs of "Zion" (from the very popular Latter Rain Revival hymnbook) come to mind. What memories does recalling the sylvan cacophony of mingled guitars, tambourines, triangles and piano evoke. Perhaps you too remember some of those old favorites:

"If I Could Hear My Mother Pray Again, God's Radio, Oh Why Tonight? Over The Top For Jesus, You'll Wish You Were One Of Us By and By (there's a real message in that one), When I Can Read My Title Clear, T 'was Rum That Spoiled My Boy," but we really swung into high gear on "When The Roll Is Called Up Yonder" and "Beulah Land." A problem of course with a dirt floor is that if a lot of people really get into the spirit, all that toe-tapping and hand slapping music can raise a good deal of dust. In a more serious vein I will tell you of the little queer.

Now my brother and I didn't know about perverts when we were children. Of course, we didn't know about sex of any kind. The delicacy of the subject prevented our grandparents from ever talking about it (I suspect our mother could have given us a few hints). But, on the whole, sex was simply a taboo of our youth. The intriguing mystery was before us in the conversation and actions of our more knowledgeable playmates.

It is very much to our grandparent's credit that we boys were definitely taught right from wrong, that we never used profanity and that we had a strict, moral code worthy of a conqueror knight seeking the Holy Grail (This did cause some slight adjustment as we grew older, particularly in regard to the "weaker" and "fairer" sex). But about the little queer. This kid definitely had "bubbles in his think-tank." As good Samaritans, our grandparents occasionally did take in some of the walking wounded of this world system. Two such were this kid and his mother.

Other than a clubfoot that required the strangest shoe we had ever seen and a right hand that went 90 degrees from the normal, the boy seemed quite average (there was also some facial disfigurement from small pox). Anyhow, they were both "shouting fundies," raging warm on the need to live "good Christian lives." This kid held my brother and I spellbound on such lively topics as sodomy and descriptive anatomy. While utterly lacking any experiential frame of reference, we did not wish to appear unappreciative in the presence of such a learned and enlightened one, and, one, who was so obviously willing to tell anyone who would listen, of his exploits into that forbidden world of "It!" On more than one occasion my brother and I felt we were listening to an episode of Inner Sanctum.

Such was the tender delicacy of our minds compared to this "august" personage; but Ronnie (my brother; also called "Dee Dee" by me and "Fuzz," by grandad because of his curly hair. Dee Dee hated that name, Fuzz) and I were well acquainted with hell-fire and damnation and did not want to intrude too far into that dark and enticing, evil world no matter how good its practitioner made it sound. Homosexuality was a term and a fact neither of us boys had ever heard or had any knowledge.

But one night during the evening Sunday service it was "Testimony Time" and the saints were popping up like fleas shouting that they were glad they were "saved and had the Holy Ghost!" While this inspiring display of religious fervor was going on, this kid was putting his arm around me and trying to kiss me. Somehow this didn't strike me as the work of The Lord, especially as his hand was feeling my leg. I moved away from him and suddenly he leaped up with an "I'm glad I'm saved and got the Holy Ghost and God's called me to be a preacher!" I was certainly surprised by this revelation under the circumstances but the kid sat down amid shouted Hallelujahs! and Amens!

and the proud, beaming look of his mother. Then he said to me, "Now it's your turn, you gotta testify!"

A rather peculiar thing then occurred. No one had ever asked me if I was saved; I guess my grandparents just took it for granted that no boy could be loved and preached at with such fervor as I had been and not be a sure fire contender for salvation. "Well," I thought, "Whatever 'saved' means, I'm not and I sure don't have that 'Holy Ghost' that knocks old lady Walker off her hinges." Nor was I at all sure I wanted that dreadful power pushing me all over the place making me cluck, spit and moan in strange ways. And, so, I remained nailed to my bench, refusing to be this kid's first "convert" to "holy-rollerism" (not that many of them really rolled much, but they sure twitched a lot). I knew I was a sinner but I also knew that being saved must be a different thing than what this kid was.

Later, as a teenager, a kindly, old man was to ask me directly, for the first time, if I was saved. I will never forget, since my grandad was present, saying I was just to satisfy him. I felt intense guilt for this deception. I still didn't know what "saved" was then. It wasn't that the Bible and Jesus weren't made prominent in the little church or that I lacked examples of real Christians. But the Gospel was so distorted by ignorance and, sometimes, terrible hypocrisy, that it was never really explained in its pure simplicity. It was not until I read the Bible for myself that I discovered this.

One of the greater things I found by reading God's Word for myself was that so much of what others had told me was "Scriptural" was nowhere contained in the Bible. The world our children will inherit will be filled with ignorance. Not the ignorance of being able to use a VCR or flip hamburgers, but the hurtful ignorance of prejudice and bigotry, ignorance of science and real art and literature, ignorance of what a clear, mountain stream and a starry sky represent.

Grandad used to work with an old fellow that claimed to be Indian. The Indian and I used to go hunting together in the mountains around the mining claim. At that time, the hills were full of quail, deer and other game. I'll never forget the time we got his car stuck in Erskine Creek and had to spend the night. It was very cold and you know how hard it is to try to keep warm when it is so cold that one side of you is "frying" and the other side is freezing. Then, to top it off, the first snow of winter began to fall. I have no romantic illusions of "roughing it" in such circumstances. It was a thoroughly miserable night. Anyhow, this old fellow had many tales and I never contradicted him or acted as though I disbelieved him. I was raised never to do this with adults. But I will recount one story to make the point.

The fellow was visiting one evening at our cabin and he told us of a pistol he once owned. It seems that this gun was used to   commit a murder. He slept with it under his pillow and in the morning, it would be covered with blood. He would clean it thoroughly but every morning it would, once more, be bloody. He finally had to get rid of it. Now he would have been grievously wounded in his soul if my brother and I had expressed disbelief over what he obviously expected us to accept as "gospel truth." Like the old lady in "Little Oklahoma" that stuffed rags into empty light sockets to keep electricity from leaking out and the old man that would never eat anything from a can that had been opened from the bottom because this "poisoned" the contents, such ignorance and fanciful imagination was not really hurtful or intended to do harm.

But the ignorance of prejudice and bigotry, the ignorance of basic skills in a technological society and the selfish ignorance of Me! Me!, Me! that is entirely something else. This together with the ignorance of real values that makes other people worth caring about, that leads to self-discipline and sacrifice; that kind of ignorance is dooming our children. We were poor in material things in Weedpatch, Little Oklahoma and Boulder Gulch, but, thank God, we did not lack in the things that make life worth living. Family, community, patriotism, faith in The Lord and our country, these were real to us simple folk; would that today's children were equally "poor!"

CHRISTIAN PERSPECTIVE

In order to give the reader a fuller appreciation of the function of our little church, Faith Tabernacle, in "Dust Bowl era Little Oklahoma," I will describe a typical "service." "Call to worship" was accomplished by ringing the bell Sunday morning. This was the only sound to be heard at this time and day in our little community. No lawns so no mowers. No loud radios or TV's. No cars so no traffic. Only in summer the noise of flitting insects and birds and the occasional yap of some hound.

The congregation filtered in, women in flour sack dresses and straw hats, children in the conventional bib overalls and, mostly, shoeless. The men tried to dress in "Sunday go to meeting" attire of miscellaneous items, some with uncomfortable bow ties and, here and there, a white shirt might be seen. Folks tried to "dress up" the little girls but the boys, while clean, escaped such nonsense. We would begin with a few "rousers" like "Come and Dine" to warm up the audience. The cardboard fans donated by a mortuary in Bakersfield that grandad did business with would begin to flutter by now.

Bakersfield summers were hot and it didn't take much to work up a sweat among the faithful. Prayer requests were taken and testimonies given of what The Lord had done for (or to) various people in the neighborhood. At prayer time, The Lord's favor was implored for all our boys overseas and His righteous judgment against the enemies of Democracy. After the people had prayed, (we had no "Amen corner," everybody had the liberty to interject Amen and Hallelujah as the spirit moved them) it was "Show time!" I do not mean to interject irreverence. We all took the service seriously. But, to us children, it was definitely show time.

While we enjoyed the singing and Sunday school lessons very much, it was the "grown-ups" that could be counted on to "gay-up the time somethin' fierce." How we looked forward to the fun as people began to warm to grandad's preaching. My grandfather's face would contort with rage against the iniquitous Philistines and Pharisees. His voice boomed out like thunder as his fist pounded again and again on the old, wood pulpit. His whole body lurched in cadence with the words and seemed to help hurl them out like bullets at the helpless spectators in the pews (actually the "pews" were ramshackle benches more or less nailed together).

Old lady Walker suddenly jumped to her feet, flang her arms toward heaven, threw her head back and with eyes closed began shouting in "tongues." To my childish ears she seemed to be spouting a kind of sound like our make-believe "Indian talk." "O lalla lalla keba o notchaway, O lalla lalla keba o notchaway" she repeated over and over, her voice growing softer until she was finally "slain by the spirit" and slipped to the ground. Another old saint, Mrs. Hall, taking her cue, jumped to her feet and took off on "Helagumba, hellagumba, hellagumba, hellagumba until this terrible force of heaven also mowed her down. I thought again for the umpteenth time that old lady Walker sure had it all over Mrs. Hall. After all, an entire sentence must be a greater accomplishment than one word. Also, old lady Walker had a certain way of falling which left her in a more decorous position than Mrs. Hall. We children took great notice of how each dear old saint fell and writhed and twitched, not just their facility with grunts, yelling, jumping, tongue clicking and enthusiasm in general.

My grandfather would halt his thunderous barrage against all sorts of wickedness from bob-hair to hug-dancing each time the spirit moved on one of the saints. I always admired my grandfather's great sense of delicate timing. When the spirit moved he had sense enough not to interfere with such a terrifying power. But, no sooner had this dread force accomplished its work and felled its victim but he would pick up as though nothing had interrupted his discourse. Up jumped Mrs. Young as though goosed forcefully and indiscreetly. "Geeda geeda lamasabathany, geeda geeda lamasabathany, geeda geeda lamasabathany" until the ambushing spirit polled her like an ox (this was one part we children really liked because Mrs. Young had the heft of a cord of wood.

We often wondered how Mr. Young, who could have posed as the 90-pound weakling for Charles Atlas ads, controlled this pulchritudinous behemoth. But Mrs. Young had class. No twitching or groaning or moaning. After the performance, she just lay quiet with flecks of spittle on her hairy, upper lip. At the end of the service (performance?), there was the "altar call." This was the opportunity for each member of the congregation to come to the front of the church and kneel and pray. If the spirit really moved, a real catharsis of sins, real and imagined, would be poured out with much crying and shouting. This was a treat for the children as we heard many things our parents and other adults would never say in front of us otherwise.

Lest the reader misunderstand, the altar call was real in many cases. People often needed the gathering together to confess and pray for one another. Many wounds were healed in this fashion and fellowship restored. On rare occasions, we would have a baptism. This was accomplished only during the summer because we had to make a day of it at the "Jordan" (otherwise known as the Kern River). "Real" baptism must be done by completely submerging the penitent in a real river; none of that sissy "bathtub" or "sprinkled Dandy" stuff for Little Oklahoma believers. And, you wore your Sunday best, not "baptismal robes." Grandad would remove his shoes and roll up his pants, but it was still Black suit, black bow tie and white shirt. A picnic atmosphere was always a part of the ceremony and a great time would be had by all. If the congregation was not so small, I'm sure many a sinner would have gone back for seconds just for the fun of it. Fried chicken, rabbit, catfish and frog legs were plentiful. Pies and cakes; in all, and with so much food deep-fried, there was enough cholesterol to make a mortician smile.

We children would be occupied catching crawdads for the feast. The summer Mrs. Young was baptized was especially entertaining. She kept bobbing up like a huge cork and grandad had to have two of the deacons help him to "get her under." At that, she proceeded to float downstream and it took half the congregation to "beach" her.

My grandfather always dressed the part: Black suit and black bow tie. He was a large, raw-boned man, over six foot and about 200 pounds. He had a commanding presence and a thunderous voice. He had actually played a gambler in a silent movie made locally and he and my grandmother had done a stint in a circus; he as a "Barker" and my grandmother as the "Fat Lady." Grandma played the piano marvelously and grandad loved music, and keeping time with a tambourine tapping it on his knee with his deep, loud and resonant voice overpowered us. Faith Tabernacle could always be counted on to make a truly "joyous noise unto The Lord."

My grandma's piano playing and the spirited singing meant a lot to culturally starved Okies and Arkies and the success of the church. The church was truly a great social need-fulfilling thing as well as meeting the spiritual needs of the poor "white trash" as they were known to the greater Bakersfield city dwellers. While it was true that the community was "dirt poor" and many were "on the lam" and had criminal records, there was no shame attached. We were all aware of the frailty of the law in understanding some of the injustices of extremity. Many were "criminals" for things like stealing food or material to put a makeshift roof on a shack.

But no deputy sheriff ever intruded into Little Oklahoma in those days. My grandad was sworn in as a "Special Deputy," complete with uniform, Sam Brown, a Smith and Wesson .32-20 (peculiar caliber), clamshell breakaway holster, handcuffs and a copy of the California Penal code. He, like Judge Roy Bean, became "The Law" and arbiter of justice in the community. His primary function was that of liaison with the powers in Bakersfield.

Grandad's preaching was dynamic. The format was to have my grandmother read from The Scriptures and when she came to a spot that hit my grandad right, he would "take off." Grandad, of course, had no formal training for his "calling." But, like many that heeded the call, knew The Lord would give him the message. Now my grandfather tolerated exaggerated behavior on the part of the saints and expected them to have a good time, and a certain flexibility was needed amid the shouts of hallelujah and amen in order for them to enjoy their religion. When one of the sisters would feel the moving of the spirit and jump up to "speak in tongues," my grandfather would halt his thunderous barrage and wait for the "fit" to pass. He did not "hold" with most of this nonsense but had enough insight to understand the need of his constituents. When the spirit finally fled, grandad would resume his discourse as though nothing had interrupted his discourse.

While grandad looked askance at women speaking in the church (believing Paul's admonition that this was a shameful thing) he also knew that human nature and culture required outlets of expression. I suspect he also realized that it was a lot of fun for us children. Curiously, it was always the women that spoke in "tongues," never the men. Years later I would read that if the women in the church stopped speaking in tongues, the "movement" would soon cease to move! But this was before the "formal" churches like the Roman Catholic and Anglicans got into the act and "legitimatised" the gibberish, even giving it a good, solid Greek name; *Glossalalia*. Too bad Amy "Simple" wasn't around to cash in on that. But Swaggart, Baker, et al. would make up for her, and then some.

My grandfather's own conversion experience needs a little elaboration. It was supposed to have occurred during a tent meeting somewhere in the South. Being a real "heller" as a young man, he obviously presented one of those challenges that so inspire the fervent, holy pursuit of the godly. As he told the story, he went to the meeting with some other "young bloods" to heckle and enjoy the show. But one dear, old saint who recognized him decided the time was ripe for his call to repentance. So enthusiastic did she become under the influence of the spirit that she literally began to chase my grandfather around the meeting place shouting the imprecations of his lost condition and his need to call on the mercy of God for salvation. No fire-breathing dragon could have so consumed its prey as effectively.

The woman, aided by several who had joined in the chase, finally brought grandad to ground. Turning to face his tormenters, grandad said that the Spirit "Suddenly took hold of me and rattled me good!" To the holy delight of his "hounds of heaven," he cried out to God in repentance. There was no doubt to any that such a Saul-like experience could betoken anything but a divine call to preach. And it was thus that my grandfather was impelled on his colorful career in the Lord's army. Buying himself a "Pharisee" Bible (these are large Bibles, usually with thumb indexing, color plates, glossary, index, concordance, doctrinal notes, maps, short histories, biographies and pebble grained leather bindings weighing enough to tire any but the most energetic "thumper" and providing a not inconsiderable weapon should need arise) a Cruden's Concordance and equipping himself further with a few well-selected hell-fire and damnation verses, he, like so many others of similar background, was in the preaching business.

While my grandfather did not believe in "Theology" and might not even have heard the word, or use any commentaries, he had a pretty fair grasp of what was reasonable in religion and what was not and preached accordingly. A curious aberration was his refusing to "take up a collection" or to ever ask for money from the pulpit. His curious response when pressed on the issue was to reply: "God never made a beggar out of any man or His church!" What heresy! Not even a "Bingo" night!

Grandad had built the little church on his own lot at the corner of Cottonwood and Padre. It was built, like our "house," of material he had scrounged from various places. The bulk of the wood was from a wrecked boxcar at the rail yard. The last couple of years we lived in Bakersfield, grandad acquired a PA system for the church. By attaching two large speakers outside, the entire neighborhood received the benefit of hearing sin denounced in the booming thunder of grandad's preaching. I'm sure the local sinners thought the terror of the heavens had descended upon them when they were first bombarded with this wrath and vengeance unleashed upon the ungodly. No doubt the local sink of iniquity (a combination cuttin', shootin', liquor and grocery store where you could steal Bull Durham by holding the bell with your hand as you opened the door) profited mightily. They must have, as they were the only ones to complain of this counter-point to their customer's lively language and cultural pursuits.

At one time, he and grandma also had a little "mom and pop" grocery store (Faith Grocery) next door to the church. It fell victim to a fire from faulty wiring. Our home, an architectural curiosity fronting Padre, was built of box car lumber, rail ties, coffin shipping crates and anything else substantial enough to use as building material. Like our neighbors, we made do with whatever came to hand. Along with the "traditional" tarpaper, you would find tin signs used as roofing material and cardboard for interior "finish."

We were considered "rich" by our poorer neighbors because grandad had a steady job at the time with the post office, had a car and such a magnificent home. The beautiful chandelier in what we called the dining room helped support this accusation. There was always something incongruous about the crystal chandelier hanging from our cardboard covered ceiling. Other incongruities included the lovely French doors in our grandparent's bedroom and living room and the marvelous tapestries hung on various walls. I understand tapestries were used in castles to ward off the chill. They undoubtedly served a like purpose in our home. In the beginning, we had no electricity and had an outhouse.

We boys discovered an interesting phenomenon once electricity came to Little Oklahoma. When you turned on the light in the kitchen, large roaches would be running like crazy all over the floor and disappear. If you waited a little while and turned the light back on, the suckers were back like magic. Indoor plumbing, like electricity, was slow in coming to the community. One of our more odoriferous chores was emptying the "thundermugs" of the nightly accumulation; no job for the weak of stomach.

Being a preacher, special deputy and having a Federal job gave my grandad somewhat unusual status in the neighborhood. His California Penal Code book was always lying with his Bible and Cruden's Concordance. His Smith and Wesson with its breakaway, clamshell holster accounted for a hole in the ceiling of our cabin when we moved to the mining claim in Kernville. I was practicing my "fast-draw" when I touched the trigger a might too much (it never occurred to me that doing this with live ammo might result in an embarrassing situation). There is something unique about the sound of a powerful handgun going off in a room. It certainly gets the attention of the occupants.

I wouldn't want you to get the impression that we did not live in a "fine" house in Little Oklahoma. Though it was built of salvaged box car lumber, coffin shipping crates and the inside was finished with cardboard, it was, nonetheless, a great house compared with the neighbors'. Some simply dug a hole in the ground on arrival and covered it with whatever they could find. If it rained, they would just move the "roof" and sit under it as a kind of "lean-to" until the storm passed and they could dry out the hole. Eventually some of them acquired tents or built tarpaper shacks with material gleaned from the rail yard or the local dump.

It was a unique time in history. WWII was our constant absorption in play as children. Superman, Batman, Captain Marvel and Captain America were doing their part to win the war and we children applauded their efforts against the "rotten Japs and stinking Knocksies." The toys of those years were, of course, guns, bayonets, savings banks that were shaped like pigs, with Hitler or Tojo's faces which squealed when you deposited a coin for the war effort. If you want to forecast the future of a culture, take a look at the "toys" of the children. Stores were filled with cute, little uniforms (my brother and I were often decked out by our mother as sailors or soldiers according to the present stepfather's occupation. Our mother, patriot that she was, tried to marry into each branch of the service during this period).

It seems incredible in looking back that children were so involved in the war that people should actually think it "cute" to dress them in such a way. But we loved it. Hitler knew what he was doing in this regard in brainwashing the youth of Germany. We too were ready to repel, with our lives, any enemy that should come to our shores. While a war raged, we children played at war, contributed our metal toys to "scrap drives," bought war stamps at school and dreamed dreams of honorable and heroic conquest. As I said, it was a unique time in history. In no other decade has the country seemed as united as in the war against the Axis powers. We had a national purpose and the enemy was clear. Tom Mix, Hopalong Cassidy, Gene Autry, The Lone Ranger, Red Ryder and Roy Rogers could be counted on to always do the right thing (kiss the horse, not the girl).

Since playing "cowboys and Indians" involved a lot of "gunplay," the transition to killing Japs and Germans was natural. I have often wondered whether our government continued to make "caps" so readily available to children during this period of time, when you would have thought gunpowder so necessary to the war effort, wasn't a shrewd way to keep us "practicing" for our eventually becoming "cannon fodder." Guns were a natural part of our culture. Unhappily, instruction in the safe use of them was not. A kid was simply given a gun, usually a BB gun, to start.

I earned my Daisy Red Ryder carbine by selling Cloverine Salve, flower and garden seed door to door. But the "real thing" was all too readily available. Grandad had, in addition to the Smith, a .25 caliber Browning, a .22 rifle and a .410 shotgun. There were no "large bores" until we moved to the mining claim and deer, quail, pheasants and ducks were available. Children and guns are, of course, a deadly combination even with adults trying to make them aware of the danger. The fascination is too much. If they are within reach, kids will try to get them. Only adult supervision is acceptable with such weapons.

But, with guns treated with such familiarity, it was perfectly understandable that I would have my "close calls" with the things.

The Browning was especially captivating since it was so small and "toy-like" in appearance. Unfortunately, the safety catch on this gun was very easily disengaged when removing it from its small holster. Grandad may have thought he had it safely hidden but children are quite expert at ferreting out grownups' hiding places. I had found the Browning and often played with it. The "familiarity breeds contempt" concept came into full bloom in this instance leading to the nearly untimely demise of one of my playmates. This occurred after we had moved to the claim and this boy and I were in the woods.

I was old enough by then to have a modicum of sense about weapons, but crazy enough to still play with them. The boy's dad had driven us out to cut wood. While he was down the canyon from us, we had an impromptu "gun-fight." I had drawn the gun from its holster. The safety came off and there was a round in the chamber. "Bang!" Fortunately, the boy had ducked behind his dad's car and the bullet put a neat, glancing crease in the trunk instead of his head. We told his dad a pinecone had fallen on the car. I'm glad he didn't look too closely.

We were lucky. Many children have not been so fortunate. I did manage to put my experience about guns to good use in raising my own children. While raising them to shoot, they would never have such easy access to guns as I had. And, while children, they never took one out without me along.

While living on the claim, I traded a Japanese sword for a Canadian Ross .303 and an old English fowling piece; a double barreled 16 gauge with "rabbit ear" hammers. The fellow I swapped with ran a "two-handed" store in Bodfish. I can't remember his name but I will never forget his idiosyncrasy of using an ink pen to stencil on his mustache. The Ross was a beautiful rifle and was used by the Canadian armed forces. But the stock needed refinishing and I removed it intending to take it to school and do the work in the woodshop.

The old fellow I got it from only had a single round for it and I had chambered it and, forgottenly, left it in after removing the stock. It was early morning and, as my grandparents were finishing breakfast, I was seated by our old piano with the gun between my legs, muzzle against the floor, examining it without the stock. On a whim, I hit the trigger with my left index finger and the gun went off with a deafening roar in the cabin. Something struck my right hand with terrific force. It was the tang on the bolt of the rifle. I felt something hit my left hand and face as well. The unexpected and mind-numbing explosion transfixed my grandparents. There are few experiences to equal the sound and concussion of a large caliber rifle in close quarters with your morning coffee.

I watched in fascination as the palm of my right hand turned all the colors of the rainbow settling on an ugly, yellowish purple. The back of my left hand was covered with a black crust that began to slowly ooze blood droplets. My face also had been powder-burned and a few grains had penetrated my eyes. I can still see a couple if I look closely, even today.

A book I was to read years later, "Fate Is The Hunter," tells of the extraordinary chain of circumstances that leads up to a nearly disastrous airplane crash. As I later examined the rifle, I was to discover exactly what had happened and why this was to be one of the most fortunate "accidents" of my life; life-saving in fact. I discovered that the bolt of the rifle could be disassembled and reassembled incorrectly. Since the Ross was a "straight-pull" action design, if you reassembled it incorrectly, the "locking-lugs" that kept the explosion of the cartridge properly contained, would not engage. The entire force of the explosion would then blow the bolt back into the face of anyone firing the weapon, the firing pin assembly passing through the eye and brain of the shooter.

Had I fixed the stock of the rifle, assembled it and actually shot it, I would not be writing this account. The National Rifleman, just two months later, had a feature article outlining just what I had discovered for myself. The story related that some 200 Canadian soldiers had been killed in just this manner in using the gun. The bolt of the rifle accounted for the injury to my right hand. I never recovered the firing pin assembly as it had gone through the roof of the cabin. My left hand had received the burning powder and gasses that had ruptured the base of the cartridge case. Some small amount of these had sprinkled my face as well. I sported a patch over my right eye for a while and felt quite the romantic figure (remember Brenda Starr's sweetheart?).

The kids at school were fascinated by the incident as you can well imagine. But teenagers are immortal and there was never any sense of what I had actually escaped. I have the ruptured cartridge case to this very day, however, as a curious reminder of things inexplicable and how, at any time, circumstances can change things in sudden, drastic and incredible ways. Since I had not taken the bolt of the rifle apart myself, I received it in this deadly condition. I have often wondered about the possibilities. Who had done this and why did some kid have a "lucky" accident thus possibly preventing a tragedy? Ecclesiastes 9:11, "Time and chance happeneth to all alike."

Having thus learned several things of value by this episode, I decided to try the shotgun I had gotten from the old fellow in a safe and sane manner. I did know enough at this time to realize that the peculiar pattern on the barrels of the gun might mean that they were of "Damascus" manufacture and, therefore, unsafe with modern, smokeless powder ammunition. Having nearly precipitated a couple of heart attacks by my earlier exploit, and being kind and thoughtful by nature, I waited until my grandparents absented themselves before conducting my latest experiment in explosive devices.

The plan was simple. I loaded the old piece with low base bird shot and secured it to a table outside the cabin. I theorized that, unlike a rifle or pistol, a shotgun would make more than a neat, round hole in the cabin. Also, only a real idiot would fire a gun in a house. I then tied a string to one of the triggers and, cocking the hammers (I have often asked myself why I cocked both of them) I proceeded to a safe position behind a big, old "digger" pine tree. A louder explosion than I would have expected of a single round of birdshot followed my tug on the string.

Sure enough, when I walked over to inspect the project, both barrels had gone off simultaneously. The breech of the gun was cocked slightly open and one hammer blown off by the force of the double explosion. Like the .303 case, I have managed to hang onto this old "wall-hanger" over the many years since (*sans* one hammer).

CHAPTER FOUR

CHRISTIAN PERSPECTIVE

DECEMBER, 1990

Proverbs 15:14

"YOUNG POOREST GROUP IN U.S. 23% falls below poverty level."

This is a front-page headline in a large, metropolitan newspaper. But it comes as no surprise to millions of struggling young people. They know all this first hand.

I quote the following by way of elaboration: "One third of (a sample school district) high school students won't finish school. In a typical public kindergarten class of 30 children, seven live in poverty, six have no health coverage, nine speak limited or no English, 15 are from broken families, and 14 meet federal standards for being educationally handicapped and are at high risk of failure in school." This is "handwriting" on the wall that does not need a Daniel to translate.

If you fail to get the point, I quote the following from the same source: "A grim, Orwellian future awaits America in the 21st century, say literacy experts. It is a future where thousands of jobs will go unfilled and businesses will fail, a third of the adult population will not know how to read or write, crime rates will soar, and the rift between the haves and the have-nots will widen almost (me: certainly, not almost!) irrevocably." For over twenty years I have often made just this point. But the "experts," primarily those with worthless doctorates in education, have just made the situation worse. I have used the auto repair business as a case in point and the following will illustrate why. "A car mechanic in 1965 needed to comprehend 5000 pages of a service manual in order to fix a car. Today, that same mechanic must understand 465,000 pages - the equivalent of 250 big city phone books!"

As I write, I can see a beautiful panorama of mountains with pure white, fleecy clouds in an azure sky free of pollution. There is a strong breeze rustling the pines. It is easy in such surroundings to forget the poverty and grief so many face today.

There is a new organization, DOOM, the Society for Secular Armageddon, with a "Hotline of Doom" (415) 673-DOOM) if you are interested. As I have said for years, and as DOOM now says, "We don't need God to finish us off. The coming end will be a strictly 'do-it-yourself apocalypse.'" Not that I do not believe that God won't be involved, but I have always known that man, left to himself and his fallen nature, can certainly accomplish his own demise without the assistance of The Almighty.

This is Christmas time. Fewer will "celebrate" the occasion in the manner they did as children. Harsh, economic realities confront us at every turn. And, of course, as a "Story Teller at Large," thereby hangs a tale.

Children have been cheated of childhood in our generation. TV has supplanted reading and radio shows that allowed (demanded) the use of our most remarkable ability: Imagination. And where are the people, parents and grandparents that so inspired children of a past generation, by reading to them and telling them stories?

Without being able to exercise (because of being spoon-fed so- called entertainment via TV) their imagination, children are easily bored and fall prey to getting into trouble. The poor excuses for toys that require no ability or challenge other than pushing buttons are a travesty. And cute as they may be, how many stuffed animals contribute to a child's learning and self-esteem?

In fact, many children are being taught to be selfish and acquisitive, possessive, by their parents "buying them off" by multiplying these things as if a room full of "things" are proof of a parent's care. A child knows better. But the message is clear: "getting and having," multiplying material possessions is important.

In lieu of time with a child how much easier to simply buy another "toy for the shelf" and delude yourself that you have shown a child that you "care!" God forbid that you buy something that will take your time to show them how to construct something of real value, both in the building and finished product.

But we live in a culture that no longer can hand a hammer and saw to a child and teach them to build. No longer are we able to give them "chores" that, like tending the livestock and vegetable garden, contribute to the family table and teach the responsibility that the demands of such enterprises brings. Somehow, feeding the resident hamster or family dog or cat, putting dishes in the dishwasher or "taking out the trash" doesn't teach the necessary values.

The "Young" that our headline heralds are not poor in material things alone, they are poor in spirit as well and, too often, without hope of anything better in their future. They are not only illiterate in the academic sense; they are ignorant of the things that give real value to life.

My brother, Dee, (Ronald) and I called our grandmother "Toady." I don't know why unless it was because she was so fat. My grandparents were in an auto-train accident. As a result, our grandmother "swole up somethin' fierce," to the degree that she was able to play the part of a "Fat Lady" in a circus and our grandfather was a "Barker" as I mentioned.

On our first day of school, dear old Mt. Vernon in East Bakersfield, Dee Dee was crying for his Toady which prompted the teacher to ask my grandfather if he couldn't let my brother bring this favorite "toy" of his to school the next day. Grandad, of course, declined.

I should point out that ours was not an "average" American home, not even in 30's and 40's Little Oklahoma. Our father left us when I was 3 and my brother 2. We never saw him again. When we got older and learned to know our mother the idea didn't seem to be such a bad one. Of course, any man that runs off from his responsibility toward children is contemptible but our mother was a real "pistol."

Not that we didn't love her or she us. But her insane temper and threats to kill us occasioned by such lapses in our behavior like washing her toaster, waffle iron, clock and iron in the bathtub or cleaning the toilet with her toothbrush left us, often, in fear of our lives. My brother and I thus became very close as companions in fear when we were with our mother. The threat of death does draw people together so, if you are having trouble with your children, maybe you haven't tried this method yet.

Because of her numerous marriages, some carping critics (our grandparents) might consider our mother incapable of a firm commitment to a life partner, even a little promiscuous. Her efforts to marry into each branch of the service did provide us with a lot of war stories and different versions of how the war was being fought. There was some confusion over the fact that while "daddies" changed frequently, our grandparents remained the same.

I have often thought that our mother's rather heterodox marriage pattern added a somewhat different dimension to my brother's and my perspective of life. Certainly if a child has a nightmare and calls out for "Daddy" and rightly expects a stampede to assistance, he has little to fear from the lesser monsters inhabiting a dark bedroom. But this is not the only advantage our mother gave us. My spelling was much improved by having to master so many names (Pospieszynski was a real challenge).

I should point out that my grandparents were not prejudiced, but the neighborhood? Whew! In fact, while my grandfather was born in Oklahoma and raised in Arkansas, he escaped the ignorant and hurtful prejudice so common in those states in those days. On the other hand, because he chose to marry a "Blue-bellied Yankee," his mother did not speak to him to her dying day. Thus grandad rebelled against his Southern heritage and married outside the Confederacy. His kindness and affection for Negroes was another quirk of his character.

Our great-grandmother was indeed a "Grand Mother." She was grand in everything and my brother and I loved her dearly. She was a rebel of her time, being trained as a nurse and well educated. She was also a divorcee, which in those days showed a rare individualism and lack of concern with the mores of her day. She made no secret of the fact that she married the second time for money. Unfortunately, the man had lied to her about his financial situation in order to get her to marry him. When he died, she lived with our grandparents. The Lord had apparently taught her a lesson.

Some of my fondest memories are my great-grandmother reading to my brother and me. She made the stories come alive to us. I can still visualize "Tugboat Annie" and others from her reading stories from the old Saturday Evening Post and Collier's.

Children of my day had radio as a primary, entertainment media. While we always looked forward to the Sunday "Funnies," and, on rare occasions, a trip to the Cartoon Matinee in Bakersfield (imagine watching two hours of great cartoons for ten cents?), it was radio that really gave us the skill to imagine. We grew up on Captain Midnight, Jack Armstrong, the All-American Boy, Terry and the Pirates, Tom Mix, Inner Sanctum, The Cisco Kid, The Whistler, I Love a Mystery, Corliss Archer, Henry Aldrich, Lum and Abner, Duffy's Tavern, Charlie McCarthy, Baby Snooks, The Great Gildersleeve, The Life of Riley and so many more. When we moved to the mountains, we still had a battery powered Zenith and a wind-up gramophone for entertainment.

After we moved, some of the old programs were already passing away but I still remember Sam Spade, Mr. X, The Green Hornet, Mr. Keene, Tracer of Lost Persons, The F.B.I., Gang Busters, The Thin Man, The Sheriff Show, Fibber McGee and Molly, The Lone Ranger, Jack Benny, Can You Top This? The Thin Man, etc. Amazing how Batman, The Phantom, Mandrake the Magician and others have disappeared or changed. And how we enjoyed L'il' Abner. Al Capp sure had the number of politicians and religious charlatans.

While living on the mining claim, I tuned in a new radio show called "Gunsmoke." It was unlike any other I had ever heard. Bob and Ray had already introduced a new format in humor, almost Phil Harris-like, but here was drama of an almost existential form.

The TV series of Gunsmoke was nothing like the beginning radio series. To me, looking back, it seems to have been the precursor of a very new concept in entertainment, requiring great attention to understanding a psychic plot. It was a very mysterious show to a child used to the usual, predictable and straightforward Lone Ranger format. Life was simple back then but complications were on the horizon, and the early Gunsmoke betokened these things for us children; but, back to my own "plot."

My grandparents were a treasure trove of folklore and turn of the century knowledge. My grandparents had one of the first marriages performed by telephone. Grandad had enlisted in the army after leaving home at the age of 12. At 14, he joined up by lying about his age (he was truly large for his age and got away with it) and stayed in the service until a cannon ran over one leg giving him a disability discharge.

While in the army, he met my grandmother and they decided to get married. But, as the day approached, the camp (Camp Beauragarde) was placed in quarantine leading to the novel arrangement via a local judge, the governor and the camp commander and my grandparents married by telephone.

In a curious way, my brother and I were raised a generation behind most of our age. Our grandparents were relatively young due to their marrying early in life and our mother marrying so young as well.

It was common to our Bakersfield community to live without electricity and indoor plumbing. Hand-dug wells were used for water. When electricity arrived at Little Oklahoma, ours was one of the first places to be "electrified." This was due to the fact that grandad was a "Jack of all trades" and could do house wiring himself.

The house was of simple construction (salvaged box car and coffin shipping crates, tarpaper, etc.). An interesting way of cleaning the kitchen floor was to simply swamp and mop, the water draining through the cracks in the boards. The combined smells of the wet wood and moist earth were marvelous, honest odors.

Washday was a communal effort in those days in Little Oklahoma. Some of the neighbor ladies would come to our place and fires would be built. Galvanized washtubs would be placed over the fires, propped up on rocks or bricks.

Once the water was boiling, lye soap (Do any of you remember a song "Grandma's Lye Soap"?) and Mrs. Worth's Bluing, for white things, were added. The clothes were then placed in the tubs and constantly stirred with broom handles as the clothes boiled.

There was a festive air and the gossip flowed around us children as we played. The smell of the fresh washed items was pleasant to us. Once the clothes and other things were properly boiled, the ladies would place them in another tub of less hot water for scrubbing on washboards. The final wash was a rinse in a tub of clean, cold water.

After the wash was done, the ladies would go their respective ways to hang it to dry. Looking back on it, I know that all this was a hard chore. But it seems that everyone enjoyed getting together and making it fun, especially for us children.

Grass was for cows and goats in our neighborhood, not lawns or for smoking. Over time, a few scraggly lawns appeared here and there. A few women tended plants of some variety and, of course, there were "Victory Gardens." But the necessities of living precluded any attempts at "finery, either in housing or dress. Feed and flour sacks were common clothing material for men, women and children.

Our little "Dust Bowl" church, built by my grandfather, was the focal point of the community. Christmas was an especially grand time for us, as children, because the only toys some of the local children would receive would be through the church. My grandparents would gather contributions from some of the Bakersfield merchants for distribution to "Little Oklahoma" children. Owens Toy Store was most generous. My brother and I spent many glorious moments at this wonderful treasure house. Any trip to the city was incomplete without us visiting this fabulous place.

I remember one Christmas, before the church was built, my grandfather dressing as "Santa" (though, of course, I didn't realize it was him at the time) and having the neighborhood children come to our house for gifts. It was a particularly bad winter that year (and they could be cruel in Bakersfield) and bitter cold. But the children came, some without shoes, to receive their gifts. I'm sure The Lord was pleased and honored more by this act of my grandparents than by many of the sermons that were preached in His Name.

I recall that grandad, in an attempt to help some of the older children avoid a life of crime, tried to get a youth group started. He was even able, by his association with the Sheriff's department, to obtain a few films and projector to show some movies. These invariably were "morality plays" that showed "crime did not pay." How times have changed!

Not long ago, I was in conversation with my old friend of nearly thirty years. We are good enough friends to love each other "warts and all." I shared with him my concern that preaching, since we both are "men of the cloth," does not meet the needs of people.

Grandad was an imminently practical man. It was practicality more than anything else that "ruined" me as a "professional educator" and preacher. In education, having earned an honest living as a machinist and mechanic for years before becoming a teacher, I faced the "fairy-tale" world of make believe that is inhabited by "Ivory tower" citizens, those without the haziest idea of the requirements of the real world and "teach" accordingly.

By far my most disillusioning experience in education was trying to teach a class of graduate students who were prospective teachers. They were incapable of writing a proper paper and had come through the "system" to graduate status, fresh B. A.'s in hand, and unable to do even adequate, undergraduate writing tasks. But their respective colleges had told them they were "well educated." I shudder when I think of it.

But seminaries have not done any better in preparing those that "heed the call" to "divine service." Is there life after Hebrew, Greek, Hermeneutics, systematic, and dogmatic theology? I'm afraid not in most cases.

The teaching and preaching of The Bible is very practical. Much of it is in the category of "If you touch the stove, you will get burned!" variety. But the flowery obfuscation of erudition will cover a multitude of sins according to modern "exhorters."

No matter how thin you slice it, it still comes out "baloney." Without application to real life, without the merit of real teaching (I am appalled by what even well-intentioned men have the nerve to call "teaching") these so-called *sermons* are too often nothing but attempts to earn a paycheck at best and ego-inflators at worst.

"You know," my brother told me on one occasion, "Stealing is wrong!" To fully appreciate this remarkable revelation of my brother's you have to understand that it came to him at fully thirty years of age. I could hardly fault the soundness of his theology and had to agree with him.

Now my brother and I had been taught that stealing was wrong but it took events in our lives to take the "abstraction" and move it to where dear old J. Vernon McGee would say, "The rubber meets the road." I suppose "abstraction" is what preachers major in. But God deals in absolutes. We are supposed to teach our children not to steal. If they do steal, we are supposed to punish them. If they are obedient and do well, we are to reward them. Simple ethics. But somewhere along the line, sermons became "professional." The minister pours over "notes and outlines," reviews his commentaries on various "proof texts," inserts his favorite "humorous story" and "current events" and he is ready to "minister to the flock."

The fact that such "sermonizing" has little or no effect in the lives of either the preacher or congregation does not seem to faze the "professional soldier of the cross." He is at his best when he can take today's headlines and, with feeling and "Scripture," convince his audience that they have done battle with the "powers of darkness" and learned something of value. What that "something" is, none can tell specifically. But the best of these "pulpiteers" leave the people feeling that something of worth, intangible as it may be, transpired.

My particular prejudice is that the professionals have never considered how God feels about all this. He is, after all, supposed to be the "Boss." Maybe, it is as simple as most of them not really caring about how He feels about it.

I do believe that most people, the "leadership" included, have a completely erroneous concept about the very nature of God. The "party line" is that God is omniscient, omnipresent and omnipotent. This is simply, by His own Word, The Bible, not true.

In sharing this with some people a while ago, I met the "party line." In good, orthodox "religionese," these people made the record quite clear; they have solid church and school background and expect someone to accept a few, well chosen, religious terms to be accepted as explanation of a position when all that has been said is a parroting of meaningless gibberish, albeit perfectly acceptable gibberish unless an explanation is insisted upon, by the faithful.

The tragedy of this was the fact that they really believed they had actually "explained" something when, in fact, had said nothing. Now I love these folks but their egos would never allow of a "pagan" like me to contribute anything of substantive value that might disabuse them of their own cherished prejudices.

The "rightness" of their own "orthodox answers" to my "heterodoxy," carefully cultivated by adhering to the party line, lo these many years, does not insist on answers to the really tough questions about the nature of God; much safer (and, seemingly, more intellectual) to parrot the "professionals" whether you really see the inconsistency in their apologetics or not.

Unhappily, the party line does not answer the really tough questions of life. Nor does it answer to the needs of people. And here is where the professionals fail. People need help; not religious platitudes, pious phrases and sanctimonious "holier than thou" pretense.

Perhaps it is my serious concern for children and young people that led me to some "unthinkable" conclusions about the nature of God. My grandparent's little church in East Bakersfield was a happy place. It took organized religion and the "professionals" to teach me that God didn't know how to have fun or appreciate a good joke.

After my years of being a good, orthodox "professional," The Lord was kind enough to make a few things clear to me. Among these "new" lessons was the fact that He would like us to be able to include Him in our laughter and enjoyment of life.

Walt Kelly was one of my early teachers in political and religious humor. Being a "Pogo" aficionado, I am reminded, when I think of those "sober brows" that try to rob us of enjoying our relationship with The Lord, of a keen observation by "Seminole Sam." He said: "Wonder what language the Romans used for the old 14 karat bamboozle?" This as a reaction to Owl's use of Latin to attempt a "scam."

In religious circles, the languages are Hebrew and Greek. But, too often, as in Law, the bamboozle is the same baloney. Of course, it helps, as Elmer

Gantry learned, to use some of those 16 cylinder words like *Eschatology* and *Supralapsarianism*, etc. to accomplish the purpose.

No one who knows me would accuse me of denigrating the hard, honest work of God's scholars. I consider them among the "Gifts" to His Church. I am speaking of the abuse of learning and scholarship by those that willingly or ignorantly, "twist" God's clear intent.

It was a simple matter for me, as a shop teacher, to teach young people the value of being able to use a lathe or mill, of being able to overhaul an engine or build a radio. But they could see such skills as desirable things to acquire; these "Learnings" had relevancy.

The abstractions of math and language were more difficult. They are also more difficult to assess in terms of immediate benefit. As adults, we know how very badly such skills are needed for survival in a technological society; but how to make them as desirable as learning to do a valve or brake job? When the skills lack the incentive of easily seen desirability and relevancy, you are left with having your students accept yours and a society's assessment of their value.

Preachers fail miserably in both cases. They not only fail to teach the necessary skills for living, they try to "bamboozle" people by religious clichés and "spiritual" nonsense.

I wait impatiently for my "peers" to really explain how you cast out demons, deliver over to Satan as Paul did, why God seems so very 'human' on occasion, why He left Job's wife to torment him, why The Lord changed His mind in several instances, and so on.

But, these "colleagues" seem determined to "explain" such things by religiosity and "mumbo-jumbo" that makes no sense to poor benighted souls like me. I suppose Walt Kelly could prick the balloons of these pompous asses without rancor but I have the disadvantage of having to have worked with too many of them personally, both in the churches and the schools.

As things grow progressively worse in the world, people are desperately looking for leadership. But it has to make sense. Those of you on my mailing list will certainly understand why the "David Duke's" are beginning to look attractive as political leaders. It is easier for you to understand why people like Charles Krauthammer can write freely about the selfishness of people with AIDS demanding they be given consideration before those with illnesses they did not bring on themselves, like breast cancer.

While columnists like Ellen Goodman can cry about the way women in congress are treated like second-class citizens, we in California are seriously considering a woman like Feinstein for governor. Insanity! A world gone mad, being prepared for "unthinkable" solutions for "insoluble" problems.

Most certainly, as a nation, we are missing a sense of history. It is easy to make "simplification" a cause, just as Hitler did so successfully. A "Gregorian" can say "Students don't fail; teachers fail!" and miss the real point that an entire society has failed.

As religious leaders have failed to impart real knowledge, have failed to call sin what it is, have failed to provide real, moral leadership and substituted situational ethics, Hollywood entertainment, their own peculiar theologies for the clear Word of God, they have led an entire nation to judgment.

Many years ago, I began to tell young people that the critical problems they faced could only be resolved on an individual basis, that answers for society as a whole, would be "unthinkable" and equally unavoidable. These young people, many with families of their own now, only have to read a newspaper to understand the truth of what I said and meant.

CHAPTER FIVE

CHRISTIAN PERSPECTIVE

FEBRUARY, 1991

II Timothy 2:15

Well, the world is at war again and the situation changes daily. In the first days, people were glued to TV and radio, shocked that such an event was really taking place. I, like many others, was watching CNN when the first air attack took place. Immediately the memories of the attack on Pearl Harbor came to mind. We were now a nation at war.

"WE'RE AT WAR!" the next day's newspaper headlined, just as I read fifty years ago. But now we have war as a media event, TV giving us instant coverage of the events that are changing, forever, the world we knew. And, people now, as fifty years ago, are in a state of shock wondering what next?

It is appalling, of course, that so many had no idea where Iraq was, that some were actually expecting Hussein to invade our shores, but these are now getting a "geography" lesson they never had before. Even more, so many are terribly ignorant of the forces that have been at work for centuries that have led to this historical imperative. While a very small number of people understand the significance of the Middle East from God's perspective, the whole world now is forced to focus upon it. Only a very few understand why God focuses so much of His attention on tiny Israel. But the majority are being suddenly informed of its political, i. e. Economic, importance.

The real importance of what is happening is open to those with a good, working knowledge of The Bible. It is in this geographical area that God closes His plan for the ages. The "Pharaohs" of the leading participants "neither know The Lord" or have any idea why they should obey Him. They are ignorant of God's plans and fight as "one beating the air."

It is ignorance that has had my attention for so long, beginning with my own. As a teacher for so many years, it was my business to educate young people (this in spite of an educational hierarchy that was working to the opposite purpose). Teaching, education, should be the dispelling of ignorance. A good education should give us an appreciation of our own ignorance and encourage more learning.

Is the world headed toward the prophesied *"Gotterdammerung?"* Undoubtedly. The time line, though, is, of course, in God's hands. When I was a child, the world seemed so huge and wondrous. There were mysteries galore. The fascination of the unknown was compounded by newspaper and radio accounts of World War. Hitler and Tojo were the "Monsters" of my childhood.

In retrospect, we know that these men were not insane monsters but they were guilty of megalomania, like Hussein. As Pharaoh of old, such men believe themselves to be Messiahs or gods; they realize that most men are of little minds, without great ambition or qualities of such greatness that leads to thoughts of destiny and immortality.

In a time that seems so long past, people had time to read and share their thoughts with one another. But in an age of "instant everything," the old paths to knowledge are no longer traveled. Unhappily, there is no "royal path," no short cuts to knowledge. People will say they wish they had more time. For what; certainly not to study and to read great literature though they will say they wish they had knowledge of such.

Whether The Bible or The Republic or The Jefferson Papers it matters little that they gather dust while minds are occupied with attempts to maintain a "living." It does not occur to such that they are "camped" in front of TVs and VCRs as their minds atrophy. Millions will spend hours watching a "Super Bowl" and complain they don't have time for anything "worthwhile." Even some who call themselves "Christian" will say this was the highpoint of their day. And, war or not, we will have our "Super Bowls!" It makes me wonder what the course of events would have been had the Apostle Paul or John Muir been sports, or other entertainment, fanatics.

Of course, there is the religious "entertainment" doing business as usual. The Pat Robertson Show is having brisk sales, accompanied by drum rolls, shouts of "Hallelujah!" and fervent "Amens." Avuncular Billy Graham (you know; the guy that discovered there wasn't any real religious persecution going on in Russia and was the religious inspiration to Richard Nixon) has offered "solace" and "prayerful guidance" to our leaders. It is all quite marvelous and silly; and all this while the missiles fly. I wonder which paper will first compare the whole thing to a "Disneyland" version of Nintendo? Maybe Gary Trudeau will undertake it.

In view of the momentous events of war, it is hard to pay attention to some of the other things going on. The fat cats (Willie Brown et al.) are busy trying to shoot down the term limitation initiative and protect their large, unearned retirements and well-endowed backsides. Assemblyman Richard Floyd says he will shut down his office and handle constituents by an answering service. He cries that the initiative has virtually ended his political career! "I'm depressed," he says, "there is no future for me! (I suspect he means his future of feeding at the public trough). There's no future for my staff." Some staff is being given cushier jobs and large amounts of severance pay. My heart bleeds for these "professional career bureaucrats" (*Tax-fattened hyenas*. Thank you, Berke Breathed). Our founding fathers would turn over in their graves at such. But, I believe the evil system will allow them to prevail through the courts no matter what the will of the people, the great "unwashed."

It was an age ago that I sat with Senator Ed Davis in Sacramento and he expounded on "Jeffersonian ideals" while I tried to warn him of the deteriorating condition of education in California. But then, I never did hear from Gary Hart or most of our other "leaders." At least Ed let me in his door and I have some of his cordial correspondence upon which to reflect.

I just returned from renewing my acquaintance with an old school chum, Russell Hand. Russ is a farmer here in the valley. I credit him, as I do most who earn an honest living, with more common sense than our "elected leadership." It was good to talk with him and the years slipped away in our conversation. He is a good and honest man and his warmth and openness, this in spite of the fact that we had not seen each other for almost forty years impressed me. I think Russ and his wife represent many who see the madness of the world's condition, who wish they could change things for the better and prevent the hurt and sorrow of others. But what can they really do but pray and hope?

Certainly there is a "secret agenda" as Hussein says. But neither he nor those he accuses really understand what it really consists of. Our "Pharaohs" think they will prevail but as Pharaoh of old, they will finally have to say: "He is The Lord!"

But, back to the subject of the ignorance that I fight against; the ignorance of those that call themselves *Christian*. This is the job I believe God wants me to undertake. I will not change minds dedicated to blind orthodoxy and prejudice. But, because some have at least indicated a willingness to listen, I am encouraged to try for their sakes.

I believe the majority of people see most of what passes for orthodoxy as nothing more than "religion." The "show-biz" types like Roberts, Cerullo, Robertson, Schuller et al. are easily dismissed as the hysterical, egotistical, greedy ignoramuses and personal empire-builders the world sees them as; "professional religionists."

Most of the so-called "higher" churches, Episcopalian, Anglican, Lutheran, Roman Catholic are dismissed as, largely, harmless purveyors of mysticism. The cults such as the JWs and Mormons have their peculiar appeal to the intellectually lazy and those that believe God has rewarded superstitious nonsense. In sum, "religion" has something to offer every whim of taste; the

Truth, on the other hand, demands personal dedication and commitment to the search "whether these things be so!"

In undertaking my own personal pilgrimage, I have had to set in abeyance many of the beliefs I had so jealously, and ignorantly, held. These beliefs were the result of actual study of famed theologians and historians, of input by men held in reputation in accepted universities and seminaries.

But, as Paul under Gamaliel, much of what I had been "taught" was little more than the result of blind orthodoxy, leaving huge gaps in understanding the answers to legitimate questions. More than that, these questions were "beggared" by attempts to "spiritualize" them away or treated as doubt, or "lack of faith" on my part.

It was not until the answers to these questions became of paramount importance in my own life, this as a result of God dealing harshly with my own prejudices and lack of intellectual honesty, that I had the courage to face them. I also knew that I would alienate many of those that I respect and love in the process. It was no easy task to choose such a course.

But God did provide a few that, while not necessarily agreeing or understanding, at least showed a willingness to listen, people like Byron McKaig who had the patience and love to hear me out without damning me out of hand. I like to think these people know me well enough to believe that mine is an honest inquiry into these things and that I am not impugning The Lord or His Word, that I am trying to gain understanding and help others in their own quests to know The Lord better.

In attempting to divest the Gospel of the superstitious claptrap that passes for "religion," it is necessary to divest your minds of the things men would have us believe and let God speak for Himself. If, with an open and honest mind, we do this, amazing things come to light.

I have often said that, the thing that impressed me so forcefully upon reading the Bible entirely through for the first time was so much I had been told was in it wasn't there! I had been the "fortunate recipient" of much religious "teaching." I had a background in Pentecostalism, Roman Catholicism and Fundamentalism. But what had been "catechized" by the "professionals" had little root in God's actual Word!

As a result, I have been a long-time proponent of asking people to read the Bible for themselves rather than taking men's word for what it says. Far better no teacher than a false one no matter how well intentioned. Having said that I must make it clear God has blessed us with men through the centuries who have dedicated themselves sacrificially to the scholarly study of His Word. I count it a rare privilege to have the years of study of these men's works in my own background.

It is a sad thing that contemporary scholarship has fallen on bad times. There are no more Henrys, Ellicotts, or Clarkes to guide us. And, while I would be the last to lightly esteem the necessity of a background in systematic theology, hermeneutics, the languages, history and mores of the Bible, it is more important to read it in its entirety than be at the mercy of those that twist and distort the Bible to their own purposes.

Having done this, you are not at the mercy of those that would tell you God has said something He has not. You have a "well to draw from" and can then undertake its study for yourself. While you will not remember everything you have read no one will be able to tell you that God has said something He has not. Hopefully, you will be equipped to discriminate in choosing your teachers. But, until you have undertaken to do this for yourself, you are at the mercy of every religious kook and charlatan, even your own prejudices.

It is well said that no one can think themselves to be truly educated who has not read the most influential book the world has ever seen. And so the Bible is. No book has come close to its impact on civilization. No one can ever surmount its influence for good as long as its principles are adhered to in honesty. And it is just that kind of honesty I ask of you and with which I undertake the following study.

I think it appropriate to begin with an example of what I am driving at. There is a most interesting account in the 17th chapter of Acts that will shed light on my own search. It concerns the Apostle Paul and his approach to the questions of people in Athens. It is just as relevant now as then:

"While Paul was waiting for them in Athens, he was greatly distressed to see that the city was full of idols. So he reasoned in the synagogue with the Jews and the God-fearing Greeks, as well as in the marketplace day by day with those who happened to be there. A group of Epicurean and Stoic philosophers began to dispute with him. Some of them asked, 'What is this babbler trying to say?' Others remarked, 'He seems to be advocating foreign gods.' They said this because Paul was preaching the good news about Jesus and the resurrection. Then they took him and brought him to a meeting of the Areopagus, where they said to him, 'May we know what this new teaching is that you are presenting? You are bringing some strange ideas to our ears, and we want to know what they mean.' (All Athenians and the foreigners who lived there spent their time doing nothing but talking about and listening to the latest ideas.)

"Paul then stood up in the meeting of the Areopagus and said: 'Men of Athens! I see that in every way you are very religious. For as I walked around and observed your objects of worship, I even found an altar with this inscription: TO AN UNKNOWN GOD. Now what you worship as something unknown I am going to proclaim to you.

"The God who made the world and everything in it is the Lord of heaven and earth and does not live in temples built by hands. And he is not served by human hands, as if he needed anything because he himself gives all men life and breath and everything else. From one man he made every nation of men that they should inhabit the whole earth; and he determined the times set for them and the exact places where they should live. God did this so that men would seek him and perhaps reach out for him and find him, though he is not far from each one of us. 'For in him we live and move and have our being.' As some of your own poets have said, 'We are his offspring.'

"Therefore since we are God's offspring, we should not think that the divine being is like gold or silver or stone - an image made by man's design and skill. In the past God overlooked such ignorance, but now he commands all people everywhere to repent. For he has set a day when he will judge the world with justice by the man he has appointed. He has given proof of this to all men by raising him from the dead."

There is a wealth of information to be gathered from this short discourse of the great Apostle, historically, eschatalogically, exegetically and eisegetically. To begin, he is dealing with a bunch of religious people, a hard task under any circumstances. As with most religious people, they were "very superstitious." But he "reasoned" with them.

Now there is no reasoning with prejudice and bigotry. Paul was not successful with all these people but his approach was, of necessity, based on reasoned apologetic. The appeal of the Gospel is its very reasonableness given the nature of God to which men do respond. God is, preeminently, reasonable. It is a shame that religious charlatans portray Him as a fool.

Paul's audience did not deny the existence of God, they were ignorant of Him. I call attention to the statement that these people "happened" to be there. They were there, not by some peculiar "fore-ordained" machination of God, some "fate," but by happenstance. Ecc.9:11

It does seem peculiar, particularly to those steeped in the traditions of orthodoxy, that chance of any kind is mentioned throughout Scripture but such is the case. Jesus Himself uses the expression. Something to think about.

Paul says a most unusual thing to these people. He states that in the past, God overlooked such ignorance of Him but now requires all men everywhere to repent. This repentance is based on the fact of the resurrection. Bear in mind the fact that John the Baptist and The Lord Himself came preaching repentance. Without repentance there is no forgiveness of sin.

But the question is; what was the ignorance Paul refers to? It seems to be the ignorance of people in their search for the truth of God. Paul gives credit to the universality of men's idea that God can be found of them, that the history of men evidences their common acceptance of His existence and their need for fellowship with, and worship of, Him.

Paul also states that God made man and had him inhabit the earth so that they would seek Him and "perhaps," reach out to Him. That word, "perhaps" is a very thought-provoking one. It gives the impression of hope, rather than certainty. Wasn't God sure? By the time of the Flood, only Noah was "reaching." Jesus said the same conditions would prevail when He returns.

God clearly says that He has appointed a definite day "... when He will judge the world with justice by the man (Jesus) He has appointed." While the passage in Acts raises some good questions, it is the ignorance of the past that God "overlooked" that has my especial attention. To open one line of inquiry, it is a given that the Law was given to teach, to instruct. But the Law was "childish" in the sense that, as with children, it largely consisted of prohibitions and commands without explanation.

There are many instances throughout the Bible where it is evident that God is dealing with people as a parent with small children. The people themselves behave, in many instances, as if they were "childish," ignorant of the most rudimentary elements of adulthood in spiritual matters. Perhaps blood sacrifice is the most glaring example of the child-like knowledge of God early people had. I think Adam was the first spiritual "infant."

Certainly, Abraham and Sarah behaved like children. While the great patriarch is given as an example of faith, even arguing face to face with God, some of his actions were anything but good examples of trust and holy living. But if we credit him with immature knowledge, these things are much more understandable.

The Apostle Peter, in the first chapter of his epistle, gives us some foundation for the position of the lack of knowledge (immaturity) of early saints, even the imperfect knowledge of angels. It may well be that God, beginning with Adam, had to gain knowledge of this being He had made in His own image. The test in the Garden, I believe, was a real test in that God Himself did not know for certain what Adam would choose to do. But He did make provision, through Jesus Christ, for Adam's failure.

There is no doubt that the ancients had many superstitions. They thought a snail or slug "melted" as it moved along (Psalm 58:8, though K&D and other scholars offer alternative renderings), Jacob thought to influence the breeding of the flocks he tended for Laban by using "striped" branches placed in their watering troughs (Jacob offers much material in support of "immaturity"), Rachel's use of "Mandrakes" in the hope of conceiving.

Multiplying wives was another point of spiritual darkness that God seems to have overlooked in dealing with those of early days. Jesus made God's feelings plain about the subject, but it did not seem so important to these early "saints."

In sum, God certainly seems to have "overlooked," even, at times such as Jacob's striped "rods," to have honored some of these superstitious beliefs. Not that "Moderns" are a whole lot better off, look at what the translators of the N.I.V. did to appease the charismatics in rendering the word "language" as "tongue." Very sad.

The curious account of Naaman the Syrian, II Kings 5 and Luke 4:27, gives us more insight into the mind of God in His dealings with ignorance. God healed this man of his leprosy in spite of his superstitions and his compromising "deal" with Elisha. For those with a "bent" for the "Typology" of Scripture, much can be made of this whole account. But the cleansing of Naaman's leprosy as a result of his washing himself seven times in the Jordan would lend credence to the superstitions and "childishness," the immaturity and ignorance that God had to deal with.

Saul and the "witch of Endor" is another curious story. The fact that evil was at work throughout this history should help us to understand the many ways that God had to deal with these problems and work with what He had. And what He had was a great deal of spiritual immaturity and ignorance on the part of His people.

David, that great man "after God's own heart," was guilty of adultery and murder. The Psalms reflect a man who struggled constantly for spiritual understanding, a man who earnestly wanted to know the mind of God, but was hampered by his own ignorance and selfishness. But when he sinned, he accepted the responsibility of his actions and repented.

Moses, that great man of God, was tormented by his own incomplete knowledge and resultant failures. Many times Moses literally did not know what to do. He made a mess of his first attempt to help his people, committing murder in the process. He lost his temper at God Himself. But God honored Him for his faith and obedience.

The miracles throughout the Bible reflect works of God that attempted to deal with ignorance and superstitions, incomplete knowledge as well as His power and sovereignty. I am certain that this is the reason the miracles of the New Testament were done. They not only provided the "credentials" of the Lord and the Apostles, the early leaders of The Church, but also were necessary in the face of ignorance and superstition.

The Cannon of Scripture being closed, the increase of knowledge, thanks to The Lord and these early saints of The Church, such actions on the part of The Lord faded away. I believe Paul made direct comment on this in I Cor. 13.

It seems abundantly clear to me that God was, and still is, learning from us as well as we from Him. Certainly He is not striking dead the many Ananias's and Saphira's that are as guilty as they were, otherwise we would need a mortician as a member of every church. But with the fuller revelation of His mind and nature, with the vast increase in knowledge we have through the sciences, histories, etc., God no longer has to work in such ways as He did with "children."

If, in fact, the ancients were so ignorant as to believe they could build a tower to heaven, if they were so quickly mired in idolatry and disobedience so soon after the Flood, it is no wonder that God had to use strong, supernatural measures (confounding their language) to have any hope of accomplishing His purposes.

Children need discipline and instruction. But it is often impossible to provide a child a rationale for the parent's commands. A toddler can be told that touching a hot stove will hurt him but he often needs to discover this for himself. It is a lack of knowledge that prompts a child to stick a screwdriver into an electrical outlet. How much easier it would be on us parents if our children would simply obey us rather than suffer hurt.

But sin, disobedience, always carries hurt with it, no matter how much learning we have acquired. Sin is always the result of a heart that is not right with God. And, since He has the responsibility of the ultimate parent, we can expect our sins to be dealt with accordingly.

There have always been those that "despise instruction, hating their own souls," but God has always been quick to teach and honor obedience. "DROPOUT RATES FOR HISPANICS STILL CLIMBING!" Thus screams a daily paper.

"What does that have to do with anything?" you yell. Well, if people, regardless of ethnicity, despise instruction, a society suffers. As a nation, we are suffering from appalling ignorance. There is a case for the cultural "macho" attitude that Hispanic males have toward education that helps explain their own educational failure, but, overall, we are declining alarmingly in education across the board.

The "dumbing down" of America is the fault of an entire society that is not able, thanks to its rejection of God, to cope with the monumental failure of values and leadership. One must have an absolute, moral imperative, for doing what is right. God alone provides such an imperative, particularly if it requires sacrifice of selfish interests to the good of others.

Thoreau would walk miles through the snow to keep an "appointment with a particular tree!" "Now that is just plain dumb!" you say. Not if you understand his meaning. In his communing with God's natural creation, Thoreau and others like him are attracted to the marvel of nature and some places, even things like a particular rock or tree, come to be familiar friends. Certainly not as "totems" or pantheistic nonsense, though that was and is common to some but as things that stir our thoughts beyond the mire of mere clay. It was the corruption of this kind of nobility that led to "nature worship" and the building of idols, to the false worship of the stars, the "hosts of heaven," leading men to worship the creature more than the Creator.

Because of such foolishness God says He "... gave them over in the sinful desires of their hearts to sexual impurity for the degrading of their bodies with one another. They exchanged the truth of God for a lie, and worshiped and served created things rather than the Creator..." God further says, "Although they claimed to be wise, they became fools and exchanged the glory of the immortal God for images made to look like mortal man and birds and animals and reptiles."

In this same place God says that the invisible things of Him are clearly seen, being understood by His very Creation, the universe and all that is within it so that men are without an excuse for not knowing Him. This is a deep and sobering concept. But it is one of many reasons that I don't "hold" with "Secret Service" or "Carnal" so-called "Christians." God has, with all His works and His Word, given us more than enough to act responsibly and knowledgeably.

But we continue to confront ignorance. We no longer have any excuse, like the ancients, for superstitious nonsense. Those that engage in "tongues" and so-called "spiritual experiences" are badly self-deceived and bring nothing but shame to the Gospel and the Truth of God.

It isn't only ignorance that is to blame for the travesties practiced in God's name. We have been told that virtually half of 15 to 19 year old girls engage in premarital sex. There are some that say of that: "What's wrong with the other half?" "You've come a long way baby!" But my point is that, the flesh being what it is, many who engage in the hysterical shamefulness of the charismatics do it for their own glory, certainly not God's.

I ask you, what was it that really unseated people like Baker, Swaggart, Humbard, Falwell, et al. from their "thrones?" Many know of these people's desires for self-indulgence and the applause of the crowd. But, like Oral Roberts' stupid claim that God threatened to kill him if he didn't raise millions of dollars, like Swaggart's claim that God told him that he was the only man He could use to save the world, these silly pronouncements of God's "special handling" are seen for the egotistical and foolish things they are.

The sheer ignorance of Robertson's and Cerullo's use of phraseology like "Word of Knowledge," can't help but make one think of Joseph Smith's "peepstone, gold tablets" and rank plagiarism of the Old Testament to supply the bulk of his Book of Mormon and the JWs, pathetic attempts at scholarship by their perversion called the "The New World Translation" and other publications.

The fact that people like Robertson and others are called "Fundamentalists" and "Evangelicals" muddies the waters further. It certainly does not help the cause of Christ to have every hair-brained scheme done in His name accepted as the work of the Holy Spirit and every shouter of "Hallelujah" in His name thought to be speaking for Him.

Yet, such is the ignorance with which Satan does his dirty work. It is most fortunate that Jesus said that even though Satan's "ministers" appear as angels of light the children of God will always be able to tell the difference. "By their fruits we shall know them!"

"Respectability" is no measure of knowing the Lord either. The most "respectable" churches, Episcopalian, Anglican, Lutheran, are noted for their "respectability." But they are also noted for their empty piety and "Making long their robes." Of such are the likes of Robert Schuller. Squeaky clean on the outside while denying the truth of God's Word.

In the institution of The Church, The Lord provided for teachers. But these are "called" men. NO WOMEN! And we are told that men are to be very careful that they know of a certainty that they have such a calling or they face great condemnation. It is largely because many have assumed this role without God's calling that the churches are in such dire straits and are ridiculed by the world. Let's face it folks, if you behave like a nut, talk like a nut, you probably are a nut.

The preaching of the cross most assuredly does appear to be foolishness to those that are too hard of heart to listen. But nowhere in God's Word does He give approval for believers to behave like fools and spout foolishness. Neither will He countenance "educated" fools.

It is most unfortunate that so many "leaders" that profess Christ give the impression of latter day Elmer Gantry's or Amy "Simple's." It really makes it tough on those that are trying to warn the wicked with the honest truth of the Gospel. But for those of us who sincerely believe in the truth and integrity of God's Word, it becomes ever more important to give heed to its study, to being able to give "... the reason for the hope that is within us" and that we do so with "... gentleness and respect" toward those with whom we wish to convince of the truth of God.

But back to the subject of ignorance; it should seem obvious to all that if God requires it of us to be reasonable in our witness to others, that "hiding" the truth behind pious platitudes, religious clichés, "traditions of elders," liturgical and charismatic nonsense is sinful and a dereliction of our honest duty toward God and others. To "Study to show ourselves approved" is a solemn command of God. The necessity of this is easily seen by Satan's success in leading so many astray, even into absolutely silly, even deadly (Jim Jones) error. If God's people would give themselves to sincere and dedicated study of the Bible, the enemy wouldn't have things so much his way.

There has always been the problem of choosing teachers. In the world, a teacher, in order to work in state schools, must be a college graduate, pass necessary tests and then be credentialed in the subject he is to teach by the state. In spite of these safeguards, we still wind up with far too many unfit as teachers. How much more likely do you think it to be to have so-called "Bible" teachers when the criterion is absent or exceedingly minimal?

Thus it is that "Sunday school teachers" are abysmally ignorant, as are most that fill the pulpits of churches. So-called "Devotional studies" proliferate while scholarship gathers dust. What Wilkerson, Roberts or Schuller purvey as "truth" is widely quoted but the silence of Alexander McClaren, Whyte and Newell is deafening.

We want to be entertained, not study. The constraints and demands upon our time are horrendous. Time to study, to reflect, to commune with The Lord and even our own souls must be purchased at a great price in our society with its insatiable appetite and demands on our time. One might envy the poor, who have the time but lack the resources to enjoy their "liberty." Unhappily, many of the poor also have to work at only being poor rather than destitute or impoverished. And, thanks to a bloated bureaucracy and ever increasing taxes, more join the ranks of the poor every minute.

But I take it as a given that if someone thinks he is a child of God and is too busy to know the Bible thoroughly, that person is deceiving himself. It may well be that those that are drawn into the ranks of deception are "too busy" to search out truth for themselves. But "Wisdom is justified of her children!"

A very dear man, Bob Daveggio, keeps in touch with me in spite of his disapproval of some of my comments. I love this man and he has been through many trials of his own faith and remained faithful. I count on such men to be honest to me and keep me from getting off the track. We all need great friends like Bob. It is a tragedy when one finds himself without a close friend and I have been blessed with several.

But friendships require the sacrifice of time as well. Jesus said that we are his friends if we do as he commands us. The "doing" requires time. Jesus, as the closest and dearest friend anyone could ask for, "commands," not as a despot or tyrant, but for our good. As a true friend, he seeks our welfare, and he does so sacrificially. In this world, the greatest sacrifice we can give him is our time.

Money is important. How is that for profundity? But no one can purchase time; it is without price. We may earn an hourly wage and assess the value of time in some such way; but how to buy back a wasted hour, a wasted life? As millions of professing Christians watch hours of football, these same will complain that they don't have time for Bible study. Some will try to "buy God off" with tithes and offerings while He suffers from the lack of real fellowship with them.

It is certainly not profound that I would choose a vow of poverty (no, it is no great honor being poor) rather than "sell my soul" for a paycheck. But to earn one's daily bread and provide an honest living is a command of God. "If any not work, neither should he eat!" is still a part of God's Word.

What I am saying, to repeat, is that it is still God's requirement that those that say they represent Him before others study to answer; and reasonably. Such a requirement demands the sacrifice of time, time to study, reflect, pray, and know the mind of God.

I have opened several avenues of inquiry into the nature and working of God. These demand a great deal of study and insight. I sincerely hope that some of what I have written will move others to give more serious thought to these things and their own relationship to The Lord. I hope some of you will communicate your own thoughts to me on these things. No man is an island and, most assuredly, no man has a "royal path" to The Lord or to knowledge that is exceptional to him alone. We need one another.

But I do ask that, if the things I have been saying trouble you, please don't find fault or curse me until you examine them in the light of God's own Word rather than the prejudices and ignorance of "blind orthodoxy." You may be profoundly surprised by what is at the root of your perplexity with the things I am discussing.

Recently, Geraldo did a program called "The New Inquisition." It had to do with some of the evil perpetrated by churches and their leaders. I have witnessed, myself, much of what was being paraded on the show. But, then, some of the most horrible and shameful acts of men throughout history have been, and are being, done in the name of God. Such is the hatred of men and the Devil for the Truth.

The Assemblies of God churches came in for special attention on Geraldo. But what can one expect from an organization that breeds the likes of Baker's, Swaggart's and others like these? It is no accident that an organization which promotes hysteria, charlatanism, self-indulgence by its peculiar teachings should provide "leaders" like those mentioned. It cannot help but suffer such men to develop from such ignorance and heresy.

The Geraldo Show, Fundamentalists Anonymous and other such things will increase as the times become more desperate and the Truth of God more obscured by the evil that "religious" men do. Hitler and Saddam Hussein are examples of men who said God was on their side.

I know it is difficult for most of you to think seriously about the things I write about when your own circumstances are so hard and the whole world seems to be "going to hell in a basket." We watch our families, our children being destroyed by the system of evil all about us, we watch as those that lie, cheat and steal prosper and we think: "Why should I bother trying to do what is right?" Remember Asaph's same complaint?

But, perhaps, Asaph saw and understood much more than the end of the wicked when he entered the Sanctuary of The Lord? Just perhaps, he saw some of the things I have been writing about. Maybe that seemingly terse statement, "the end of the wicked," contains volumes of meaning.

Certainly if one understands the end of the wicked, one of necessity must also understand the end of the righteous which gives the patience to endure wickedness; that motivates to do right no matter what others do, to obey God regardless of the sacrifices. It also means that you will sell all for that "Pearl of great price," that you will put your hand to the plow.

God has not given us an easy road. What He has given us, if rightly understood, is purpose with joy in the work and, as pilgrims, a "land" that He says is beyond our imagination that requires extraordinary beings to carry on His eternal work and purpose.

I stand accused of being guilty of Rationalism, Progressive Revelationism, Arminianism, Pre-tribulationism, Dispensationalism and a host of other "isms." Not only do my "accusers" not understand what I am saying, most are too lazy, ignorant or blindly "orthodox" to search these things out for themselves. I can only hope that some will be as the noble Bereans and look into God's Word "whether these things be so."

But no honest inquiry into The Bible can help but lead the reader to the conclusion that much of what is written proves that God dealt with early people as "children" in their understanding of Him and His creation. The Psalms and other writings have a child-likeness to them that cannot be mistaken. They show a very simplistic understanding of The Lord and His workings.

Jesus, in His earthly ministry, dealt with this "childishness" constantly, even losing his temper on occasion. How very much like an older brother with his younger siblings. The Lord's question of them is most provocative: "How long will I suffer you?" That the Apostles and others exhibited "childishness" in understanding Jesus is beyond controversy. But he rightly expected them to "grow up" and be men.

With the the cannon of Scripture complete, with the vast increase in knowledge and science, none of us have, any longer any excuse for the ignorance and childishness that, once, God "winked" at. He requires, now, that all men everywhere repent and study to be approved rightly dividing the word of truth.

CHAPTER SIX

CHRISTIAN PERSPECTIVE

MARCH, 1991

Isaiah 1:18

The response to the last few issues of CP has been gratifying. I am encouraged by the thoughtful remarks of those that have taken the time to communicate. I hope more of you will give me your input.

With the chaotic conditions prevailing in our nation and the world, it is difficult to find the time to give serious attention to the things I have been writing and speaking about. And yet, if you really care about the things close to the heart of God, if you care about others and the work, time must be given to study and prayer.

The demand on our time is crushing. It seems almost impossible to draw away for a few moments to gather our wits and enjoy some degree of respite for our soul's (sanity's) sake. In spite of the best intentions and sincere desire to simplify our lives, the "beat" goes on and we find ourselves in continual frenzy to just get through another day. And, as we fall asleep, we wonder if anything we have done makes any difference or whether we have gained any ground.

"Toxic World Spreading Mysterious Chronic Fatigue Syndrome!" screams one headline. "Try separating out the stress of a baby crying at home from the strain of waiting for the computer at work to blink *On Line*, or determining whether today's headache was spurred by the office photocopy fluid, recycled air, sinus congestion or last night's glass of wine." The list of possibilities for "just plain tired" is seemingly endless.

I cannot accept from anyone that they are "too busy for God!" If you are that busy, something better be done about it, and quickly! No one understands the stress of "busy-ness" better than I do. And I know all too well the price of making the time for The Lord. But I also understand the far greater price for failing to do so.

I also understand that many are losing the "battle" of "just trying to make it!" from one day to the next. But if you think you are "trusting The Lord" and you are too busy for Him, you are deceiving yourself. He commands that we seek Him and His righteousness first and He will then meet our needs.

No one just gets up one morning and decides to become a "Dumpster Diver!" No, it takes time to become impoverished. In many cases, this is accomplished by failing to meet just one month's bills. But the decisions that bring people to such a miserable existence usually occur over a period of time. We are quick to agree that people must plan for success while never giving attention to the fact that people "plan" for failure as well. Of course no one consciously plans to fail; it just "seems to happen." But we can accept the fact that if one does not plan for success, a plan for failure is already assured, whether in our spiritual or physical lives. If we say we believe and have faith in God then deny Him of our time and resources, we can most certainly expect Him to call us to account. Our fellowship with Him, our honoring Him as God, our Father in heaven, takes time.

I wonder why kids don't play marbles anymore? As a child in "Little Oklahoma," I lived for shooting marbles. Any child worth his salt, to be acceptable in our company, had to have a good collection of "Puries, Boulders, and Stripies." A couple of "Steelies" had to be included as well. One had to be on the lookout for "Doughies," only used by the unscrupulous and "Cheaters." How many of you remember the incantation of "Here's the river, here's the snake, here's where you make your big mistake!" while kneeling in the dirt, drawing the appropriate symbols to foil your opponent's shot? Or, do any of you remember throwing a marble over your shoulder in order to find a lost one? This was one of the hazards of playing "chase."

In order to give the reader some idea of how serious I was about marbles, I came in second in the Bakersfield Championship in 1943. Such was the innocence of the times that a city could have a marble-playing championship for children while the world was plunged into war. Yes, there was a citywide championship for "marbles." But, then, there was no such thing as TV or gangs of kids shooting bullets at each other. Shooting marbles was certainly preferable but, then, children had a chance to be children in those long ago, simple days. I could read the papers, listen to Gabriel Heatter and Walter Winchell, hear news of battles over the radio, but bombs were not dropping on Little Oklahoma. Therefore, the "War" was an exciting and far-away thing, made real only by Superman, Captains Marvel and America doing battle against the "dirty Japs" and "rotten Knocksies." And even Bugs Bunny was doing his part alongside John Wayne, Humphrey Bogart and others.

There were the numerous military personnel in and about, the little flags in windows with blue stars indicating some loved one in the military (and, of course, an occasional gold star, commemorating the ultimate sacrifice). We children could see AT-6's and an occasional P-38 overhead from Minter Field.

Sometimes we were entertained by them engaging in mock combat. But God was sparing America from an enemy invasion.

I remember Ted Martin and I attempted a revival of playing marbles in high school at old Kern Valley High. But the times, they were "a changing" and we met with little success. Too bad.

Cap and rubber band guns, marbles, slingshots, the good, warm, honest alkali dust under our bare feet; and there was a truly marvelous place called "The Dump."

None of us had ever heard the word "Landfill" as children. The Dump was its progenitor. There were few as exciting places to visit as the Dump. Whenever grandad had to go to the Dump, I was quickly in the truck with him, all eagerness to explore this wonderful treasure trove of people's cast-offs. Truly, one man's trash is another's treasure but to us children, it was all hidden riches only awaiting discovery.

I still remember the time I became "wealthy as Croesus" as a result of my finding an entire, dollar bill. Nothing escapes the sharp eye of a child. No eagle is a match for the gimlet eye of the child seeking treasure. I was making my way up a hill of paper, cans, broken wood and glass when I spied it; a fresh, crisp, new, one-dollar bill. It was folded into a square no larger than about one inch. But I saw it.

To understand the magnitude of such a find, one must remember that at that time "penny candy" was really a penny, bread was five cents a loaf and an entire peach pie could be bought for fifteen cents. Pepsi, Coke and Nehi were a nickel. An entire dollar was real wealth.

My strict, religious up bringing caused me to give ten cents (a "tithe") of my treasure to the church (The church was the small one my grandad had built himself and pastored in Little Oklahoma in Southeast Bakersfield). But what was a dime to insure that The Lord would undoubtedly "bless" me in finding even greater wealth? Such is the innocence, as well as the often superstition and greed of children.

But, then, I had little acquaintance with the Holy Spirit except when that dread force would "knock old lady Walker off her hinges" or Mrs. Hall would jump up as though she had been "goosed" shouting "Hollogumba, hollogumba, hollogumba!" in our Sunday Service. I think it was a real tragedy for the churches when such good, clean fun was legitimized by the "respectable" Anglicans, Episcopalians and Catholics. As the "Glossalalia," it forces poor, simple Pentecostals to compete unfairly against "Bishops, Priests" and other "Swells."

As a man of simple tastes, I will still "hold" with the "stompers" and "thumpers" when it comes to just having a good time with your religion. Only when it is taken seriously does it begin to really hurt people. The simple ignorance and superstitions of us "Okies" in our little church was never, consciously, a pretense of Truth, but, rather, a social thing. No one was really deluded that God was so foolish as to think that others would ever be honoring God by such shenanigans.

The work of the Holy Spirit is to take the things of God's truth and make them plain to us. He makes His Word real and effectual in our lives. He does not glorify Himself or in any way behave unseemly or irrationally. "Let all things be done decently and in order" is one of the hallmarks of an honest and God-honoring church. The Church is an orderly institution with designated leadership that has proved itself in service and knowledge.

The "childishness" of the ancients required a "Tabernacle" and, later, a "Temple." In God's learning of men and their learning of Him, many changes took place. "In the past God spoke to our forefathers through the prophets at many times and in various ways." The Tabernacle was a necessary thing at one time. But it was only a "shadow" of the reality in heaven. Hebrews 8:5. At one time men needed a material, tangible evidence of God's work and location. But with the coming of the Holy Spirit to indwell believers, we became "The Temple of God!" Childishness was to give way to adulthood. The complaints, even peevishness and pettiness of the Psalms were to give way to the "New Covenant." God had brought men through the infancy of Adam, the childhood of Abraham, Isaac and Jacob, the adolescence of Moses, Samuel, David and Solomon, the Jesus and the early immaturity of young adulthood of the Apostles to those who would be responsible, knowledgeable and of mature age.

I have not forgotten how to "shoot" a marble but I no longer "live" to play marbles. The "treasures" of the Dump are things of long ago. The things of my childhood were exciting and great joy in their times. My memory is stirred by the preciousness of loved ones gone on to be with The Lord, my grandad, grandma, great-grandma, my daughter Diana, and others. Life has gone on in spite of joys and tragedies. Life is a changing thing. The hope is that through it all, one grows in knowledge and in the ability to accept greater responsibilities, to apply wisdom in helping others in the growing process.

A Negro woman, Abiola, has written a book about what Negro men ought to know about Negro women. Her thesis seems to be that Negro women are to blame for the failure of Negro men to lead families. Her solution, in part, appears to be that "The hole in black women's faces needs to be shut by black men."

Now, while a "punch in the mouth" might seem a tad extreme, it cannot be denied that women have a peculiar talent for "getting to" men by their words. To quote a man who, through his own foolishness ought to know, Solomon: "A foolish son is his father's ruin, and a quarrelsome wife is like a constant dripping. A quarrelsome wife is like a constant dripping on a rainy day; restraining her is like restraining the wind or grasping oil with the hand. Better to live on a corner of the roof than share a house with a quarrelsome wife."

Job certainly had his trouble with his wife. "Are you still holding on to your integrity? Curse God and die!" was his wife's solution to Job's troubles. Job's reply: "You are talking like a foolish woman!" One may well wonder why God had to even warn men about "multiplying wives" to themselves.

Holding out the ideal of a wife who is a gift of God, one who submits to her husband's rule, is diligent and cooperative in teaching and caring for her children and house, Solomon laments: "A virtuous woman who can find, for her price is far above rubies!" And just exactly what did Jesus mean by His warning to "Remember Lot's wife!"

And the complaint of most women today: "Where are the men who deserve my obedience to them?" The problem is theological. God commanded, in judgment of Eve's sin, that women would obey their husbands. He then commanded, in judgment of Adam's sin that he would have to accept responsibility for Eve! It should be patently obvious that to comply with God's command, both would be required to cooperate with the other. Each would have to accept God's judgment and obey for the whole thing to work out.

We are told in Romans that Adam was the "pattern" of Jesus. But unlike Adam, Jesus would be obedient in everything God had commanded. In Jesus' own words, he came to do the will of the Father and to please Him in everything. And so He did.

It may well be that God had hope in Adam which was not realized. This presumes a lack of knowledge on God's part for which He accepted all the responsibility. Adam's complaint against God for giving him Eve is, in part, justified. But Adam's own failure to obey is without excuse. It therefore remains that Adam was intended for great things, but in his sinful failure to obey God, became a "pattern" for God's ultimate hope of man even as the Tabernacle on earth was only a "pattern" of the things in heaven.

I have remarked to some that what is required in these days is a whole, New Systematic Theology based on the increased knowledge that men have, or should have, of God and His Word as opposed to the incomplete knowledge and Word they had in the past. The "childishness" should give way to adulthood, the mind of God in us as well as His Spirit. What exactly did Jesus mean when he said that: "The Kingdom of God is within you!" Unlike the need for "Tabernacles" built with hands, we are the "Temple of God" due to the indwelling Holy Spirit and because of this fact we are supposed to be "discerners" of The Truth, rightly "dividing" (understanding) God's Word.

It is obviously God's hope that we be "as infants concerning evil, but as men in understanding." (I Cor. 14:20). I ask all of you with access to a concordance to read each and every verse of Scripture that has the word "understand" and its derivatives. I believe you will be astounded at all that God has given us and expects us to know and understand.

In regard to our need of a new, systematic theology, a few examples will suffice. At the outset it is well to remember that the End of the Age there will be a "Famine of God's Word." This "Famine" will consist of a lack of teachers who really believe and know The Truth and can therefore teach accordingly. It is the paucity of such teachers that leads to the darkness (a nearly, total lack of knowledge and understanding of God and His Word that will be all-pervading, that leads to only a few believers living in this world at that time.

There will be, of course, many that say they believe in The Lord, that say they have knowledge and understanding, but their actions will betray them to real believers. Our own President says, for example, that he strongly believes in God. Not that naming The Lord saves anyone or vouches for saving faith, many charlatans do that, but President Bush won't even risk that much for fear of alienating millions of unbelievers (Liberals, Jews, A.C.L.U., perverts, etc.). After all, a real testimony and witness for God is a dangerous thing today even if you are not the President of The United States.

The root of the problem is in the self-willed ignorance of all the "Adam's" who will do as they please in spite of God's Word. The childishness of such an attitude is easily seen. It is childish to be a "spoiled brat" who demands his own way and, in flagrant disobedience, insists he knows better than the parent. Such "children" won't believe they are hurting and robbing themselves of any "inheritance" by their willfulness.

But the "children of the promise" will always be known by their obedience. They are the ones who seek always to please the parent. Their obedience is based on the knowledge that they are loved and will never be asked to do something that is not for their own welfare, though they may not understand the command.

For those that entertain some hazy idea that they would be "leaders and teachers of others" and have no need that "one should teach them," I ask you to thoughtfully consider some of the following things that I believe demand a new, systematic theology. And, I want you to consider whether, in view of God's Word and His natural creation, if you are not prejudiced by "orthodoxy" in regard to His "perfection," whether, in fact, He has attributes that belie the "party line" of some hazy concepts of omniscience, omnipotence and omnipresence. I also ask that you keep in mind the fact that God is reasonable and purposeful in all He does. I ask you to heed His admonition to us to "Come and reason together with Him." Isaiah 1:18.

In II Kings 13:21 we read that a dead man "touched the bones of Elisha and came alive!" Why would God do such a thing at the risk of promoting superstitious nonsense? In the same vein, why would He allow the appearance of Samuel to Saul at the conjuring of the witch of Endor? I Samuel 28:7

Why did God "take" Enoch and Elijah in a supernatural way?

Why the Shunammite's son, the daughter of Jairus, the widow's son, Lazarus, those that came out of the tombs at the crucifixion and their appearing to many in Jerusalem, why Dorcas, and Eutychus?

Why did the ax head float, was the stew "healed" by Elisha, the cruse of oil and the meal extended, the "burning bush," the plagues of Egypt, the cloud by day and the fire by night, the Manna and the quail, the serpent on a staff for healing, Aaron's rod that "budded," and so many other such "miracles"?

Why the casting of lots being seemingly honored by God?

Why and what "Urim and Thummim"?

Why did Jacob "wrestle" with an "Angel"?

Why did God honor beliefs such as the "healing" by Peter's shadow, and the touching of "aprons and napkins" that had come into contact with Paul?

If, in fact, as I believe, "...everything that was written in the past was written to teach us, so that through endurance and the encouragement of the Scriptures we might have hope" (Romans 15:4), if the Holy Scriptures are, in the words of Paul, able to make us "wise unto salvation," if the "times of ignorance God "winked at," if, by all the things The Lord has done and empowered others to do, if all these things were in the purpose of God to bring us to knowledge and understanding, to carry us through infancy, childhood and adolescence to adult men and women, I am utterly appalled by my own ignorance and lack of understanding!

If, as I propose, we come to The Lord, confessing our ignorance and, with sincere hearts, ask that He lead us in understanding, I believe He will answer us. He says that if any lack wisdom let him ask and he shall receive. But the qualifier is to ask in faith, nothing doubting. I have a mental picture of The Lord reaching out and desperately seeking people to come to Him. But what I see all about me are people behaving like children, acting as though God is blind or a fool!

In a discussion with a dear friend recently, the question of the "Sacraments" came up. These were developed through church councils of time past. They include the "Sacraments" of marriage, "The Lord's Supper," baptism.

A Sacrament, by the churches' definition, means a conveying of God's "Grace" supernaturally; they are the "rites" of the church, supposedly instituted by Jesus.

Now no one would dispute the fact that God instituted marriage, that Jesus commanded us to gather together and eat and drink in remembrance of Him, and that all believers are to be baptized in His name.

My friend is a "high churchman" of Episcopal persuasion. I do not doubt he has a heart for the things of God and wants to serve Him in truth. He recognizes the fact that the Episcopal churches are presently going through many troublesome battles. I think he recognizes the superstitious nonsense of the Roman Church's doctrine of "transubstantiation" and the "mystic nonsense" of "Baptismal Regeneration" but he is a believer, nonetheless, of some "mystical grace" being conferred by "communion" and baptism.

I do not say "mystical" in reference to my friend in a derogatory way. It's just that so much of the "traditions of the Elders" seems like religious "hokum." I believe putting away some of the so-called "mysteries" of such things is a perquisite to putting "childhood" behind us and going on to full understanding and adulthood. The fact that the Holy Spirit is a miraculous and supernatural work in our hearts in no way forces us to accept something as a "mystery" of which He expects us to have full understanding.

Can it be so hard to accept "communion" for just what it was in the early churches, a simple gathering in Jesus' name for the sake of fellowship, breaking of bread together, sharing, teaching, and learning? And baptism, why not a simple ceremony whereby you make a public declaration of your beliefs?

But for the early superstitions of those with a bent, and need, for "mysteries" it seems they "hit" on these to satisfy the on-going need of future generations with the same proclivity for emotional "experiences" and "magic formulas." Not unlike the "secret" rites of Mormons and Masons.

There are enough legitimate mysteries in God's natural creation to satisfy my needs of a lifetime. To simply look out into a star-studded night is to feed any need of imagination or, even, fantasy. The mind of man is a virtually unexplored universe of mystery; and the relationships between men, women and children? Now that should satisfy anyone's need for "mystery." So why hang "religious baggage" around our necks and invite the world's ridicule of The Lord and His people? But, sadly, there are always those that see the ridiculousness of "pope-blessed waters and medallions" and fail to recognize the same mentality in the "worship" of their own "icons."

It is one thing to enjoy "magic" as an illusion and quite another to cloak superstition with what is nothing more than religious prejudice or blind orthodoxy. The Lord may get a "kick" out of the one but certainly not the other.

The miracles of God throughout Biblical times, like the destruction of Sodom and Gomorrah and the walls of Jericho, and the "shadow going back ten steps" for Hezekiah at the prayer of Isaiah are to be understood in their historical framework of God's dealings with "children," this too in reference to the miracles of the New Testament.

The Lord, in both Old and New Testament times, lost His temper with the lack of faith and understanding on the part of people He expected to know better. God chose men who failed to live up to His hopes a number of times. One only need think of His hopes for Adam, Abraham, Moses, David and the Apostles to recognize this fact. But our children often disappoint us and we love them nonetheless for it though we do, at times, become exasperated with them.

The Lord has a temper, a sense of humor and righteous wrath; He hopes, dreams, loves and hates, plans and builds for the future, in short, is and does just like the creatures He created in His Own image but without sin, without selfishness. He is, in fact, our Father in Heaven.

Above all God loves and He loves perfectly. The love of God hopes all things, endures all things, bears all things, never fails, is not easily provoked, seeks not its own satisfaction but that of others, does not envy.

But it is hard to grow up and put away childish things at times. The "Old Adam" in children is "naturally" selfish, self-important, demanding, envious and rebellious. Sound familiar?

It is hard to accept adulthood with all its responsibilities. In the normal course of events we have so little time to enjoy the privileges of childhood. I so very much miss the "mysteries" of childhood. I miss being able to experience wonder at viewing the sun through a piece of colored glass, of laying on the ground or grass, observing the various insects go about their secret business, I miss the warm, secure lap of a loving grand and great-grandmother, the stern but reassuring presence of a "real man," my grandfather, a "rock of responsibility" I knew could not fail.

Such is the most fortunate childhood, wrapped in the security of being loved and cared for. Nothing is impossible for such children; they weave fantasies of castles and adventures, of distant lands and creatures of strange shapes and behavior. Santa Claus, the Easter Bunny, the Tooth Fairy, invisible playmates, these are the "rights" of children: I'm a real cowboy, you're a real Indian and this is a real six-shooter! There are real ghosts in the haunted house, the boogey man can get you, Lady Bugs do fly away home, little girls are very strange creatures and little boys are silly.

Inner Sanctum and Charlie McCarthy, the fun of being scared and laughing, wrapped in the security of loved ones, letting your imagination fill in all the pictures. Feats of derring-do and adventure with Robinson Crusoe and The Last of the Mohicans, And the blessedness of being surrounded by grown-ups who always knew what they were doing, and they could do marvelous and mysterious things, and they never hit or yelled or screamed at each other. The teacher, preacher and policeman were your friends; they were "helping" people, to be trusted as authorities. If your folks or the President said it, it was true. Frogs gave you warts and Santa knew whether you had been naughty or nice.

As children, we were free from the knowledge of mortgage or rent payments, utility and other bills, food "materialized" as did clothes and shoes, toys. We were "free" in our "blessed" ignorance. And this was true regardless of "privilege" or economic status. A child may know "want" but he does not understand it.

Then, seemingly suddenly, childhood is behind us, the "excitement" of becoming adults absorbs us and demands attention. The marbles, cap guns and dolls are making way for a job and accepting responsibility for other children; ours!

While we often think wistfully of the simplicity of our own childhood and long for the lack of complexity and joy of just being able to dream and watch the clouds, to enjoy going barefoot and pass the time "just doin' nothin'," the world with its demand for our time and resources wont go away. Now we face the rent, the bills, making the food, clothing and toys "materialize" for others.

And so it is that we begin to realize how we "had it made" as children and couldn't understand or appreciate it. We begin to realize how those loved ones that cared for us sacrificed their own wants and interests, ambitions and dreams for us. We begin to appreciate missed opportunities and, as we grow older and, hopefully, wiser, are able to appreciate what wisdom has to offer the young. And, sadly, too often tragically, have our wisdom despised.

The parent of a rebellious child begins to learn the heartfelt cry of The Father in Heaven: "Ye have set at naught all my counsel and would none of my reproof!" God does, in fact, just as any parent who loves and experiences the hurt of a child's rebellion, cry.

Are you the parent of a child old enough to make you understand what I am talking about? Have you had the bitter experience of having your counsel despised by a rebellious child to their own hurt and your grief? Then you are in a position to understand the heart of God as He reaches out for our understanding, for our acceptance of His counsel.

You know you would give your best in love to that child if only he would accept it. But, by despising your love, your authority, he reaps the whirlwind and breaks your heart. If only adulthood were not so painful and so full of responsibility. But, the real pain is in loving and caring for others only to be rejected; worse, to suffer over and over again as the object of your love continues to despise, to reject, to suffer shipwreck because of their "childishness" and selfishness, "Ever learning but never coming to a knowledge of the truth!"

And so God asks us to come to adulthood, to be men and women of The Truth and put away "childish things." He does not ask that we not enjoy the memories of childhood or forget its lessons.

No matter how old I get, my sons and daughter will be my "children." Though they be adults and have children of their own, they remain my "children." God has not given up parenthood no matter the maturity of His "children; though He literally cries out to us to "grow up!" even as we do to our own children at times, the element of position remains.

In my statement that we need a new, systematic theology, there is the idea that in this age of The Church, there is knowledge and understanding available that was lacking in previous decades. I say decades because the past fifty years alone have been "packed" with new learning from histories, languages, sciences, archaeology and experience beyond the imagination of the ancients or, even, scholars of the 1800's.

Yet, there have been no recent scholars of the caliber of a Henry or Ellicott. Harking back to my own studies of the systematic theologies of Strong, Warfield, Chaeffer, Hodge, they are filled with religiosity in an attempt to "answer" the hard questions; in so doing these men, though good men, failed, even misled many.

Others, leaning on these "weak reeds" for their own foundations, have only succeeded in muddying the waters of understanding further. The cry of today is for leadership that will put aside "childish" things and teach the things that lead to understanding and an ability to do God's work, the things that, by the power and authority of the Holy Spirit, excite the heart AND mind.

Though it was over thirty years ago, I still remember the excitement of earnestly committing to begin memorizing many verses and passages of God's Word. The old, familiar passages of John 3:16, Romans 3:23, 6:23 and 10:9, Ephesians 2:8,9, Isaiah 1:18, Psalm 103:12 and 107:2 and oh, so many others. It was, as David learned, that early "hiding" of God's Word in my heart that has kept me all these years. Good Book, Precious Book!

Even now, after all the years, the excitement of sharing these old, familiar promises of God with others has not abated. But the years have reinforced the truth that God has limited Himself, as II Corinthians 5:20 declares, to the use of "Ambassadors" to save others, those of us who possess the "Keys of The Kingdom," those of us who have the "power" to "Loose and to bind" men's sins, those of us who speak for God Himself solely by the authority of His Word and the indwelling Holy Spirit.

It is a sad and tragic thing to see so many "Sons of Sceva," so many "Simon the Sorcerers" doing business in The Lord's name and not called to account by a Peter or, even, unclean spirits. But God expects us to be adults, to have learned the "whys" and "hows" of the past and utilize the learning, knowledge and power He has made available to us.

It is not that Ananias and Sapphira are no longer among us, that "Judaizers" are not still plying their trade, that Diotrephes no longer "loves to be first," that Hymenaeus and Alexander have given up "blaspheming," but where are the men of God who can "deliver over to Satan," who can tell the "young men" to take out the bodies of liars and hypocrites in the middle of the church service? In short, where is the fear of God against wrongdoing even in the churches? Does no one any longer believe or care that God has said: "Be sure your sins will find you out!" or that: "It is a fearful thing to fall into the hands of the living God!" that: "It is appointed unto men once to die and after this the judgment!"

"Ichabod" may well be already written over the door of the Church. It is certain she no longer says: "Silver and gold have I none, but what I have, I give unto thee, in the name of Jesus Christ of Nazareth rise up and walk!" And certainly the likes of Oral Roberts cannot make such a statement.

"I sought for a man and I found none!" God once said. What do you suppose He is saying today if we but had ears to hear? Where are the "Elijahs" and "Nathans" of God? Today's "wannabes" seem to be too busy building their own empires and reputations, too busy begging for money and prestige to see even their own pride and foolishness. But ask Rex Humbard, Jim Baker, Jimmy Swaggart what they have learned, if anything, about mocking God or making Him look like a foolish beggar! These are definitely not the "stuff" of a Luther, Knox or, even, a Spurgeon.

For the many who stand in doubt of our need for a new, systematic theology, for those that think my statements about blind orthodoxy and its comparison with the "Phariseeism" of old to be too strong, to those of you who think you know something of God and His Word, I invite you to a study of the book of Romans. This alone should convince anyone with a heart for understanding and a love for The Lord and His Word. The eighth and ninth chapters alone spell out what I am driving at. Paul was given "visions" and "revelations" that he said, "man is not permitted" to utter. II Cor. 12:4. Daniel plainly said at the close of his writing that he was told: "Go your way, Daniel, because the words are closed up and sealed until the time of the end. Many will be purified, made spotless and refined, but the wicked will continue to be wicked. None of the wicked will understand, but those who are wise will understand."

But if the book of Revelation, The Apocalypse, is a reading of the end of the age, Jesus says: "Do not seal up the words of the prophecy of this book, because the time is near."

Given the few examples I have offered, I think it is clear that while "prophets and angels" desired to look into these things in times past, that it falls to those living at the end to understand and act on that understanding. Else how to know the signs and preach and teach knowledgeably without appearing the fools like Oral Roberts, Pat Robertson, et al.? How not to fall into the trap of even good men like the great theologians of the past?

The entire Word of God should now be plain to us, devoid of "mysterious clap-trap." We are called of God to be, to live and speak, as men and women of understanding and knowledge. And, to be effective, our speaking should be with the power and authority of God's Holy Spirit within us. No matter what knowledge and understanding a person may have, The Word, no matter how true, will have no effect for God's purposes in the mouths of those without the Spirit of God indwelling them. The sons of Sceva had the right "formula" but did not know God and the Devil and his servants know the difference.

No amount of "preaching the Gospel" in the mouth of unregenerate men can save others. People are brought under conviction of sin, are brought to true repentance by God's Word and The Holy Spirit only through one who himself knows God personally; so much for so-called "mass evangelism."

We freely grant that people who refuse to learn are fools. A person who makes the same mistakes repeatedly is a fool. We accept that people are supposed to grow out of childhood, accept the responsibilities of adults and behave with increasing maturity and wisdom.

Why should it then be so difficult to accept the fact that God expects the same of us, that He rightly expects us to learn from all the ages past, to learn in a growing and maturing way, to accept the responsibilities of knowledge He has provided, to seek wisdom and apply all He has given us to do so? But, of course, only those with a true heart for God will do all this.

And what is so unreasonable about God expecting us to have a fuller understanding of Him and His works and Word than those of the past? If, as I believe, there is a "famine" of His Word, if people are perishing for the lack of knowledge, it is not God's fault, it is the fault of those that know better but are not doing better. Certainly "Where there is no vision the people perish." But it is not a "vision of angels" etc. that is needed; it is a vision of the work and what is required to accomplish it.

I am maintaining the position that unless credence is given to the call for a new systematic theology, no progress against evil is possible. I will not accept the "Doom-saying" of so many that only try to call attention to themselves. I will maintain hope as long as there are those that will listen, will try to understand and prove it by their lives, as long as there are those that read their Bibles and pray, that try to "witness" and continue to tell others of what God has done for them.

God has warned that His Spirit will not always strive with that of man's. Now there has to be conflict in order to have strife. An omnipotent, omnipresent and omniscient "force" or "entity" does not strive. God has made it plain that He needs us, that He is limited in reaching the hearts of others through His "Ambassadors." That is the "high calling of God to those of His own. It carries with it immense privilege and responsibility, it makes of us, "joint heirs" with Jesus, it makes us "priests and kings" but it requires our putting on true humility in service to others, faithfulness, commitment and consistency. And it requires grown-ups, not children, real men and women who, with knowledge and understanding, can minister to others.

"Let all things be done decently and in order" is God's way. He is not a fool and His people do not do foolishly. God is not only loving, He is preeminently reasonable. We need, desperately, men and women who understand Him in this way and will study to serve acceptably. While I may privately believe the "night" is fast approaching when no man can work, we are to continue, right to the very end, as those that walk in the light, as those that have that "certain hope."

Paul said that: "I consider that our present sufferings are not worth comparing with the glory that will be revealed in us. The creation waits in eager expectation for the sons of God to be revealed. For our light and momentary troubles are achieving for us an eternal glory that far outweighs them all." Anyone who has this hope cannot but show it in their lives, honoring The Lord in all they do, constantly trying, no matter the failures, the "battering" and "hammering" of the evil one and his servants, no matter the evil of his system that seeks, always, to destroy them.

But Bunyan said it so well. It is either "Pilgrim's Progress" or you are none of His. I sincerely pray you are "progressing."

CHAPTER SEVEN

CHRISTIAN PERSPECTIVE

APRIL, 1991

John 17:3

"Life is a crap-shoot!" The philosopher who made this profound observation is forgotten to me but his point is well taken. It reminds me of the short time I lived in Las Vegas when I was a young boy. We lived within six blocks of the Golden Nugget and it was during the time of the premier of "My Friend Irma Goes West" with Jerry Lewis and Dean Martin.

I will never forget the sight of Jerry being towed on roller skates behind a Cadillac convertible down the "main drag" or the stand-up comedy routine with Marie Wilson. Nor will I ever forget the little ditty she gave about fishes: "Of all the fishes in the sea, my favorite is the Bass; he climbs up in the seaweed trees and slides down on his hands and knees." Children remember some of the most amazing things, often to the chagrin of their parents.

"Mama was a pistol!" (Not to be confused with the very popular "Pistol Packin' Mama") is more than the catchy title of an old song. It fairly describes my own mother. While I was raised, primarily, by my maternal grandparents I am grateful to my mother for adding an important dimension to my early childhood and teenage years.

It was during one of the periods my brother and I would visit with our mother and the latest stepfather that I enjoyed the cosmopolitan flavor of Las Vegas. The stepfather, Jim Blaine in this case, had a job as a Disc Jockey at the local radio station. That was a most important and interesting position. My brother and I enjoyed our visits to the station and I have fond memories of that period of time in my life.

I love the desert and the combination of the excitement of Las Vegas and the wilderness close at hand was hard to beat. Our mother always entered the equation as a promoter of excitement in her own right. While she had a violent temper and my brother and I were, many times, partners in fear because of it, she made life interesting for us.

Mom loved music, as did my grandparents, and I attribute my own ability as a musician with a wide range of musical tastes to the combination of my grandparents and "Little Oklahoma" and travels with mom. No matter where we lived, music was always playing and I listened with equal enjoyment to Ernest Tubbs, Fats Waller, Spike Jones, Vaughn Monroe and Benny Goodman.

But one impression of Las Vegas troubled me as a young boy. Going to the local grocery store, I watched as a young woman with a baby in her arms take the change from her purchases and deposit it in one of the ubiquitous slot machines on her way out of the store. I'm not sure why this troubled me, I only know it made a vivid impression and I still recall it clearly.

The lure of gambling is well known. I learned early on that I could never be successful at it. Given a fifty-fifty chance, I will usually pick the wrong number. Maybe I was bothered by the idea that a young mother with a baby in her arms had better ways to spend her money than throwing it into a "one-armed bandit."

Sometimes, it is worth it to take a "chance." We read in The Bible about an archer who drew his bow at "random" and struck King Ahab, mortally wounding him. (I Kings 22:34). Personally, I believe God Himself directed that shaft. If so, the bowman certainly could take no credit for marksmanship.

It may be that Augustine, the great and venerable, early theologue of the church read this story and decided to "box" himself in with his theory of predestination. Though he faced a lot of "fancy foot-work" in trying to maintain this position in spite of its paradoxical conclusion, he held on, as far as we know, to the end of his life. The "gamble" explicit in the theory is that if men are, according to Augustine and, later, Aquinas and Calvin, "predestined" to "election," how to make sense of any moral imperative that would be incumbent on mankind as a whole? Why not, if God has already decided who is saved and who is lost, "Eat, drink and be merry for tomorrow we die!"

Over the years, many an interesting discussion, sometimes violent, disagreement has been waged over the issue. "Predestination versus Free Will" is always an interesting "philosophical entertainment." But reason dictates that if God has already decided you are going to hell, eat drink and be merry. In fact, rob, cheat, lie, steal and do as you please; how can you make it any worse for yourself?

Ah, well, there are always those that think they have the liberty to be astute in the affairs of this world and leave their brains at home when talking "religion," and, "blasphemous" as the statement may appear to some, the same thing can equally apply to Augustine, Aquinas and Calvin. What, one may well ask, did Aquinas really believe he had accomplished when he came to the end of his life and pronounced all that he had done as "... nothing but straw!" If true, a whole lot of theologians built their systems of just such "straw" and I suspect they will make a satisfactory "fire" in the end leaving nothing but ashes.

But, what can one expect of those that hold the reputations of men in more esteem than the plain Word of God? By what standard do we judge Calvin the arbiter of God's Word and accept his approval of burning Servetus at the stake? It is no accident that Dante, Milton, et al. had such ignorant and superstitious views of God and His Word having been obscured by such well-intentioned "defenders" and "exegetes"

It almost seems that many of the church fathers were intent on "out Pauling Paul" when it came to Peter's comment on things "hard to be understood." But, of course, Peter was talking about the "unlearned and unstable," not men of such stature as Augustine. However, I do wonder what Augustine might have done differently if he, as Luther, could have foreseen what others would do with his teachings?

A "happy wandering" through light reading like Strong's Systematic Theology gives us a clue to the extent of "propagandizing" points of view. It is not that Strong was not a worthy exegete, but he, like Augustine, Aquinas and Calvin could be just as guilty of taking a book to say a paragraph, and, even drawing a wrong conclusion.

If it were truly the objective of Aquinas to avoid "...frequent repetition [which] brought weariness and confusion to the minds of the readers," and to "Endeavor.... to set forth whatever is included in sacred doctrine as briefly and clearly as the matter itself may allow," he missed the mark by a considerable distance.

"Plain manna" just doesn't do the trick for those that have "their mouth set" for more exotic fare. When dear, old brother McGee said: "It is time we speak the Word of God in the language of the peoples of the world. This is the kind of 'tongues movement' that I'm interested in," he must have meant more than a slap at the gibberish spouting of the charismatics. I believe he meant more, also, than the outreach of Through The Bible Radio.

McGee was a simple teacher. Though well educated, he did not vaunt his schooling. He tried to glorify Jesus and make God's Word plain to others. Those are hard goals upon which to improve.

If "mysteries" are wanted, life is full of them. A "pet" one of mine is my accumulation of socks that lack mates. Too bad some of our latter-day "theologians" couldn't turn their attentions to things of such a practical nature. I'd give a "pretty" to have an answer to such real mysteries. Come to think of it, I'll bet you they have the same problem with their socks. And why on earth don't we just throw them away; another worthy mystery.

You see, practically speaking, washing machines and dryers do not "eat" socks. Yet, at any given time, these nefarious machines can receive a bunch of perfectly matched socks and, when you least expect it, one will come up missing; a real conundrum more than worthy of an Anglican or Baptist seminary teacher to expound upon.

My point, silly as the example may seem, is that many of these worthies might better spend their time on such practical issues than continue to muddy the waters of understanding by their "pilpuls" not far removed from the number of angels dancing on the head of a pin or what to do if a filament of cotton finds itself inadvertently mixed in a batch of wool. A good, Talmudic scholar will have a more reasonable answer to such problems than some other theologians. Perhaps all of this goes back to some very fundamental basics of what Jesus and the Apostles tried to teach, particularly in the area of being good "servants" of God.

The night of the "Last Supper," Jesus himself washed the feet of the Apostles. He says he did this as an example of the attitude we are to have in service to him and to others. We are never to be "too good" to serve in any capacity he calls others to. No work he gave as an example is to be "beneath" us. Now the "Old Adam," the "Flesh," the Ego, hates this and is in rebellion against any such thinking.

The attitude of a real child of God is to seek ways to serve. In Psalm 123:2 we read: "As the eyes of slaves look to the hand of their master, as the eyes of a maid look to the hand of her mistress, so our eyes look to the Lord our God." Unhappily, this is not the attitude of most professing "Christians!" On the contrary, most seem bent on avoiding work for God unless it fits their fancy of being meant for "better things." Far from asking: "What can I do?" let alone actually anticipating the desires of The Lord, these try to avoid any manner of work that is "beneath" their "vaunted" status (beneath and vaunted in their eyes alone).

When I was a boy and we had recently moved to the mining claim in Boulder Gulch, I had the whole Sequoia National Forest as my playground. Ecstasy! But grandad didn't quite trust me to take a gun and immediately set out to claim this wondrous domain. He knew that at eleven years of age, I had a few things to learn first.

But I knew grandad. Children are marvelous "cons" when they put their minds to the task. I desperately wanted to get out and explore this treasured wilderness but, I also wanted to take a gun with me in case of the usual Indian uprisings or any other practical and anticipated menace that might arise like a bear or lion attack.

My plan was elegant in its simplicity. There was much work to do to make the cabin habitable and firewood was always needed. I set to with a will to show grandad how seriously I took these responsibilities. I cut wood, fetched water from the well and even looked for other things to do. And all this without even being asked or threatened! I actually asked grandad if he had any other chores I could do! Looking back, I know I risked my grandparents' questioning my sanity but, so intent was I on my goal, I didn't even stop to think how utterly disquieting my behavior must have seemed.

Now grandad didn't hold with loafers or laziness. I was always taught, and made, to carry my share of the load (there were the usual thoughts of rebellion and hazy concepts of abuse and child labor laws in my mind but, in the end, I didn't fail to carry out orders). But to actually ask if there was any work to do? That is childhood heresy! An act that would get any self-respecting kid drummed out of the corps! Fortunately there weren't any other kids around to witness my apostasy; except my younger brother.

Now Ronnie, my nemesis (read: younger brother and fink), was not taken in by my newfound religion of obedient industry. At the end of the day, and what a day it had been, grandad made the kind of pronouncement which all parents think is praise. He said to my grandmother and great-grandmother: "A certain young man really made me proud of him today! He did what he was supposed to do without being told and even asked if there was anything else he could do to help!"

The "fink" then piped up: "Yeah, he just did it so you would let him take the gun out by himself!" There is no wrath such as rises up to confront the truth when you have been found out in a well-executed plan to deceive.

Now, while I have never been one to hold a grudge, and while this only happened forty-five years ago, I have recently forgiven my brother his base canard against my integrity. Of course, I assume the proper degree of repentance on his part for so nefarious a calumny. If not, forget it! In time, I was entrusted with the "artillery" (no thanks to "you know who") and was able to claim my rightful place with Kit Carson and other worthy, mountain men but I never forgot my attempt to deceive grandad by my "good works."

As I have pointed out in other writing much of The Bible, particularly the Old Testament, makes no sense unless we take the position that God was learning about people and they were learning about Him. That much of what God has done is only understandable in a context of His literally dealing with children as a parent should be equally obvious.

Ah, parenthood! The bitter-sweetness of raising children (too often, these days, little "devils"), but when a parent faces the hoosegow for even spanking a child, what should a society expect? The total asininity of laws that on the one hand make parents responsible for their children, and on the other, deprive them of the means of exercising any authority. Such a society is obviously doomed to raising devils, not children.

Under the present laws both my mother and my grandfather would have been cooling their heels in the local gaol. But I survived and, in retrospect, deserved "most" of the discipline I received. The very imperfection of parents prevents me from saying "all." While it is true that I would gladly put the noose around the neck of any monster that truly abused and hurt a child, we have inherited the whirlwind in going so far in allowing the "State" to dictate to parents.

It was during WWII and another episode with our mother that Ronnie (you know, the "fink?") and I, with the usual child's love and familial affection decided to do a really nice thing for Mom. We were living in San Pedro at the time and it was exciting to watch the great, gray ships of war going through the harbor.

Mom was a late riser and without adult supervision, two little boys can be quite creative. It occurred to us that it would be a very kind thing to show her our appreciation for all she had done for (to?) us. Now how were two, small children to be able to do something really grand for their momma, early in the morning, with no adults around. Boggles the mind, doesn't it?

Inventive and imaginative little chaps that we were, we finally hit on "doing the dishes." Now, gentle reader, I was about five years old and my brother, four. If you have had the inexpressible joy of raising children through those early years, you might wonder how two children, four and five years of age, "do the dishes" without adult supervision? I will, of course, explain.

There were the usual plates and silverware but those items were simply too pedestrian to warrant our genius and industry; simply too unworthy of the zeal we had to really impress our mother with our "good works." And so it was that, filling the bathtub, we submerged Mom's toaster and waffle iron in its depths along with a copious amount of bubble bath. Of course, there was a lot of water and soap and the two appliances hardly made a dent in the tub's capacity.

Casting about for more items that were obviously in need of "cleaning," we tossed in a clock and electric iron. I think a curling iron also made the tub and some other miscellaneous items too mundane to recall; lastly, how to do the actually "washing?" Well, nothing but climbing into the tub ourselves seemed reasonable. And thus it was that Mom, finally awakened by the joyful sounds of her little "darlings" splashing and laughing, hard at work in their worthy occupation, and came into the bathroom.

The scene in my mind's eye, after lo these many years, shifts somewhat. I seem to recall our mother's jaw hanging open, the most amazing look of horror on her face as I raised the waffle iron from its soapy depths in salute to our labor of love. I do recall, specifically, that one of her girlfriends had spent the night and mother, to her undying credit, asked her to please take a hairbrush to us, as she was afraid to.

"Love's Labor Lost" is more than the title of a musty, old novel. It was quite real to my brother and me. Not only didn't Mom appreciate our act of affection, she actually seemed to respond in a very negative way. That we survived with our "heinies" intact was a miracle.

But our intentions were honorable (well, partly, at least) and we were slow to show such industry again. There was my scrubbing the toilet with her toothbrush but I have found that a rather common misstep among the more responsible children. In retrospect, maybe it isn't so hard to understand why I was raised, primarily, by my grandparents?

Well, what is God to do with such children? If earthly parents are any example, and I believe they are, God has a tough row to hoe. His "children" often mean well but good intentions are worthless. There is actual work to do and the laborers, in the words of Jesus, "are few." Of course, Jesus also said only a few are going to enter through that straight gate to life. That makes the work of even more importance and the burden on workers even heavier.

It certainly complicates matters when professing "Christians" make The Lord look foolish with childish attempts at the work He wants done. Often, such "work" is simply "religious" and is recognized as such. Most of this stuff is rightly seen as relatively harmless, like the charismatics waving their arms and hollering gibberish, but some of these things, like churches contemplating, in some cases actually, ordaining homosexuals is downright destructive and spitting into the face of God Himself! There is no sin in God's sight as abominable as sexual perversion including adultery, I might say especially adultery. For this cause He once destroyed the world by a flood. He destroyed the cities of Sodom and Gomorrah as an everlasting testimony to His hatred of this abomination.

At a time when our nation is basking in the "easy victory" of Iraq, when "patriotism" is once more "fashionable," it is well to remember that nothing I have written about has changed in regard to God's judgment. Men may think God is "asleep at the switch" but remember He has warned that when He has had enough, His judgment will come swiftly.

And there is nothing that has shamed Him and our nation as much as the perversion of homosexuality. Hardly a day goes by that we don't read or hear of some new "progress" of the perverts and their father, the Devil, have made in "legitimizing" their damnable perversion. The two most recent have been an attempt to pass legislation putting perverts in the same class as ethnic minorities. If this legislation passes, it will be a felony to write or speak about these perverts, as God requires His people to do. The other thing is a Master Card stamped "Dallas Gay Alliance." This Alliance of Satan was granted a Texas credit union charter in 1988 and was given a Master Card license after passing a financial audit late last year. The interest rate will only be 14%.

We already know that, because the very halls of Congress accommodate perverts, they have political clout. It is Satan's intention to do as he has always done in promoting this sin by giving the queers financial clout as well.

As I have always pointed out, God hates prejudice and bigotry. But He also hates perversion. God does not give His people license to harm others. "Gay bashing" is a sin as far as actually, physically attacking another human being. But God commands us to warn the wicked and I choose to make the warning indelibly clear. This not only gets the attention of the wicked, it invites the enemy to see me as a clear target in his attempts to legitimize this perversion. I wish to make myself as clear a target as possible so there will be no mistaking my own position; no mistaking any seeming ambivalence or equivocation on my part.

Now, of course, there is always the accusation of being "homophobic" directed at people like me. Were it not such a somber subject, it would be laughable to think that any Christian should have a phobia, clinically an irrational fear of something and thereby homophobic being a nonsense word contrived by Satan's servants, and about standing up to the Devil and his children in this regard. Sexually normal people are not afraid of perverts, a claim by perverts which is patently silly; they have a very legitimate revulsion towards sexual perversion. The consequences are entirely in God's hands as long as we do what is right and nothing could be "righter" than fighting against perversion.

The Apostles were whipped and thrown into prison for being obedient to God. Eventually, all but John were martyred. Are we to risk less? I think not. But only The Holy Spirit will give us the courage of our convictions even as He did for them. We believe that or lead lives of fear and God has "...not given us a spirit of fear, but of power and of love and of a sound mind."

Satan is a liar and the father of liars. A certain "Bishop" Spong has been one of the devil's more recent tools. He is quoted as saying that he doesn't know of "any biblical scholar today who takes the birth narratives (of Jesus) as literal truth" and asserts that attempts to defend the scientific truth of the Genesis accounts of creation "have absolutely no credibility in the world of biology." He further declares that the Apostle Paul was a homosexual. While he admits this is not an original idea of his (he is aware that the Devil has tried this lie a number of times), he does take a lot of credit for his attempts to "Rescue the Bible From Fundamentalism."

This deluded follower of the "That Old Deluder" is the Newark Episcopal bishop. He rebukes Biblical inerrancy and fundamentalist theology as "hopelessly outdated and unrealistic." Naturally, Spong plays fast and loose with all sorts of things like his ignorant use of the term "fundamentalist." But there are a lot of "crazies" like the charismatics that supply the "ammunition" for the enemy. He also appears to be totally ignorant of biology and the work of the Creation Research Society. He also seems to be totally ignorant of an entire spectrum of solid Biblical research that easily refutes his own opinions.

It is tragic that, because of "denominationalism," some continue to be called after "Cephas, Apollos, and Paul" (read: Baptists, Lutherans, Nazarenes, etc.) and that some, like the charismatics, make God look foolish. With such divisiveness, foolishness and arrogance, Satan has a field day.

It is not surprising, when the "trumpet gives an uncertain sound," that the enemy can have his own way. The silly "Jesus Seminar" that calls God's Word untrustworthy, the Presbyterian task force recommendation that the denomination ordain perverts, the law in San Francisco permitting perverts get "partnered" with the legal sanction of normal, married people, a doctor censured because of her legitimate fear of AIDS, all this and more is part of reaping the whirlwind of unbelief.

"Anti-gay violence escalates in major cities, reports say," is a recent headline. "Homosexuals' children fight taunts, stigma" is another. One wonders what is to be expected when perverts are not only allowed but encouraged to flaunt their perversion; a pat on the back? And what is to be said about a society where perverts are able to flaunt their perversion and then ask that same society to protect them? Yet, a society that condones adultery, that passes legislation making God's thoughts on the subject look like a quaint anachronism is doomed to chaos and His righteous judgment.

Both perversion and adultery were capital offenses punishable by death according to God's Word and commands. He has not changed His mind about these things and no laws of men or changes in a culture will make them less of an abomination. It is a fact of God's Word that He considers two people married when they "come together," to use the euphemism. A marriage is not a ceremony or "piece of paper" in His eyes. He requires the commitment of absolute faithfulness to one another in the relationship and gives no room to equivocate short of death or its spiritual equivalent, adultery, in regard to divorce. "The two become one" in His sight; but people find that laughable in today's world but God does not! What do you suppose would happen to the preacher who insisted on this requirement of God's Word today?

TVs and VCRs are marvelous inventions. But they have made every conceivable abomination known to men available to the smallest child at the press of a button. I recently learned of a grandmother who bought her three -year-old granddaughter her own VCR! This is one woman who either cares nothing about the little girl or was out of town when brains were passed out (since I have the unhappy "privilege" of knowing this adulterous woman, I suspect both reasons).

I minister to a few people and families that know the truth of all these things. I know that George and Cathy, Steve and Julie, Jude, Ross and Teri, Bob Daveggio and others would be appalled by anyone suggesting that a three-year-old should have their own VCR. But such is the perversity of sin that sinners do not distinguish between the welfare of children and the capacity of the enemy to use these devices for their destruction.

Madness! A world plunging toward Armageddon in its madness yet it will not tolerate a "God-mad" man! "Away with such a man!" the world howls. The problem is that the only hope people have is such men, men who will count their lives for nothing because of their love for God and His Word. But it is the "madness" of "reason" that the world hates. The God-mad man is the sanest and most reasonable of men. But only, as the Apostle Paul points out, if they truly believe in God and point to Him as the only hope of this poor, sin-soaked and weary, old world.

The closer we walk with The Lord in the light, the more His Word dwells within us, the more Spirit-filled we become, the more obedient and useful in the work we will be, the more reasonable we will be in contrast to a mad world sunk in the darkness of evil. "Children of the light" should not be an empty or "religious" phrase. We are called to be the most reasonable and practical of all people.

Part of the "Crap-shoot" is having to contend with the W.V. Grant's, Peter Paul's, Peter Popov's, Jim Baker's, Swaggart's, Ken Copeland's, Mario Cerullo's against whom even the Robertson's and Schuller's look good by comparison. And look at Jerry Falwell ordered by a judge to pay off a foolish "bet" ($5,000) to a pervert because of his ignorant remarks! But I do applaud his trying. Small wonder the term "fundamentalist" has fallen into disrepute when all these people claim to be "fundamentalists!"

Dear old brother McGee and I agree that faithfulness and obedience should characterize the Christian life. He would also be quick to agree that reason and practicality would also mark such people; but how few there are in positions of authority. Who do we have? Billy Graham? a man who preaches a good, simple message but who refuses to confront the real evils tearing a world apart, a man who allows rank unbelievers to share his pulpit?, a man who would credit the pope with spiritual insight and "Christian" leadership?

Where were you, Billy, when poor, Anita Bryant was taking a stand against perverts as teachers? You were silent as these "abominations" destroyed her. You showed you had no backbone for a real fight with the devil!

The "Sanballats" constantly try to interfere with the work, constantly try to discourage and tear down. But we are called to fight evil, to build for The Lord and encourage one another and our families in the battle. Concern for others will drive us to prayer and hiding God's Word in our hearts, will cause us to love The Lord, trust and depend on Him as we see answers to our prayers. Remember at all times that Jesus came not to save the world but to save a few out of it. He came as a "Testimony" against the evil and wickedness of a lost world, to bring a "sword," the Gospel that divides the "sheep" from the "goats." Only in that sense are we "peacemakers."

"Meaningless! Meaningless!" says the Teacher. "Utterly meaningless! Everything is meaningless. What does man gain from all his labor at which he toils under the sun?" Ecc.1:2,3. Reminds you of the words of Aquinas at the end of his life, doesn't it? Yet Solomon voices the very thoughts that solemnly intrude into most men's minds. And, apart from the truth of God, what else is there?

Those that say and do not have made it a life-long habit to rob God of His tithes and offerings and are not likely to change; their treasure consists of a library of VCR movies, etc. and where their hearts are, there will their treasure be also. Somehow, though, I don't expect God will have much use for the "treasure" they have stored up for themselves in the day of His wrath.

The "tithe" is not a part of the "Law." Anyone who teaches this is either just plain, Biblically ignorant or simply trying to cheat God. Tithing comes from the earliest times of God dealing with people. For those that think they know something of the "typology" of Scripture, look at the example given us of this whole subject in Hebrews and try to make something else of God's clear intent in this regard.

But, as the old saying goes: "Preacher, you have left off preaching and gone to meddling!" Besides, if a person has no true heart and motive for giving to God's work, if they lack even enough interest in the subject to seek out God's Word in this regard, nothing I have to say will be of any consequence. But it is truly an enigma that so many that I have met over the years can claim to love God, can claim they know something of The Lord and His Word, and yet do all they can to get away with robbing God!

It all does point up the fact that I have tried to stress that much of God's dealing with people in the Bible is that of a parent with children. Paul points out that the "Law" was intended to be a "tutor." As such, it was to teach, as with children, obedience. Wouldn't it be wonderful if our children would ask what they could do to help us, if they didn't have to be disciplined and corrected, trained in good manners and consideration for others? Ah, well, wishful thinking. Children just aren't that way by nature.

A continually, rebellious child, one that refused to be obedient, was commanded to be put to death under the law. That is God's attitude toward rebellion, refusal to comply with the Law. But such training and obedience was essential to the survival of the whole nation and the honor of God.

"Faith cometh by hearing and hearing by the Word of God." Romans 10:17. Now the "hearing" is meant in the sense of believing and being obedient to God's Word. Read the epistle of James in this regard. The Law consisted of commands and prohibitions, the manner of parents and children, "childish." I am sure The Lord was relieved when by the Gospel we were made free from the "Law of sin and death" and, by His Holy Spirit, are now able to do in love what was not possible by "legalities."

But children may, at times, feel like "prisoners." As a child, didn't you often think things like: "Boy, wait till I grow up and can do what I want! Boy, will I be glad when no one can tell me what to do!" Childish, of course; but look at what the difference should be between the grace of God and the Law! And look at the "childishness" of most "professing Christians." What does the comparison remind you of?

You can't have it both ways. If you love and have faith in God you will live like it, in all the requirements of love and obedience. If not, you will be like the rebellious child who wants all the freedom and "goodies" without any of the responsibilities. The utter disaster that such selfish thinking leads to! "Better to give than to receive!" Not on your life, according to such "children."

There was a time, not so long ago, that the air was dark with clouds of a bird called the Passenger Pigeon. Not long ago, the prairies were covered with the Buffalo. Due to ignorance and selfishness, the Passenger Pigeon is now extinct, the Buffalo was nearly so. "Help, Lord; for the godly man ceaseth; for the faithful fail from among the children of men." Psalm 12:1. The cry to people for repentance by such men for a nation of idolaters and whoremongers is stilled. They are nearly extinct. Certainly we cannot credit the "show and tell" artists like Oral Roberts, Schuller et al. with being such men.

When Elijah's, Jonah's, Isaiah's and Nathan's are the only cure, we get the Graham's and Falwell's or shameful charlatans like Baker and Swaggart. No such "men of God" are likely to be believed by reasonable people. Real men of God will speak out reasonably and fearlessly to the issues. And they will not use religious clichés and "pious platitudes" to blunt the plain speaking of God's Word!

Small wonder the "Godly man ceaseth! Away with such a man!" is the cry of the crowd. Never mind the fact that God says He will begin His judgment with those of His own house. If revival is ever to come to this nation, it will be at the preaching of Elisha's and Jeremiah's, not Cerullo's.

No small part of the problem is the fact that there are many "ravening wolves" in among the "sheep." These ministers of Satan, disguised as "angels of light," are masters of counterfeiting. An example is a "tract" on the subject of "Grieving the Holy Spirit" I recently received from a very dear friend.

My friend and I love each other and we love The Lord. We have sweet communion in our relationship and though we disagree on the subject of the so-called "gifts of the spirit," he is kind enough to continue to try to "set me straight."

The tract this dear friend sent to me is characteristic of many I have read on this theme over the past thirty odd years. This particular one has God making "class distinctions." If you are "filled" with "the spirit," you are an "upper-class" child of God. If you are not "filled," you are a "lower-class" child of God. Ridiculous, isn't it. But that is exactly the point the writer, a Mr. Wm. B. Young, makes.

Now if the Holy Spirit is to be glorified above God the Father, who is trying to delude whom? Jesus expressly says that the Holy Spirit is to glorify the Father. But deluded followers of the hellish doctrine of charismaticism not only try to make the Spirit supreme, they make God appear foolish by their circus antics and devilish twisting and distorting of God's Word.

In this respect, the worshipers of charismaticism, "spirit-olotry," are in nothing any different than any other idolaters and they might as well join the Roman Catholics and add Mariolatry to their list. They don't pray in the spirit, they pray TO the spirit. But they are deluded in thinking it is the Spirit of God to whom they pray.

Now if you had rather have a good time with your "religion" than go to a football game, go ahead and whoop, holler, shake, rattle and roll, wave your arms and hands, froth at the mouth and shout gibberish to your heart's content. I won't find fault with you in any of this unless you blame such idiocy on God's Holy Spirit. If you do so, I am your bitter enemy for shaming Him so. God is not the author of confusion (or idiocy). I Cor. 14:33.

Recent rain and snow has the "green" sprouting everywhere. The streams are running and the "critters" are glorying in the abundance God has provided. Quail and deer are moving about. Marvelous; I begin to dream of Bull Run creek and the trout. I have much of which to be grateful. "All this and Heaven too!" brother McGee would say, and to think that the situation in the world and our nation should ignore God and plunge deeper into "wars and rumors of war; poverty and homelessness, the abuse of authority and the utter futility of trying to solve "insoluble" problems, insoluble without the blessing and help of God.

CHAPTER EIGHT

CHRISTIAN PERSPECTIVE

MAY, 1991

Deuteronomy 8:3

I have just moved, temporarily, to Frazier Park. It's beautiful here in the hills, there are quail galore and a gray squirrel that fights with an "uppity" ground squirrel and insists on walnuts and pecans. If he is given a Brazil nut, he throws it on the ground in disgust. I thoroughly enjoy the antics of the various "critters." There have been as many as 35 quail at a time taking advantage of the "free seed" along with a few Jays and various other birds.

And just what did Jesus mean when He said to seek God's Kingdom first? I have asked this question of many people over the years and have gotten so many different answers that the point is well made: People are very confused about the issue. But the basic problem is that they confuse Jesus' statement with "religion." It is not a "religious" thing. It is an imminently practical thing; but how so?

When I ask someone: "What practical value do you place on my ministry to you?" I get all kinds of answers. None very satisfactory; in fact, if one were to assign their consideration of my work in The Lord a monetary value, I would soon starve to death. Fortunately, I have never had to count on their support of the work. Like Paul, I have learned to "make tents."

But if people were to really think about the "practical" value of The Gospel and the ministry of God's Word, they would soon come to some fascinating conclusions. The truth of it is that much of such "practical" value is too easily taken for granted. And, as a consequence, men give little thought, through their naturally ungrateful hearts, to the tremendous debt they have to God and His ministers. But ingratitude and selfishness are, sadly, the "Hallmark" of the age.

To begin with, what is the "practical" value of a soul? According to The Lord, a soul is of more value than the entire wealth of the world! Not according to the dark minds of those that have no knowledge of The Lord. But you would think those that claim to be "saved" would act as if those that brought them to knowledge of The Truth would be owed a debt beyond anything they could ever pay. Sadly, this is seldom seen to be the case.

Of what "practical" value is it that a person is saved, through The Gospel, from a life of crime, drug addiction, homosexuality, beating a wife or children? Of what "practical" value is it that a husband or wife is faithful, loving of children and others, that they become people that can be trusted to keep their word, be honest, hard working, concerned for the poor and the helpless? Of what "practical" value is a hope that brings people through every dark, circumstance of life, of a hope that hopes in the face of absolute calamity that hopes in the face of "hopelessness?" Of what "practical" value are the "Words" that bring comfort and joy in the darkness of the evil that surrounds us at every turn, that promises riches beyond our wildest dreams and an eternal future that is exciting and fulfilling beyond our imaginations? And what "dollar" value have you proved all this is to you?

In the context of The Sermon on the Mount, Jesus obviously meant that in order to seek God's Kingdom first we must first have a heart for the things of God, represented by His Holy Spirit's work in our lives. This is evidenced by our sacrificial love for others, a desire for God's Word and prayer, a holy grieving for the lost, an intense jealousy for The Lord and His honor, a "dying" to the old "fleshly Adam." Jesus says the tree is known by its fruit. It's easy for any man or woman of God to be, as old brother McGee would say, "Fruit inspectors. "By their works shall ye know them."

I have just finished proof reading my book and hope to have it ready for you all in a few weeks. I'll let you know when copies are ready for mailing. It finished up at 270 pp in the selected, pocketbook format. A follow-up book will be ready sometime in the summer. The cost will probably be around $20 and this pilot edition will be by subscription only so be sure to let me know if you want a copy.

For those that haven't heard yet, the title of the book is: CONFESSIONS AND REFLECTIONS OF AN OKIE INTELLECTUAL or Where the heck is Weedpatch? Sure, it is largely a "put on" designed to "prick the balloons of pompous asses" but I do not want it mistaken for the drivel you find on most Christian bookstore's shelves. I suspect the "Okie Girl Brewery" just down the road "a piece" would be a more likely spot. The title and the picture of me in full "Okie" garb posing in front of my '64 Chevy pickup is probably worth the price of the book. You'll love it. Since many have asked: "What the heck is an "Okie Intellectual?" I include some clarification in the book.

But, for example, an Okie Intellectual wears shoes and socks. Of course, the socks don't always match and the shoes have holes in the soles. He is also conversant in the language and knows what a "Two-handed" store is and can distinguish a "rich Okie" as one with two-mattresses tied on the top of his car. The car, of course, will be in the class of my '69 Dodge Wagon, complete with multicolored paint job, a radio that doesn't work and suitable dents. The book is full of "Chirkers" like this. What's a "Chirker" you ask? Obviously, it's something to chirk you up (cheer+kid =s Chirk). Unhappily the "i" sometimes comes from some wet blanket's response when they misconstrue some of my "leg-slappers" as "irk" instead of Chirk. There's just no accounting for taste among some people.

People, especially children, like a good story. I have told some that have made eyes pop like a trod on toad. It's a lot of fun to watch jaws drop open and faces reflect joy, horror, fear, amazement; to hear the gasp of those that cry: "What did he just say?" Ah, the wonder of it all.

A good storyteller has to have all the attributes of a ham actor- the ego, the flair and the obvious enjoyment of moving and manipulating the emotions of his listeners and readers. While my speech and writing often injure the "finer sensibilities" of the "churched," the "common people" hear me gladly. I fear, as a result, I will have to forgo the bookshelves of Bible bookstores and settle for Walden's or Pickwick.

Having had more than the "usual" childhood, I love to entertain children and adults with my "humor" which is often directed at my earliest years. Not that I haven't had my share of laughs as an adult (like nailing your "buddy's" lunch pail to the work bench or the time I tried to cut some idiot's Chevy in half with my motorcycle), it just seems that the things of those early years in "Little Oklahoma" and Boulder Gulch were funnier.

Take, for example, the time the whole family had a real donnybrook involving my grandad, grandma, great-grandma, and the "principle," my latest stepfather, Dan Pospieszynski (what a time my brother, Ronnie, and I had trying to learn to spell that one). But he was an excellent mechanic and he loved building model planes. I am grateful for his teaching me some of these skills.

We had just returned to California after an abortive attempt to live in Cleveland Ohio with our stepdad's parents. We just didn't take to the Polish Ghetto and the snow and ice of Cleveland after the sunny clime and culture of Bakersfield.

I will never forget the train trip from Bakersfield to Cleveland. It was wintertime, VE day was only just past and there were many military personnel on board. Of the many things children of today have missed is the glory of travel by train. There are few methods of travel to rival the trains of the past. To watch miles of varying scenery slip by to the "clickety-clack, clickety-clack" of the rails, the gentle, swaying motion that lulled you to sleep in the comfortable and snug Pullman births; sheer luxury.

Eating in the dining car was marvelous. The sparkling cleanliness and beauty of the table settings, the courteousness of the waiters, all to the continuing, rocking motion of the cars and the variety of the scenes slipping by. The aura of it all was beyond description. Fellow travelers were friendly and companionable. It was a whole different world.

We arrived at Cleveland in a blizzard. Ronnie and I had never experienced any degree of snow and were entranced by the sight. As with life in general, I have bittersweet memories of our short tenure living in Ohio. My brother and I saw our first fireflies there, wonderful little insects with their entrancing ability to flick their lights on and off. We also celebrated VJ day in Cleveland; whistles blowing and people running out into the streets shouting and hollering up a storm.

Since the stepdad and all his relatives were "Old-world, Polish Catholics," nothing else would do but that Ronnie and I should become indoctrinated into the church as well. I suspect some motivation on our mother's part in rebellion to her parent's religious persuasion. It was quite educational and certainly a contrast to our experience with our grandparent's Pentecostal fundamentalism in Little Oklahoma.

It was in Florida (St. Joseph's Military Academy, a place that parents "dumped" their kids so as not to be bothered with them) that Ronnie and I were "catechized" into Catholicism; quite a change from the boisterous "Pentecostalism" of Little Oklahoma. Culture shock; but a more "convenient" religion you couldn't ask for; more of that at another time.

WWII Vets faced a difficult problem of jobs and housing. I wonder if any of you recall a song called: "No Vacancy!" Even after all these years, I still remember the lyrics:

Not so long ago when the bullets screamed, many were the happy dreams I dreamed

Of the little nest where I could rest when the world was free.

Now the mighty war over there is won, troubles in thousands just begun as I face that terrible enemy sign No Vacancy!

No vacancy, no vacancy

All along the line just the same old sign a waitin' for me.

No vacancy, no vacancy

And my heart beats slow as I read on the door No Vacancy!

Since the stepdad was a returning veteran with a family, housing and jobs were a real problem. So, California and the grandparents beckoned. Because the stepdad was a mechanic, my grandparents were persuaded that he could make a go of a garage in Little Oklahoma. So, after purchasing a venerable "Terraplane," we were on our way back to California. Unhappily, Ronnie and I now had a baby brother and the trip was made in the summer to the aromatic accompaniment of dirty diapers and the proclivity of the Terraplane for breaking down in every state we passed through. This was particularly difficult as we tried to get through desert climes. I'm sure this is why mom still hates the desert.

Never let it be said that my maternal family didn't know how to have a good time. I say "maternal" because my father, Oliver Glendell Heath, left us when I was three and my brother, two. We never saw him again. As a result, I never knew any of the relatives on my father's side of the family.

My grandad was a big man, over six feet tall, large boned, real "line backer" material and about 225 pounds. He was also a "special deputy" for Kern County. Grandma, as the result of a car-train accident, must have weighed about 300 pounds and she was only five-feet tall (it was said that her glands went "haywire." As a result, at one time, grandad was a "Carny Barker" and grandma played the circus "Fat Lady"). Great-grandma, saintly old lady who walked with a cane due to a bad hip, was also only about five foot tall and probably weighed 95 pounds. Our step-dad was six-foot and about 180 pounds. Height and weight stats are important to the story about to unfold.

I must have been about ten years old and my brother, Ronnie, nine, when this sordid event took place. And what an event it was. It is said:

"It takes uh heap uh livin' tuh make uh house uh heap." And the folks sure knew how to "heap it up somethin fierce." Fun and frolic all the time; but, I digress.

Ronnie and I were awakened by tremendous crashing sounds accompanied by shouting and screaming from the participants of the family disagreement. It wasn't Sunday so I knew it couldn't be "church practice" by the congregation of my grandad's little Pentecostal flock (grandad had his own church which he pastored with great enthusiasm. I'm reminded of the time grandma prevented him from taking his pistol to one of the congregants. But that is another story having to do with the gentler subject of church "polity."

Even at our tender ages, my brother and I had become accustomed to a certain degree of mayhem and life threatening interchanges between mom, our grandparents and various lesser "contenders," acquaintances and stepfathers. All this and World War Two at the same time made for a good deal of excitement in our young lives; never a dull moment.

By the time Ronnie and I were out of bed and at the doorway of the living room where the action was in progress, it was obvious that our stepdad was getting the worst end of the discussion. He was on the floor, grandma was sitting on top of him (yep, all 300 pounds), grandad was struggling to get handcuffs on him, great-grandma was flailing away with her cane, and great-grandma could really wield a mean cane, and managing to hit grandad more often than Pospieszynski. The step-dad was screaming, "I surrender, I surrender!" at the top of his lungs. Small wonder; I bet a lot of you folks have had just the same kind of thing happen to you. Well, at least close to it.

It was all very interesting and Ronnie and I were careful not to intrude our presence into such a spirited and enthusiastic display of "adult entertainment." But we did wonder where mom was. It wasn't like her to miss out on one of these exchanges of differing viewpoints (particularly when she was often the prime instigator of them).

Finally, the battle was ended, the cuffs were on the miscreant and grandad hauled him off to the pokey. It later was discovered he had landed a "sucker punch" on grandad's nose and this precipitated the wholesale battle. To this day I don't know where mom was at the time or what part she played in the whole affair. I do recall Ronnie's and my fascination at the amount of blood and hair all about the battleground afterward as we examined the floor and broken furniture. It was all quite interesting to our young minds. My brother and I were suitably impressed with the enthusiasm of the participants. It isn't every day that kids get to observe grown-ups at play in such spirited fashion and children greatly need adult role models.

I have often found myself pitying those that have been deprived of the cultural advantages my brother and I have enjoyed. It is a truism that there are two kinds of people: Okies and those that wish they were. And, while I am only an "honorary Okie," I take great pride in my nativity of Weedpatch and raisin' in "Little Oklahoma" (Southeast Bakersfield, to the uninitiated) with all its refugees straight out of the "Grapes of Wrath" from the "Dust Bowl" and the "Great Depression." Steinbeck and the "Joads" would have been right at home. It is easy to feel sorry for those that have been denied such a rich and "interesting" heritage.

With the "Recession" that is currently hurting so many, I have to wonder what families without the necessary "survival skills" are going to do. It makes me think of some of the old songs of my own "Dust Bowl" days. For example:

Dear Okie, if you see Arkie, tell 'em Tex has got job for him in California
Pickin' up prunes, they're all out of oranges

Of course, the recent "freeze" makes such a job in California academic. Also, with the current budget disaster and California leading in the growth industries of Welfare, prisons, security guards and alarms (not to mention fatter paychecks for our elected "leadership,") the entire picture is reaching purely "academic" status anyhow. There simply is not enough money to pay the bills. So long middle class, it's been good to know you.

As I sit writing, warmed by a good, wood fire, (Still in the Kern Valley at this point) I can gaze out my windows at the snow-capped mountains all about. There are snow flurries and the whole scene is one of contentment-particularly since I don't have to be out in the cold. The secret, by the way, to a good fire in the fireplace is like the way to treat a good woman: "Once you've got 'er hotted up good, don't let the coals die down!" I know, I'm the bane of all those that think I ought to have more respect for all those letters after my name. But, sometimes, I just have to have fun with those pompous asses that think decorum is a matter of looking somber and pronouncing, seeming, "profundities" that they mistakenly equate with gray hair and the "wisdom" of the "literati."

We've had a series of storms that promise a goodly amount of water in the lake and, with an improved snow-pack in the high country, good fishing in the river and streams this spring and Summer and plenty of quail and deer. I'm reminded of that famous song by O'Dell Johnson:

Snow-capped mountains, ripplin' streams, It's not heaven though it seems in Kernville, California U.S.A.

(OK, so it's not so famous, but it ought to be).

I have taken some friends out to my "secret" Indian campground and introduced them to the fascinating search for artifacts, primarily arrowheads and fragments of obsidian. I have even found some in Kelso Valley. I have enjoyed seeing them get the "bug." They walk around now, permanent "crick" in their necks, looking at the ground wherever they go, hoping to see that wondrous glint of light that betrays the marvelous, smoky, volcanic glass the natives worked with such consummate skill.

It is a shame that the government, in its "infinite wisdom," had so little regard for this site when they decided the old mining claim would be a dandy place for a campground. So much for government's real regard for the riches of a culture that was so much more attentive to God's creation.

But, sadly, if the Indians had had the "advantages" of the "conquering hordes," But I doubt we would have found them much more conscientious about preserving their own heritage. It takes time to learn wisdom. There was a time, as a young boy that I would shoot those beautiful, gray tree squirrels. They were good eating and I hunted for our "pot." It's quite something to eat squirrel and frog legs until you're "swole up like a pizened pup!" I can still enjoy a good platter of frog legs but I now just enjoy watching the gray squirrels. The ground squirrels I still shoot. I have never known an animal with so many fleas or so industrious in procreating and digging holes.

Of course, for those of you with the unhappy experience of learning how quickly you can be up to your neck in hamsters, the ground squirrel is a eunuch by comparison. You would think that any animal with a gestation period of 16 days would one day rule the world. Fortunately, it is also true, that any animal that thinks running an endless wheel endlessly is its calling in life cannot be too great a threat to civilization. On the other hand, look at what most people do for a "living!" Maybe the hamster isn't so stupid after all. At least he doesn't punch a clock or worry about the rent. The flip side is being eaten by the family cat. Alas, it seems there is no Utopia.

The snow has been falling heavier as I write. Flakes as large as silver dollars: "The angels having a pillow-fight." The area is now a winter wonderland as the feathery flakes softly drifting down, filling the quiet air. It's enchanting and thoroughly delightful as long as you don't have to be out in it. I recall making "snow ice cream" as a kid. We simply scooped up a bowl of fresh snow, added a small amount of vanilla extract, sprinkled in sugar, mixed and ate. Marvelous; might do that now. "Simple folks got simple ways."

And speaking of frog legs, "Im 'a never forget the time" I almost caused mom to croak. Therein lays a "frog-tale."

Our second stepdad, Mahoney, a soldier, was courtin' mom at the time. He had picked us up and taken us to a nice restaurant. When Ronnie and I were told to order what we wanted, I ordered frog legs. I'm sure the poor man didn't suspect what elegant taste I had for a poor unsophisticated little "Okie" kid. But, in truth, frog legs were common "Bill of fare" for me. How was I to know that they were frightfully expensive when ordered in a "high-tone" restaurant? Us "simple folks" were used to eating the critters and certainly couldn't understand anyone placing them in some "high-falutin" epicurean category. Certainly I wouldn't have understood their being the most expensive dish on the menu.

Mahoney took it like a man and over my mother's protestations, said: "Ah, let the kid have 'em." And I "had 'em." I'm not sure what the bill came to but judging by the soldier's and my mother's expressions, I'm sure he was sorry he let me "have 'em." I'm sure mom would have liked to have let me "have it." I do recall, that, after he and mom married, I never ordered frog legs in a restaurant again. And, in truth, restaurant frog legs lacked something. They just weren't as good as "fresh-gigged."

I'm not sure how I got started on this line of reminiscences and I'm having trouble making some profound, theological point of frog legs. Maybe The Lord enjoys stories also.

When I think of my tenure in Little Oklahoma, I remember many things that belonged to our culture. Particularly the role of Negroes one of whom taught me this little ditty:

See the little bunny, shoot 'm in the head
Pop 'm in the skillet when he's good'n ded
Stir 'm up, stir 'm up, stir 'm all around
Fry 'm up, fry 'm up, til he's good'n brown
Put 'm on the platter, serve 'm with some peas
See how he lay there, nice 's you please

Some like taters some like fish
Some like the bunny, he's their favrit dish
No matter how you cook 'm, no matter how he kick
Mr. Bunny's sumpfin you caint beat with a stick

Maybe it doesn't do much for the Easter Bunny to think of his kin turning a golden brown in the frying pan. But he's sure good eatin'.

Gen. Powell made the comment that schools would work better if educators taught students the way the Army trains recruits. His perspicacity can't be faulted. His South Bronx schooling, like my years of teaching in Watts, gives him some insight into what works in education. No Negro gets to Gen. Powell's exalted station in life without learning what it takes to make it in the "System."

But the General's military career may have sheltered him from some ugly facts. For example, the fact that discipline cannot be enforced either in the home or the school. As I have said so many times over the years, when it comes to "education," we couldn't have designed a system for failure any better if we had done so intentionally.

The fact that we "kicked" God out of our schools and government guaranteed failure. Unhappily, so many religious charlatans abound God became something "religious" instead of the Creator and Righteous Judge of the universe.

Everywhere I go I hear the same, sad refrain: "What can we do about our children?" They are going to hell in droves and the best parents seem incapable of enforcing proper discipline and instruction. The schools stopped trying years ago. We live with an evil system that, inspired of Satan himself, demands our children be sacrificed on the altar of the "State." It is the "State," Caesar that will continue, with the aid of perverts, the ACLU and the government, to support a welfare nation, already bankrupt, thereby destroying any vestige of morality, personal integrity and property.

It is sad to see Mr. Bush making inane proclamations about educational "reform." Watch as he gathers the same idiots, largely those with worthless "doctorates" in "education," to "solve" the problems. No, my friends, nothing short of a national call to repentance led by real men of God, leading to true revival will save our nation. And, since this eliminates all those like Roberts, Schuller, Robertson, Cerullo, Graham, et al., who is left to call this nation to repentance?

True "religion" as God puts it, is not religious activity; pious phraseology and certainly not acting as though you had taken leave of your mind ala the charismatics. Revival, under the present "leadership," and notwithstanding II Chron. 7:14, does not appear to be likely. This leaves "solutions," as I have long pointed out, possible only on an individual basis.

Too many people, their backs against the wall, are losing jobs, homes, talking of "running off" to "somewhere simpler" (wherever that is) and just plain dropping out. Tempting and seductive as such thinking is there just isn't any "Utopia." The whole world is in a mess.

Small wonder Jesus said only a few were going to be saved; particularly when the whole "world" is against those few. Too many professing "Pilgrims" are like turtles, trying to carry their earthly "homes" with them into eternity. It ain't gonna happen that way.

As a little "Dust Bowl Okie," it was my privilege to attend second grade at old Mt. Vernon Elementary in Bakersfield. The teacher had a few problems. She had trouble with some pronunciations. This caused her and the class a real disaster on one occasion.

We were having a class Spelling Bee. I was an excellent "speller" and often won these events. But this time the teacher created a terrible situation due to the fact that the word she asked for, "accept," kept coming out of her mouth "except." Now there were several other excellent "spellers" in our class. When the first one tried to answer her with the correct spelling of except, exactly the way the teacher pronounced it, the kid was told it was wrong. The next kid did the very same thing, and so did a third. It was my turn and I didn't know what was going on. In spite of the fact that each of us was told to sit down as soon as the "x" came out of our mouths, none of us could think of any other way to spell the word she was so obviously saying. I failed to answer and the teacher was tearing at her hair by this time. It never occurred to her that she might be to blame due to her poor pronunciation.

And, so, as with many things, we think we are saying things easily understood and only succeeding in exasperating our listeners and ourselves. As a teacher, I have learned that some lessons can only be mastered by the repetitive method- saying the same thing over and over.

But I have never forgotten that episode in second grade. When something is so obviously clear to you and others are not "getting it," you better re-examine your teaching. But I did get even, though not through any motive of revenge; some things just seem to work out that way. Happy circumstance, like the early demise by a heart attack of one of my adulterous, ex-wife's "lovers."

The school was having a talent show. I was "volunteered" by this teacher to sing in front of the whole school. She had a few selections for me to choose from but none of them seemed to "hit" me quite right. They just didn't fit my mood. Bakersfield radio stations carried many good musical programs. I was always listening to music from the radio, the church and mom's records. I had memorized many old favorites such as "Cocaine Blues." As a result, I had an extensive repertoire of widely diverse songs and decided to do one of my own favorites. But I failed to share this decision with the teacher. And so it was that good, old Mt. Vernon was treated to my rendition of that great and famous ballad:

"Cold Icy Fingers!"
Now Bill Jackson was a fellow that believed in hainted sights
He used to dream about them when he went to bed at night
And when he dreamed about them you could nearly always tell
He'd just pull back his covers and jump right up and yell
Keep them cold icy fingers off 'a me
Keep them cold icy fingers off 'a me
I don't mind your naked bones
Don't mind your hollers and your groans
But keep them cold icy fingers off 'a me

One night as Bill was passin a graveyard on a hill
Somethin dressed in white jumped out and made a grab at Bill
Bill said you may not catch me but I'll make you do your best
But for we start to travel I'll make one last request
Keep them cold icy fingers off 'a me
Keep them cold icy fingers off 'a me
You can chase me out of breath
You can scare me half to death
But keep them cold icy fingers off 'a me

Bill went to see a doctor with a misery in his chest
The doctor looked at Bill and said take off your coat and vest
He started tappin' on Bill's wrist, which gave Bill such a shock
That Bill just jumped right back and said now wait a minute Doc
Keep them cold icy fingers off 'a me
Keep them cold icy fingers off 'a me
You can cure my aches and ills
With your powders and your pills
But keep them cold icy fingers off 'a me

The teacher was most unforgiving. Little did she realize how lucky she was that I didn't treat the school to Cocaine Blues (circa 1942), my alternate choice. Looking back, I think it was the reference to naked bones that got to her. She was quite the "old maid." My cultured tastes and refinement knows no bounds and I am always anxious to share the bounty of my childhood with others who have similar, discriminating tastes.

I hope you all realize that the point of my childhood stories is to try to help folks realize that it takes all we can do to help raise our children in righteousness. This means that we have to agree and work together in obedience to God for them to have any chance at all in this evil world. Children today face things that I certainly never had to deal with and neither, probably, did you. The single most important thing is the consistency of the love they need to see in their parents for The Lord and for them. It takes a lot of effort for parents to be consistent in both love and discipline but it's the only chance the children have. A loving environment among people that cared for one another and us blessed my brother and me. In spite of the turmoil of incidents such as I have described, we were never left in doubt of these people's love for us. We also had the very great advantage of the Bible and The Lord being held in reverence by these folks.

We can't help wishing things were different, that our children didn't have to face the ugly realities with which they have to deal. But wishing won't make it so. The church must be there to be the helping institution God intended where we can cooperate with The Lord in these dreadful times.

CHAPTER NINE

CHRISTIAN PERSPECTIVE

DECEMBER, 1991

Luke 2:1-20

As I write this, I'm not sure where Christmas will find me. It's hard not having a family anymore, especially during the holidays. I certainly understand the depression this brings on in others in similar circumstances. But the Good News of The Gospel remains and is there for all that will come to God and He "Sets the desolate in families."

We've had some showers in the Valley and the nights have turned cold. A light dusting of snow shows on the surrounding mountains. The Canyon is resplendent in the variegated colors of the leaves of the trees and the sun shines with crystal clarity. The air is sweet and crisp.

With so much happening throughout the world, I'm apt to suffer information overload. Also, so much of what is happening is bad news that I have to "stretch" to get some humor to share with you and lighten the load. So, I went out to the cabin and took a walk among the pines and rocks and concluded that my best source of humor is still myself. I love to tell stories on me. And a great source of humor is in life's embarrassing moments.

An adolescent can endure just about anything but embarrassment. If I didn't know this as a youngster, I certainly learned it as a high school teacher. Its judicious use as a teaching mechanism proved useful. But, you walked a fine line in its application. Never, did I exercise this option without recalling an incident in my junior high years.

Girls, at this innocent period of my life, were strange creatures indeed. They were not unlike "Martians," intriguing, but suspect. And, for all my acquaintance with the fair sex, they may as well have come from outer space for all I knew about them. They smelled nice, seemed to be preoccupied with their appearance and cleanliness and I never saw one of them spit; altogether peculiar.

They traveled in groups and spent a lot of time whispering to each other and giggling. They would look at a certain boy in a peculiar fashion, go into a huddle and giggle; bizarre behavior but fascinating.

Those of you who have read my book, "Confessions of an Okie Intellectual," will recall my talking about my being raised by my grandparents. Sex was never mentioned. Much of my reading was Victorian and novels like "The Last of the Mohicans" and other such works led to my thinking of the opposite sex in terms of mystery and purity. My moral code in this regard was worthy of a Knight seeking the Holy Grail; utterly chaste, naive and ignorant.

My favorite sport in school was baseball. It was lunchtime and three or four of the boys and I were having our usual, loose game of pitch and hit. I happened to be pitching at the time.

Three of the "strange creatures" wandered onto the infield and, in their inexplicable humor, called out to me: (They seem, like sharks sensing blood, to intuit who is easy prey) "What do you want to be when you grow up?" In a vain attempt at nonchalance, I was actually quaking at being singled out for their attentions, I replied: "Useless!" There, I thought, that ought to get rid of them.

To my utter dismay, they broke out laughing and giggling, and one of them, I would swear, was actually blushing (Some girls really did that a long time ago). Now, as "sharp" as my retort had been, I could find nothing in it to warrant such a reaction. But, as I've said, they were strange creatures; one never knew how they would respond to anything. Some things, at least, have never changed in that regard since time immemorial.

But, to my further consternation, the afternoon found several of the girls and boys looking at me and smiling in a peculiar fashion. What in the world was going on? There was, obviously, a joke being shared about me of which I had no knowledge.

During the afternoon recess, J. L., my buddy, took me aside and, with admiration, said: "You really have a lot of guts! You really put those girls in their place." Now, while I was not immune to praise, I hadn't the slightest idea of what in the ever-loving-blue-eyed-world he was talking about. So, I asked: "What in the ever-loving-blue-eyed-world are you talking about?"

J. L.: "You know when those girls asked you what you were going to be when you grow up and you said 'A NUDIST!' " That marvelous computer known as my brain suddenly went into a crash mode. "Whether in the body or out of the body, I could not tell." To a painfully shy youngster, to have to come to grips with such a story going around the entire school among his peers was too much for me to grasp.

How I got through the, mercifully few, last minutes of the afternoon I don't know. I remained in mortified shock, unable to look at anyone. Eventually, as I maintained my innocence and defended myself at such vile calumny best I could, it was too good a story for everyone else and I remained a reluctant "hero" to my buddies and the girls continued to look at me with "new eyes" thereafter.

Having had more than a casual education in the mechanisms of the female mind lo these many years, I have come to the conclusion that either The Lord has a perverse sense of humor reflected in His creature's appreciation of practical jokes and slapstick humor or He wishes He had done some things differently in His creation of men and women. I don't allow of any middle ground such as the religious nonsense that God is incapable of error. His own Word bears testimony of the opposite case. My religious friends have the burden of proof on their own heads as they try to "fancy-dance" their way to an apologetic for Jesus' command that we are to be perfect just as God is perfect and, that, if any two agree they can ask and God will bring it to pass. As I have said many times, He must have something else in mind when it comes to a definition of "perfection" than how religious people, particularly, construe it.

Back to women; while some of my detractors, a base lot all, seem to think I'm a bit stiff-necked in regard to the distaff side, let me point out that I like women, why "Some of my best friends are women.

It seems the "Topfree 10" have had their "Day in court" and the judge, a woman, Patricia Marks, has found that there should be no distinction between the bare breasts of males or females. Well, now, I have never responded in quite the same fashion to the sight of bare, female breasts as I have to men's. In spite of the judge's decision, I think most men will agree with my own thoughts on the subject. There most certainly is a distinction. In all my years I have never found myself attracted to a man's breast or considered one "lovely."

But suppose a number of women, just to celebrate their "new emancipation" decide to go "bare topside?" How many men, do you suppose, will be able to resist "reaching out and touching someone?" If the fallout from the Thomas/Hill fiasco results in more "harassment" claims, just think of the possibilities in this new insanity?

Perhaps a recent letter to the editor by a senior citizen says it best. He claims, in view of the recent flap and his experience with women in general, he will start dealing with men only! If he has to deal with a woman, he will keep his mouth shut (good advice in any case), not even engaging in the customary pleasantries at the grocery checkout if the checker is a woman. It just doesn't pay to take any chances any more. Better safe than sorry. And furthermore gals, if you decide to "take it off," hanging a "Don't Touch" sign on your chest won't help. The great majority of men will still believe you are "advertising" and "asking for it!"

A group of Brigham Young University women propose a curfew on men! Members of VOICE, BYU's Committee to Promote the Status of Women say such an action is needed so women can walk the campus safely at night. All I can say, "ladies," is that as long as women deny history, dress provocatively, buy into the "youth and beauty lie," continue to agitate for special privilege, "equality" confusing this for equal value and a sham for "I'm better than you," as long as you continue to emasculate men through the judicial process, so long as you persist in the insanity of denying the difference that God Himself established, so long will you suffer that "itch" you can't scratch. Continuing on this same course will, inevitably, lead to more and more frustration and anger on the part of men. Small wonder so few men are willing to trust you and put a noose around their necks and the end of the rope in your hand.

There is no arguing the fact that men victimize women. But, really, who "sells" sex? Women! As long as they devalue themselves, selling their "product" through pornography, commercial advertising, etc., so long will they have no right to bash men for responding accordingly. You "ladies" better get your act together before you cause a really reactionary revolution among men! Men are to lead and protect. To deny this historical imperative is to renounce your own contribution of femininity. And to give that up makes you of no unique value in any society. As a Deputy Sheriff recently said, a Hispanic one, by the way, "The lady who couldn't climb over a six-foot fence fails the testing process and she claims sexual discrimination! I suppose the man who couldn't climb over should file too... I ask what good is that person to me or any other deputy who is getting his or her tail beat on the other side of that fence? Come on people, don't use sexual or racial discrimination as a tool to try and make something of yourself in this world. Make it because of who you are on the inside, not on the outside. Society would be a lot better off."

Is this deputy prejudiced? His remarks aren't. They exhibit rare common sense and the anger and frustration that most right-thinking people have when faced with all the cries for "special privilege" that discriminates against hard working and responsible persons that try to make it as law-abiding citizens.

Phil Wyman has caught a lot of flack about his use of the term "wetback." Among whites there are "white trash, honkies, rednecks, etc. Among Blacks there are "Niggers, Oreos, and Sambos." Among Mexicans there are "wetbacks." Will these appellations go away with the constant demands for so-called "Affirmative Action" laws? Most certainly not! Whether black, brown, yellow, red or white, most people, regardless of race or gender, have a sense of fair play. None of these "bleeding hearts" would have the temerity to stand up in any crowd and actually say: "Hey! Treat me different (better) because I'm a different color or gender than you! That would be, admittedly, asinine. Then why the hypocrisy of trying to sneak in the back door of "law" to gain what you don't deserve or have any right to?

Imagine the hue and cry if I were to set up a "White Scholarship Fund," if I were agitating for special privilege as a "White Male Single Parent," (the actual case by the way) or a "N.A.A.W (white) P., and all with the special consideration and protection of the so-called "Judicial" system?

It is no accident that Hitler is getting a lot of play these days. From the neo-Nazis of Germany to newspapers, periodicals, movies and documentaries on TV, there is a tremendous revival of interest in the subject. Jewish groups recently demanded to know why files used to round up Paris Jews have been secretly kept by the French government for five decades. A "heckled" motorist writes that she was harassed by some young men who reminded her of the "Brown Shirts" she knew as a child in Nazi Germany. And everyone hears about the "Skinheads" and others espousing the praises of Hitler's doctrines in this country. California Lt. Governor Leo McCarthy: "Hate Crimes Rise As Economy Falls!" How's that for a recent headline? Here's another in the same vein: "Study Shows Homeless Children Hold No Hopes Of Realizing Dreams!" Remind you history buffs of another period in time?

"The New Order," edited and published by one Gerhard Lauck, is being distributed randomly. It includes a long list of mail-order Nazi memorabilia and an opinion/editorial page entitled: "Fun Under the Swastika." The "movement" is growing so fast in Spain that the government is threatening a crackdown on the neo-Nazi group, Spanish Circle of Friends and its secretary-general, Christian Ruiz.

Sheriff Sherman Block threatens to pull 800 officers out of security for the Tournament of Roses unless Pasadena officials apologize for remarks about neo-Nazis in his department. The accusation involves a purported "White Supremacist" group operating within the Sheriff's department. Sheriff Block, anybody with half a wit knows that police agencies are nursing a lot of hurt from the insanity of laws that make their jobs, like those of teachers, impossible, that reward the criminal and penalize the victims. The "mixed signals" like that of judges that can't make up their minds, make the job of so-called "law enforcement" a tragic joke. For example: "Judge Angered by Slayer's Third Appeal to High Court!" Everyone is disgusted with this man's (Robert Alton Harris in this instance) continuing to make a travesty of a legal system that cannot meet out justice. I'm glad the judge, Arthur Alarcon, is angry; we all are. But, now, look at what another judge, D.L. Graham just did! He has halted the return of Haitians that were attempting, illegally, to enter the States. No matter the extreme circumstances that forced these desperate people to attempt to flee their homeland, "The Law" in the person of D.L. Graham says it doesn't apply in this case. If not in this case, why in any case would be a logical conclusion?

Ex-INS chief: "Crack Down on Illegal Immigrants!" Alan Nelson says:

"California should cut off jobs, social services, driving privileges, college educations and tax refunds to illegal immigrants. They cost California taxpayers millions of dollars, they seriously hurt all areas of California society - employment, welfare, health, crime, housing and our basic values."

Now, I'll bet some of you feel the same way, in fact, I'll bet some of you didn't even know the illegals were getting all these "perks" as a reward for flaunting the "Law." The response of the media to such a reasonable complaint? An example: Teresa Puente writing for the Bakersfield Californian says such statements are "evidence" of "Racial Intolerance!" Now I suspect Ms. Puente's surname might "color" her objectivity but, really now, Ms. Puente, are you willing to jump into bed with a D.L. Graham and look equally foolish by saying your race should be "accommodated" at the expense of law and order? All you have accomplished by your lengthy, name-calling and racism is engendering more "red-neck" hatred, anger and frustration. As with perverts demanding "special handling," you certainly cannot expect anything but a violent reaction to your own bigotry, can you? The majority are madder than hell because of all such "special cases" demanding to feed on the tax-dollars of those that still hold such anachronistic views that people ought to earn a living and the law should apply, equally, without regard to color.

An editorial in the same vein from the same newspaper: "Even in defeat, David Duke personifies the most dangerous threat facing Americans in these unsettled times - a drift toward the political far right where fascists flourish and freedoms evaporate." The "editor" who wrote this garbage would have done well working for Goebbels. Attempts at propagandizing those who are madder than hell because of the system rewarding criminals, and that is exactly what illegal immigrants are, when you cannot even support your own family because of their depredations is not going to work. It is just such vain attempts to white-wash your own bigotry that is going to destroy you and contribute the most to just the kind of thing you, stupidly and selfishly, try to hang around the necks of hard-working and legal citizens of this country! It isn't David Duke you have to fear, it is an aroused, law-abiding, tax-paying multitude that damns you and your kind.

I cannot, for the life of me, believe the stupidity of some of the media! Imagine the inanity of a statement made by Richard Martinez, managing editor for the Bakersfield Californian: "Duke Represents Rebirth of Racism!" Mr. Martinez, is your head so far up where the sun never shines that you actually believe such a ridiculous statement or are you, as the media usually does, only "propagandizing?" To be charitable, maybe you are only reacting to your own racial heritage, like Ms. Puente, vis-à-vis your last name, and jumping on the bandwagon of "Duke-bashing" as the latest, racist sport of the media. Don't pride yourself on attacking such an easy and safe target. You will only be believable when you pick out an equally racist Negro, Hispanic or Jewish leader. The Arabs don't count; too many easy targets. Maybe, Mr. Martinez, you, like so many others, are simply jealous.

Here is another "beaut" from the same editorial page of this paper: The writer tries to equate the "Dust Bowl Okies" with Mexican illegals. The writer, just like Dr. Goebbels, tries to twist and distort the conditions of history to suit his own, evil agenda. Imagine trying to use the Edwards vs. California decision to vindicate illegal immigration! That law simply stated the fact that no state could obstruct interstate commerce or violate CITIZENS rights to travel! Then, like many women who have an equally lop-sided view of their "rights," the writer tries to equate the Okies of that time with the illegals now.

I'm a product of those Okies and proud of it. I was raised among them in "Little Oklahoma" in Southeast Bakersfield. One thing that might be considered "noble" about the folks was the fact that they didn't have their hands out constantly demanding the government take care of them. They didn't demand a "free lunch" on the backs of others. They subscribed to the philosophy of "If any not work, neither should he eat!" But that was a simple time and a simple society. Sin was sin and children didn't worry about being abused. We had "heroes" and the issues were black and white, not some shade of gray.

It is just the kind of propaganda of these "journalists," with their "liberal" posturing, that is leading this country to the "Hitlerian solutions" that I fear are coming. They are the ones that are advocating the flaunting of our laws, they are the ones advocating the overthrow of our government, they are the ones that want anarchy and condemn the common sense of our Constitution and founding fathers, who have made, with the politicians they have "bought," a mockery of justice for all. They are the ones that distort statistics showing most prison inmates are colored while ignoring the fact that they are criminals who have preyed, primarily, on their own people.

I applaud Mr. Bush's directive that all federal agencies phase out regulations authorizing the use of racial preferences and quotas in hiring and promotions, to get rid of regulations that show preference based on either gender or color. It's about time! "Affirmative Action" by any other name is still racist and discriminatory. But, Mr. Bush, would you have taken this action if a David Duke hadn't rubbed your nose in such common sense fairness? And, will you be able to "stick to your guns" when the "liberal Congress" gets through bashing you? I doubt it. Maybe you are only "posturing." Certainly that is how any reasonable person will see it if you cave in on this issue.

"Hunting Season" is right around the corner! What, really, can we expect history to show of a nation that calls fornicating "Super Stars" like Magic

Johnson "Heroes," that teaches its young that such "status" places one above the laws and morality demanded of the "unwashed?" I am no fan of so-called "Super Stars" but Martina Navratilova certainly put "Magic" Johnson in perspective when she said: "If it had happened to a heterosexual woman who had been with 100 or 200 men, they'd call her a whore and a slut and the corporations would drop her like a lead balloon ... The public would say 'She had it coming!'" Good for you, Martina, I couldn't have said it better and it's about time someone besides myself did.

All this has caused me to re-read Mein Kampf. It has been some thirty years since I have done so and I certainly have not enjoyed the exercise. But to understand the man is to understand his agenda and to do that, you have to read his equivalent of the Communist Manifesto.

No one can possibly discount the importance of Mein Kampf, no matter how scholars deride Hitler's writing ability. And, of course, we cannot discount the "help" he received in the writing. But the agenda was clearly Hitler's. And, further, if you read beyond the obvious "politicking" and "scapegoating" you find a man who is supremely confident of his "righteous" cause and knows how to bend people to his own thinking. And, in many cases, his thinking was supremely concise and accurate. If you can possibly get past the evil his agenda led to, you are faced with a man who exhibited real genius and could have, easily, gone down in history as one of its great statesmen rather than a disciple of Satan.

The same man who could say: "Hence today I believe that I am acting in accordance with the will of the Almighty Creator: by defending myself against the Jew, I am fighting for the work of the Lord," also said:

"Political parties are inclined to compromises; philosophies never. Political parties even reckon with opponents; philosophies proclaim their infallibility."

It was not Hitler's politics that led him to power. His politics were constantly evolving. It was his philosophy and his charismatic ability to draw others, as with other "fanatics," into its vortex that gave him authority. While Jesus did not say much that was really new in His preaching, He acted and spoke "... as one who has authority." Unlike Jesus, though, Hitler was not speaking for God but he spoke as one who had authority.

Neither Hitler nor Judas suddenly got up one morning and decided to become a stench and byword for evil to the rest of humanity. It happened a little at a time and each betrayed themselves long before they betrayed others. The sore point of which little is brought into question is the fact that they had betrayer's hearts. Each had to contend with their fleshly egos and both lost the battle; reminds me of Oral Robert's latest scam to fleece the flock and Jimmy Swaggart's fall from grace. My personal note to Oral & Son: Bankruptcy, as a

Samuel D. G. Heath, Ph. D.

ploy, might convince some of the fools that support your so-called "ministry" but you have never fooled God. You delude yourselves if you think it is a "satanic conspiracy" that is attacking you; it is God Almighty! Quit giving the Devil the credit for The Lord's work against you!

The Scrolls might "clean the clocks" of many of these charlatans. Speaking of which, the importance cannot be over-emphasized, I quote Hershel Shanks, publications editor for the Biblical Archaeology Society regarding the Catholic Church's monopoly on publishing the material: "What enormous hubris and greed it was for eight men to think that in their lifetime they could edit and write commentaries on all of this material." But, Dr. Shanks, you miss the point of what was really at work here. The point, which I have maintained all along, is what were they trying to hide?

Not even the most devout, Hard-shell Baptist, Roman Catholic, Episcopalian, etc. dares look too deeply into that part of his religion that constitutes the "Nobel Lie" or "Fairy Tale." I believe God's Spirit moves throughout the Bible and speaks to those who have a heart to discern this, a heart that at various points of reading the Bible knows "This is the truth." I am content to believe what God says for Himself and not what religion teaches. All I can say is: Good luck to you Fairy tale addicts once the historical truths and the "interpretive lies" of the Scrolls are made public. The Bible still tops the list of books with the greatest impact on people's lives but it has been so distorted by the lies of "religionists" that people are not going to know what to do with the Truth!

A recent study makes the point that it is usually futile to take a heart attack victim to a hospital. A certain Dr. Kerber says if the patient has had an adequate and full attempt at resuscitation in the field "The Further efforts in the hospital accomplish no good, are dehumanizing for the patient and the family and are costly." Now that certainly makes good sense (cents) and who would disagree? Unhappily, it easily falls into the case for euthanasia as well. Better to declare the victim dead at the scene rather than burden the family and hospital with fruitless debt. Imminently reasonable; but it is the reasonableness of it that can so easily be used for a further, and diabolical, extrapolation.

In my last "epistle," I mentioned the option of George Bush taking his lead from F.D.R. and "spending" us out of the present depression thus making us a nation of "serfs" on the government's payroll. But I have always held out the potential for a "war-time" economic "solution" as well. Will an attack on Khadafy do the trick? Poland and Pearl Harbor certainly gave Roosevelt a blank check. But how overcome the fact that we must "call Khadafy and Hussein to account" while North Korea and Israel refuse any kind of nuclear

110

inspections? Most certainly a double standard exists but we don't like our noses rubbed in it. After all, "We are doing the work of the Almighty!"

And now that Mr. Bush has been forced to succumb to Congressional demands (read: Blackmail) to extend unemployment benefits, what other extremes will he submit to with his popularity plummeting? With the threat of people like Pat Buchanan and David Duke tossing their weight into the political arena, just what will he do? Whatever it is, it will seem politically "expedient" and we must keep in mind, at all times, Judas, Hitler and the Khmer Rouge all thought they were doing the "right thing."

Goethe showed real insight into the nature of man and the extremes he is willing to go to in "cutting a deal" with the Devil. Few men at the pinnacle of power or in reach of it can resist making such a bargain. In truth, most men and women sell their souls for bargain basement prices. Jesus asked: "What profit is it to gain the whole world and lose your own soul, or what will a man give in exchange for his soul?" How you view the question depends on your real belief system; that "philosophy" by which you actually live, not pretend or simply give lip service.

It reminds me of the story told of a Northern Captain during the Civil War. He had a station on the Mississippi keeping watch for smugglers. One night he was approached by two prosperous looking "gentlemen" who offered him $5,000 to "look the other way" while they took a load of cotton down river. He refused. They offered him $10,000. He still refused. Discovering that they were dealing with a man of devout principles, they offered him $20,000 at which the Captain shouted: "Sergeant, come in here and throw these scoundrels out; they are getting too close to my price!"

For most, the Devil seems to pay better than The Lord. And, though we are warned that: "The wages of sin is death," death is far off and what we want is usually right now in this world rather than "nebulous promises" of future reward in the "hereafter." Too bad preachers don't understand this concept. It is far too easy to discount the glory of evil, to deny its attraction and pretend that the accusations against David Duke don't apply to our own dark sides.

Will Governor Wilson actually try to "close" California's borders? He is suggesting it. Why? Because we cannot afford to take on more welfare cases from the hoards of illegal aliens (I wonder why he can't follow Michigan's lead?). He has suggested a three-year residency requirement in order to be eligible for "Social Services." Imminently sensible but will it be taken seriously? Not likely. In spite of the lack of a "White Sheet" in the governor's closet, such suggestions are sure to draw the fire of the satanic A.C.L.U. But what is the answer to California's woes of budget-busting "services?" We have already cut our own throats by taxing businesses out of the state?

Dan Walters is right. The Demand-based deficit may last forever. The demands on the budget are sure to worsen as long as the phony "liberals" like Martinez and Puente, Willie Brown, Rangel, et al. continue to flourish. To quote Walters: "But slashing services deeply would have overtones of class rivalry. The only certainty is that long-term conflict is real and absent any bold policy initiatives, it will make this year's budget crisis seem like kindergarten squabbling."

Is it "Jap-bashing" to point out the obvious? Our "leadership" has given away the "store" and now our own computer technology is bowing to the "Rising Sun." Nintendo has a lock on the games to which our young are addicted and Toys R Us, largest toy retailer in the nation, won't even carry games of American manufacture for fear the Japanese will cut them off. Mac-Douglas will "cooperate" with Asians in the manufacture of airliners. We can now "proudly" display "Assembled In the U.S." rather than "Made In the U.S." on products!

With the chaotic insanity of our "leadership" is it any wonder that credence is given to some of the, seemingly, cockamamie stories on gonzo-TV? Like, for instance, the question of UFO's. Has our government "cut a deal" with Aliens? Is part of the deal involved with underground bases doing genetic experiments on missing children? Given what our government has done in the past, is anything too difficult to imagine it capable of?

Ten per cent of our population now receives food stamps. A recent poll indicated that more people are placing more value on "Family" than being rich. Of course, it hardly needs mentioning that more people have given up just getting ahead let alone rich. And, it does no good to point out the obvious fact that divorce laws need changing and women have to get over the habit of jumping into bed with any man who promises them a "better deal" than the present husband offers them. But the poll does offer some interesting prospects, for instance: The "New American Family" scenario. The setting: Two young people deciding to have a family.

Him: "If we just live together and have a kid, you can get $700 a month welfare. That with our food stamp allotment and what I can steal should keep us pretty good."

She: "What would I do without you? Sounds like a plan!"

Some time ago I mentioned the need of a book of "curses" that showed imagination because it is so lacking in the English language. To our shame, most "cursing" in English is simply vulgar, profane and unimaginative. Well, a retired professor of medieval literature, Rheinhold Aman, publishes "Maledicta, The International Journal of Verbal Aggression." A couple of samples: "May you become famous - they should name a disease after you.

May you inherit three shiploads of gold - and it shouldn't be enough to pay your doctor's bills." The good professor has performed a valuable service.

To my own sense of humor the following belongs in the "curse" category as well:

It seems a California State Senator, one Alan Robbins of Van Nuys, has "sort of" admitted to being a crook. In any event, he was found guilty of Racketeering, tax fraud, extortion, accepting bribes and a few other things, in short, of "doing his job as most politicians see it," and is going to prison. His "admission" of guilt is a veritable "jewel" of political language. I quote: "A number of my actions have failed to meet the standards of the Law!" Only politicians, "educators" preachers and rabbis seem to be able to pronounce such "curses" in language approaching that of Yiddish. Now anyone can, without any imagination, simply and vulgarly say: "I'm a crook and I got caught and I'm going to jail!" But it takes a "Robbins" to put such a civilized and polite face on it. If those German "war criminals" had answered in such language, maybe some of them wouldn't have been hung. But the Germans, like us, don't show the creativity in language that oriental cultures possess.

And speaking of crooks, how about that Alan Cranston? Imagine his standing in front of Congress after that "august" body had censured and rebuked him for doing only what comes naturally with his office and saying: "But for the grace of God, any of you might be standing here!" Now I grant you that his all-encompassing remark might have been just a tad overstated, but, really, why should we have to be left wondering if he wasn't more right than wrong in such a statement? Especially in view of the fact that the best our "leadership" can come up with is a "rebuke" for one of the "Honorable Senators" responsible for allowing Keating and his ilk to plunge us, our children and grandchildren into massive debt to bail the bastards out! You know, if someone robs me, I call him a thief! And I want him to go to jail and pay restitution. Does the fact that Cranston's "Peers" let him off with a slap on the wrist give credence to his condemning all of them, to his cutting remark that they are all crooks? What do you think?

At some point in time, thanks to Mr. Bush's use of Willie Horton, the Thomas/Hill debacle, David Duke's campaign, etc., the problems of "discrimination" in many other areas is going to have to be addressed. I foresee Jewish organizations like The Anti-Defamation League brought into question as "racist." How about B'nai B'rith, the N.A.A.C.P., and, even, churches that are exclusive to "certain" groups? When it comes to "racism," the "Kluxers" don't hold a candle to the Moslem or Jew. This is such a dangerous area of inquiry that few are even willing to discuss it. Carried to its extreme, it is madness. By his "exclusivity," the Christian invites the enmity of the whole world as Jesus warned would happen. Of course, there aren't that many real Christians around so the world isn't too concerned about them at present.

Ray Bradbury blames TV media for the recession! Quote: "Do not ever again look at local television news. If you do, you'll think the end of the world really is coming." Ray may seem a bit extreme but you have to admit he has a point. But, you have to equally admit the fact that it's the bad news, as with sex, that sells. People aren't interested in the "news" of a boy scout helping the little old lady across the street (I wonder if they do that anymore?). The problem is that the media too often distorts and twists things to its own agenda, often "liberal." It should also be admitted that the media's distortion of "liberal" is more devastating than most conservative views. It is the kind of "liberalism" that Hitler used with the expertise of Goebbels for the advancement of his own agenda.

Carried to its extreme, Man's Law is madness; Insane: "Elkhorn's schools have canceled dances until the state attorney general decides just how much slow dancing or kissing can occur before teachers must report it as sexual contact!" It has to be admitted that the present, evil system of "laws" have made the schools responsible for most of what society, the home and the church used to be responsible. As a result, there isn't a school in the nation that doesn't break the law on a daily basis in some way or another. It is simply insane to try, by mystical fiat of "law," to make the schools responsible for the entire training of children. The Lord knows how guilty the schools are for failing to educate children. But, they are asked to do the impossible, to do what only an entire society, working together, can hope to do.

To add further to the problem, ten boys at Piedmont Avenue Elementary in Oakland were subjected to a strip-search, actually being forced to drop their trousers, when a girl in their class accused them of taking some money. The money was later found in the girl's own purse. No girls were searched but think of the humiliation of those boys! Madness!

I just caught the news about Bush's "flip-flop" on his "directive" banning special attention on the basis of race and gender (special consideration for coloreds and women). Mr. Bush, Trudeau was right, you are a wimp! As a leader you are a consummate zero!

I am so angry about the wishy-washy, self-serving special privilege of the so-called "leadership" I am tempted to toss my own hat in the ring. One more "Crossfire" with that Ass (with my apology to that animal), Kinsley and his cohorts like Benjamin Hooks and his constant hand-wringing about how all us Caucasians should still be in sackcloth and ashes over keeping slaves and maybe I will. Move over Buchanan and Duke, here comes Heath!

Here is a sample of my "Platform:"

Revoke all laws that grant special consideration for employment on the basis of race or gender.

Repeal all laws that give special consideration on the same basis for college scholarships.

Make all able-bodied people do work of some kind in return for public assistance.

Enforce all immigration statutes regardless of race.

Get rid of the bureaucratic "laws" that prevent people from using their own land to provide for their families.

On that basis, let families settle some of the millions of acres the government "owns" which it now plans to eventually sell to a favored and privileged few.

Make Education accountable to the public it is supposed to serve. For example, no high school diploma should be granted until the pupil demonstrates proficiency in the basic reading, writing and arithmetic skills. That will quickly show who is doing the job and who isn't. Require a national test for students and prospective teachers and administrators.

Cause every statute that is obviously in conflict with the intent of our Constitution, The Bill of Rights and Declaration of Independence to be reviewed and submitted to the people.

Call for a Constitutional Amendment setting the salaries of Congressmen and judges at the median income of the rest of the country; further, how about returning "Citizen Representatives" to Congress by eliminating all retirements for politicians. This must be done!

Call for a national health plan that will not penalize wage earners, doctors or employers.

Enact a national no-fault auto insurance plan.

Get rid of National Deposit Insurance.

Make it a felony to export or sell the technology we develop in our own country. Stop making nations like Japan rich at the expense of our own citizens.

Make it illegal to give any form of foreign aid as long as our government does not have a balanced budget.

Enact tariffs that discourage any business that exports jobs overseas.

Get rid of the minimum wage law.

Enact reasonable term limitations on legislators. For example: no more than three terms of office in any capacity.

Put convicted child molesters in prison permanently!

There is, obviously, a great deal more that I could add but this is a sample. It is certainly enough to scare the pants off most politicians. And, no, I know many of these things require a great deal of discussion and research to make them fair and workable. But I also know that if these issues are not faced honestly, there is no hope for our nation or our children.

I also know that things like letting people build on their own land without bureaucratic constraints, letting them grow some of their own food and teach their children how to provide for themselves will result in the solutions of a lot of other problems in the areas of education, crime, and welfare.

CHAPTER TEN

CHRISTIAN PERSPECTIVE

JANUARY, 1991

Psalm 12:8

Well, the New Year is upon us. The "greed factor," i.e. "Christmas" as this nation practices it, is past once more. By the time this edition of CP comes out, we may be at war. Certainly many of you will see a drastic reduction of income via new taxes. Some who receive this letter will join the "new homeless" this year.

Many have spent money they did not have, robbing creditors, in order to satisfy some twisted sense of "giving" loved ones "gifts." Many of these will curse the landlords, banks, merchants and others they have cheated by their own perverted idea of what Christmas is all about. They will curse the "lack of understanding" of those whom they would rob: "The miserable SOB doesn't care that we had to have these things so we could have a merry Christmas and that is why we can't pay the rent, MasterCard, etc.!"

"What can the righteous do if the foundations are destroyed!" Psalm 11:3. Not much! But we are responsible to do what we can and we are responsible, always, for doing what is right.

Too many headlines read like pages out of the book of Revelation: War, famine, drought, disease, earthquakes, false "Christ's" etc., but some are humorous in a distorted way: "Rich got richer in 80's, Census Bureau Reports!" The part of the article that is not as well known is the fact that while the median wealth of all households in 1988 was $35,750, the median was $43,280 for Caucasians, $4,170 for Negroes and $5,520 for Hispanics! How do you think that will "play in Peoria?" (Or for that matter in Pretoria?).

If you were Negro or Hispanic, what would such a vast disparity of income tell you? Make way for Louis Farrakhan! But such headlines ignore the pertinent fact that the mostly Caucasian middle class is paying for all the welfare minorities enjoy, they pay the car insurance that enables the wetbacks to run into them at will, for the poor, mostly black and brown, babies to be born in hospitals and receive medical care at no cost.

A judge who recently made a most sensible demand that a child abusing, drug addicted welfare "mother" have birth control implants is castigated by the satanic A.C.L.U. and a liberal press. It seems it is her "right" to continue to "breed" more welfare and abused children. The fact that she is black only leads to the cry of "genocide!"

The largely white middle class gets the "privilege" of bailing out the S&Ls and the Bush administration is actually considering a plan to have taxpayers bail out failed Banks! The estimated cost of this plan will make the S&L scandal look cheap by comparison! And, of course, here come my "colleagues," the "Academics," howling in righteous wrath that their "Efforts to battle white oppression and sexism" are being "curbed" by those that think history should be taught truthfully and that college students should be a notch above high school dropouts academically.

Experts warn of the global fallout and catastrophic pollution of oceans that will assuredly result from the Persian Gulf oil fires and spillage that will occur in the event of war. The whole world is holding its breath wondering what will happen. Our president (remember the fellow that said "No new taxes" and "A kinder, gentler America?") has said of Saddam Hussein that: "We're going to kick his ass!" a statement that couldn't be more calculated to prevent any hope of even a temporary, diplomatic approach to a resolution of the crisis. Not that he doesn't need his ass kicked, but for a head of state to use such gutter language of another?

It surely is God's judgment when world leaders, which He has said He appoints, make foolish mistakes. Pharaoh really did not, though it may seem he did, get up one morning and say: "I think this is a good day to kick some Hebrew (Moses) ass!" But he may as well have. Pharaoh did succeed in stiffening his neck, attempting to defy God, and bringing total destruction upon Egypt, such destruction that it never again became a world power. Hal Lindsey and others have missed the mark by several miles but those with a solid knowledge of God's Word cannot but shudder at today's headlines.

The nations are indeed gathered together for war and in just that particular area God said they would be. Lawlessness does indeed abound and apostasy is the order of the day. Every religious kook that still holds sway via the "electronic church" is having a field day.

I have always contended that if there is to be a Rapture it would involve so few that their absence would not be noted. The status of the churches today only reinforces my belief in this regard. Not only did Jesus say only a few are going to be saved, that he does not expect much real faith at his return, but that those few remaining at the time of the Rapture would know, not the precise day nor hour, but how to "discern the signs of the time," so that his coming will not catch them unprepared.

A recent study by Princeton University pointed out that the Bible is very little read and even less understood in our society. So-called Bible "experts" have continuously muddied the waters of understanding by their "blind orthodoxy." They have little interest in the heart and mind of God and seem bent only on furthering their own prejudices and empires.

Because of a great deal of ignorance and prejudice, many that are guilty of blind orthodoxy misconstrue my statements and questions as an attack on the honor and integrity of The Lord and His Word. Nothing could be further from the truth. Many would rather resort to religiosity, pious platitudes or just plain intellectual laziness than really give attention to these things.

God said many centuries ago that His people perish for lack of knowledge. How true that is today. Worse, even those I know personally that name the name of Christ seem to have little interest in the things of God. Yet these same folks fret and worry about the things that will pass away rather than how they should please The Lord. This is a problem of skewed priorities. "Seek first the Kingdom of God!" was his command.

Thoreau was correct in his dictum that; "A wise man lives simply." Of course "If you don't want much, you don't need much." But then I have been both blessed and cursed as a man of simple tastes.

Those like me who have vivid memories of WWII, Korea. and Vietnam are knowledgeable of what war does to a nation. Unhappily, if world war does come through conflict in the Middle East, it will assuredly be the beginning of the end! There will be no nostalgia because there will be no future for looking back.

You may not realize it but the time is now here when The Lord is requiring His people to take a stand. For example, if you take the position that God means what He says, you now have the "opportunity" of going to jail for acting on that belief. Satan has ordered his system in such a way that a parent can be jailed for obeying God in the discipline of children, you can be imprisoned for standing on a street corner and passing out tracts or preaching, for attempting, as a father or husband, to "rule your families well", for taking a stand against the evil that surrounds us by the actions of corrupt laws, legislators, and religious charlatans.

No matter how you slice it, AIDs is an infectious, fatal disease. Yet, we read that the U.S. will end the immigrant ban on those that carry the disease. In other words, you and I have been told that our government has decided that it is all right to invite ever more of these people to come into our country and pass the disease around.

As obviously insane as such a policy appears to responsible minds, our "leadership," as Pharaoh of old, seems bent on destroying us. When we read, "God hardened Pharaoh's heart," it must be that God, as He said He did, placed Pharaoh in that position of leadership to accomplish His purpose of judgment against Egypt.

When we are told by our leaders that allowing AIDs carriers into our country because: "...the (old) policy is an unconscionable intrusion into the lives of people who carry the virus," what are they actually saying? That we are to be "charitable" to known carriers at the risk of killing more innocent people? Only Satan could so successfully blind people to such rot.

But don't you sometimes wonder how the perverts have such financial and political clout? Only by God's permission and Satan's system of government in judgment of this nation! We, as a nation, have rejected Him, and, as with Israel of old, He has rejected us.

Homosexuals prey on the innocent, infecting the young, even infants, with their perversion. If a factual, statistical study could be done, how many who remain silent could tell of these perverts approaching them? I'm sure the number would be staggering. I have experienced such myself, both as a child and adult. But, like most, I remained silent. By God's grace I escaped their depredations but how many don't? The harshest language in Scripture is reserved for these perverts (and their religious counterparts). As God Himself points out, He brought the flood and destroyed the cities of Sodom and Gomorrah as an everlasting testimony to the fact that He holds those that practice such abomination a "stench" in His nostrils.

And here they come; in increasing numbers, flaunting their perversion under the ACLU's guise of "civil liberty!" Teachers, politicians, "ministers," Boy Scout leaders, "soldiers," etc. Even now the Boy Scouts of America have to go to court to "prove" a pervert is not an acceptable role model for young boys. And some dare to say God is not right in His wrath against such a nation?!

How do you suppose God feels about our allowing "Gay churches" and "Gay believers" and "preachers" to be accepted in our society? He has made His feelings very plain. But we are inviting His wrath and judgment as a result of legislating these perverts into acceptability.

God, in His mercy and love, has made it possible for all manner of sin to be forgiven, even that of homosexuality. But it still requires the sinner to repent and forsake his evil ways. Nowhere does God approve us taking prejudicial action against perverts, Those that are enslaved by Satan to such perversion are to be warned, as all sinners, that they will answer to God for their sin. We are to warn, not take a club to all who deny God. I often wonder at Calvin's action in burning Servetus at the stake. But I have many controversial thoughts about the so-called "Reformation".

"Joseph" is unknown to our "Pharaohs." While God is judging His own first, there are many who think they can get away with their sin, saying in their hearts, as they have ever done, "God does not see." Baker, Swaggart,

Roberts, et al., even Falwell, have learned that men cannot, of their own egos, please Him by building for their own self- aggrandizement.

In my work with the churches and schools over, lo, these many years, I have noticed that the "Christian leadership" falls into, primarily, three categories. One: Those that like to engage in metaphysical nonsense, mouthing pious platitudes, liturgical hokum and making "long their robes." Two: Those that preach the "prosperity gospel" (prosperous for them), engage in hysterical nonsense like the gibberish (tongues) speakers who put on a great emotional show (Cerrullo, et al.). Three: Those that practice the "gospel" of "love everybody and keep a smile on your face and a song in your heart," and "God is too good to send anyone to hell (it doesn't exist anyhow, they say)".

Iniquity abounds because the love of many has "waxed cold". Lawlessness in the face of ever increasing laws and the fast-paced production of prisons for, largely, minority inmates; in an attempt to stem the tide, legislators are, insanely, trying to legislate morality; at least their idea of morality. In Kern County, half of the highway deaths involve Hispanics yet they comprise only one-fourth the population. Most are without insurance and were driving "under the influence." Now how about that for a "racial bias"? Yet I am quoting from the newspaper.

We have a new, national leader. A Negro woman is now the mayor of Washington D.C., our nation's capitol. I certainly see God's hand in this. It ought to shame men who are supposed to lead. It should shame a nation that built so much of its wealth from the labor extracted, against every principle of the Gospel, from slaves. I cannot help but bow to the irony of God's justice in bringing such things to pass. Neither can I help thinking that it would serve all those men right, who think they can do things their way instead of God's, who think they can avoid God's command that they are to accept responsibility for leadership, if we should have a woman president. What an extension of the shame of so-called "women preachers"!

Martin L. King. What an example of the best Negro people have themselves to exalt. A man notorious for his infidelity and unbelief of the Scriptures (I can easily dismiss the accusations of plagiarism since so many in academia are guilty of the same thing. After all, what is genius but saying old things in new ways?), yet he shames many Caucasian leaders who profess to believe as he did. But what fools to deceive themselves that a movement born of such a "leader" can result in any lasting benefit (apart from a ridiculous national holiday and chance to skip school).

As a qualified "Okie Intellectual," an oxymoron to those prejudiced against anything good coming out of Nazareth or the prophet from Galilee, I am easily dismissed as a harmless "Curmudgeon" by most. My soul- brothers,

Thoreau and Solzynetzian, understand. And, unhappily, I do not hear the audible voice of God or angels directing my actions.

Seeming inconsequential things bring a nation to its knees. I was one of the lone voices, as a math teacher that opposed the use of calculators by pupils that didn't even know the multiplication tables. We now know the folly of the so-called "new-math". Having forsaken the time-proven methods of learning, we live with some interesting results. If your doctor or some other professional has trouble with the English language due to their foreign extraction, you can lay it at the doorstep of people like Honig, and our universities. I fear Grace and Damerell were correct: Get rid of 535 people in Congress and abolish all the schools of education on every university campus.

Our children see the idiocy of what passes for education in our schools. They have learned being taught by the "leadership", that "getting," no matter how, is the main thing. If you lack the skills and a job, steal. We have succeeded in teaching an entire generation of young people that might makes right, stealing, pornography, homosexuality, lying, cheating, refusing to work if you can make it on welfare, incompetence, disrespect for parents and authority in general, burning the flag, all these and more are acceptable by the very models of leadership they are given.

A nation that worships at the throne of King Sports and Queen Entertainment (How many homeless and truly needy could have been provided for by just the cost of the Rose Parade, etc? Was Caesar correct in giving them 'Bread and circuses'?), that worships money no matter how acquired, whose material interests are more important for the moment than any sacrifice of present desire for the hope of future benefit, which teaches its young that number one is of paramount importance, whose president can say, "We're going to kick ass" (of course, that might be considered an improvement over his predecessor's "Let's dust Moscow", or another's "I am not a crook!"). Such a nation cannot look for God's help in its extremity.

That great city, Nineveh, was spared when it hearkened to the preaching of Jonah. The people, led by their king, repented in sackcloth and ashes. Can it happen in our nation? I think it can. But it cannot without "Jonah's," men, even though reluctant, who can stand up for God and His Word and be taken seriously. That automatically eliminates the charlatans, pseudo-spiritual, the "show and gibberish" charismatics and Pentecostals, the egotists and "social gospel" proponents, all who think women have the same responsibility and "equality" as men in the church and family, all who think God doesn't really mean what He says, etc. Who does this leave? Only the handful that really believe God's Word! It's a most sobering thought! As crisis upon crisis hits us from every quarter, it is a marvelous thing to have the hope that God alone never fails. But where are the men of God who are to warn a sinful and adulterous generation of the wrath to come?

The greatest disappointment of my life (apart from my own failures) has been to watch so many who started well and fell away. I worked with a group of young people once that showed great promise. They are all adults now and not a one is doing anything of consequence for The Lord. Yet every one, once, was enthusiastic and devoted to the study of God's Word. "Ye did run well, who did hinder you that ye should not obey...?" But, since so many, like myself, have a largely "Baptistic" doctrinal orientation "Blind orthodoxy" gets in the way. I am easily dismissed as a leader of "doctrinal purity" because of my convictions that the mode of baptism is unimportant, that Jesus made "real" wine, that I question men's ideas of God's perfection, and, as if that wasn't enough I smoke and am multi-divorced; so much for my being an "example" of "perfection."

There have been friends who have fallen away, grown men of whom one expected much. But, they lacked the spiritual "backbone," the "Holy Steel," to confront evil. Some have failed by pride, their own egos getting in the way of the Holy Spirit in their lives. I grieve to see some of these still thinking nothing is wrong and all the while they are blind to the fact that they produce nothing of consequence for The Lord. In the worst cases, I see some that actually believe they are teachers when they know nothing of real value to teach others.

Prejudice and bigotry feed on ignorance. It was not that long ago when Negroes in the South were treated as sub-humans, forced to ride in the back of busses, separate, public toilets, drinking fountains, schools. The shame of this to a nation! And, now, by attempting to legislate fairness, all men, in their miserable attempts, have succeeded in doing is to further the alienation and racial hatred.

It isn't law that will change men's hearts; God alone can do this. But they will not repent of their wickedness and turn to Him and He warned that He will not always strive with them but bring judgment. I fear His judgment is now here.

Jesus said that the entire Law is fulfilled by just two things- to love God and others as ourselves. Those "others" are amplified by the parable of the "Good Samaritan," keeping in mind the historical basis of the parable and the fact that God does not require us to love those that love evil and hate Him.

Our love for God is proven by obedience, as Jesus said, to His Word. Not one single individual can point to another and say, "I failed to obey because of such and such a person." Certainly none can use such a one as myself as an excuse for their failure. I have often pointed out the fact that, while God's ultimate purposes cannot be thwarted by men, the work of God often fails where God's people fail. The precedent for this was set in the Garden. The truth of this is the fact that God will require it of us, individually, when we fail to obey. God could not, in justice, judge us so if we were not responsible and given the means and authority to individually obey if His purpose in our lives, and the work He has given us to do, could succeed without our cooperation.

Do I limit God by such a statement? Yes. But it is not I that can possibly limit God. It may be that He Himself set these limitations, I don't know; but I do believe the limitations exist. It is men's faulty perception of God, a failure to understand His real nature I call "blind orthodoxy," that claims attributes of God that He does not claim for Himself.

"K'sara, sara" may do as a "cop-out" but God will not condone it and it cannot be made to fit Him. Neither fatalism nor nihilism will fit. That only leaves the fact that we have been woefully misled by many theologians who have skirted and danced away from the really tough questions we have every right to ask of God; questions He Himself wants asked by His people. The basic problem is that the questions must first be from a sincere heart, a heart that has proved itself. And how is this done? God gives us the answer. We must seek these answers as the unsaved seek worldly wealth, with the same energy, resources and diligence. Thus Jesus' remark that the "children of this world are wiser in their ways than the children of light!"

Far too may think that God will reward less than a whole-hearted and earnest effort, that He is some heavenly beggar to be satisfied with the crumbs of our lives rather than the whole loaf. Woe to those that believe such heresy! "Let not such a one think that he will receive anything of The Lord!"

I would strongly urge all of you to re-read your Bibles with this thought in mind: that God is not, and does not claim to be, omniscient, omnipresent or omnipotent! He is God Almighty, the "I Am," and nothing can detract from his power and sovereignty. What I am saying is that we have been led to believe things about Him that are not true, things that naturally lead to half-hearted service.

Since man was created in God's image, He Himself must have attributes that are reflected in us, but without sin, without selfishness, without the pride of the flesh that plagues us. But He is the ultimate Creator and as such is not satisfied that He has reached His own ideals of perfection in His creative acts that are on going.

If we are called to be priests and kings, judges of angels, God has a monumental task in mind that requires exceptional beings- beings that like Him are able to do mighty things. Now ask yourself, have you any real thoughts or hope that your present lives or work are equipping you for such an exciting and responsible future? Does "Going to be with The Lord" excite your imagination and fill you with joy? If not, you know nothing as you ought to. And I lay the ignorance that leads to your lack of joy and excitement directly on the doorstep of "blind orthodoxy," you are not seeking The Lord with a whole heart. That is not my opinion; it is what God Himself says.

Since war is a present fact that has the world's attention, let's talk about the "real war!" the warfare that God's people are supposed to wage against Satan and his evil servants. Immediately there comes to my mind the advice of Paul to Timothy: "Endure hardship with us like a good soldier of Christ Jesus. No one serving as a soldier gets involved in civilian affairs - he wants to please his commanding officer." II Timothy 2:3,4. Paul also tells Timothy to reflect on the things he has learned and been told and that The Lord will give him insight into these things.

I have made the point in my book that there is a battle between the sexes that began in The Garden and continues to this day the woman's spiritual battle is to obey God's command, in judgment, to submit to the man. The man's battle is to accept the responsibility of leadership. That is it in a nutshell. The suitability and irony of God's judgment is easily seen. God knew how difficult it was going to be for both. But the command is still there no matter the difficulties and God expects obedience of both men and women to His command.

We have been disastrously misled to think that just because God has promised eternal life to His children, to those who are born of His Spirit, not because of some emotional experience, some kind of "decision," joining some organization or some other such folly. The heart of a child of God desires to obey and has the power to do so. We are known as "believers" to others and to ourselves because we obey God. Even children know in their hearts that they are "accepted," loved, because of obedience to their parents. If they are rebellious, if they are disobedient, the relationship suffers and will continue to suffer until the child repents and does right.

The "warfare" involves personal relationships, as Jesus pointed out. Nowhere is the failure of men as abundantly clear as in the relationship between them and women. I have gone into this subject in depth elsewhere and won't belabor it here except to point out the obvious; that Satan has been more successful in this way, just as he was in The Garden, than in any of his other efforts.

In our sinful obfuscation of the commands of God, in vain attempts to set His judgment aside through "legal" maneuvering, blurring the distinctions that God Himself set between the sexes, we are reaping the whirlwind. In our hedonistic, materialistic and "equality" society, we deny God's Word and substitute men's judgment thereby incurring His righteous wrath and judgment.

Ever since Adam blamed both God and Eve for his own miserable failure to obey, men have tried in various ways to avoid God's commands that they should be responsible for ruling their wives and families. In a society such as ours, the price is too high for the weak-hearted. But you men have a choice; obey God at the risk of losing your families, or disobey and suffer God's judgment.

The example God expects you men to set is the hope of your wives and children. Now neither a piece of paper (marriage certificate) nor so-called "vows" of fidelity will keep a woman from defiling the marriage bed; my children and I have been the victims of this adulterous activity and suffered because of it. But God still requires it of me to obey Him even at the cost of infidelity or even the loss of children, friends or anyone else.

You women have a right to expect a husband who will be faithful to God and you regardless of the cost. God has made provision for a marriage partner to separate, even divorce, another who is unfaithful. But you had better make sure you are right. A husband is not "abusive" because he insists on obeying God by exercising Godly leadership and ruling you and the children, you endanger your own soul by refusing to submit to him.

Bullets fly in this warfare, sometimes quite literally. Given the enormity of the problems facing families today it is little wonder that, shunning God's way, people are in constant conflict over money problems, discipline of children and a host of other things.

I just returned from a quick trip out to Kelso Valley. It is quiet and peaceful out there. On the East there are the rugged, sere mountains of the high desert. Looking South and West, there are the heavily forested and, at this time, snow-capped Piute mountains. Today I saw actual Blue birds out there, a rare phenomena and quite a treat. The small, chipmunk-like, California ground squirrels are also plentiful as well.

How I wish I could have more people share such wondrous things rather than the anguish and turmoil of their city existence. But the jet aircraft from Edwards passing over on occasion disrupts my reverie; a reminder that wars and rumors of wars are inescapable.

I am ever grateful to The Lord for allowing me to live in an area where, in minutes, I can be alone in desert or mountain solitude. It is in these solitary ventures that I am able to commune with The Lord and seek His wisdom, stripped of the "advantages" and distractions of "civilization."

Did judge Broadman really know when he rendered his sentence of Darlene Johnson that Norplant might be a way of controlling run-away child and welfare abuse? Was his judgment only directed at a 27 year old drug addicted Negro woman on welfare with five children and pregnant with a sixth, who had been found guilty of beating her four and six year old little girls?

The Philadelphia Inquirer suggested that women on welfare be encouraged to use Norplant. The paper later ran an apology saying its original opinion was "misguided and wrong-headed." Why? Because it might lead to the impression reducing the number of Negro people could cure that poverty. The paper said birth control should be a matter of choice. Dr. Michael Grodin, a professor in Boston University's law, medicine and ethics program is quoted as saying: "People have reproductive liberties in this country and we don't take that away from them. We just don't do that in this country."

Nowhere in the Constitution do we find your "Reproductive Rights" Dr. Grodin, But we will eventually be forced to limit mindless reproduction of "human weeds" and we will do it because we no longer have the privilege of allowing crime and abuse to run rampant, because we no longer have the choice of good and bad, but bad and worse! because the taxpayers are fed up with being ripped off by social programs that not only are horrendously expensive failures, but are constantly divested of any salutary benefits by the greed of fat bureaucrats in politics, education and business that build empires for themselves on the backs of both the poor and the middle class.

Statistically, three of Darlene Johnson's children will be career criminals. Two will be on welfare all their lives. Only one will go to high school. This one will probably not graduate; five of six children to be cared for by taxpayers. And those five will breed and multiply additional social-care recipients. Racism? No! Statistical reality. Cold, hard fact.

Now all the pious, professional liberals and religionists will wring their hands and curse me, the satanic ACLU and not a few of my peers will castigate me for seeming like an ignorant "redneck" in my rubbing their noses in the truth. Historically, the only "answers" to insoluble problems have been born of expediency. You do not have to be a professional historian to know this.

Because of the tribulations ahead, "stop-gap" measures will be imposed; by force of arms in some cases. "Hitlerian solutions" will be the norm, born of necessity. Again, these are the subject of some of my other books so I won't dwell on it here, I will only repeat that when circumstances are right, the "unthinkable" becomes, not only "thinkable" but downright attractive. Tragically, the end of such things is death and destruction and the abrogation of all freedom and liberty.

Those of you that think yourselves to be saved, you had better give the more earnest heed to seeking the face of The Lord while He may be found. You had better get your priorities straight and your houses in order, regardless the cost.

But to do this, you have to understand the very nature of The Lord, and in this, as I have said, many have been badly misled. Our notion of God's perfection is terribly flawed by our own sinful nature. As He declares, such a skewed view leads to some that think He "... is one such as you!" But if we could unload ourselves of the "baggage" of prejudice and "religion," if we could begin anew to read exactly what He says of Himself, a whole new world of understanding opens to us, provided of course that you are in fact a child of God.

Having had the rare privilege of wandering and exploring many marvelous places, having been able to hark back to a time of much simple honesty and living, having been the fortunate recipient of Godly learning by humble and unpretentious people, I am able to confess my own folly in following many things that, in the words of Paul, "Were not so." There is much to be learned about how the early churches "cooperated" with The Holy Spirit in the work. Acts 15. Now cooperation is not what the churches practice. They don't even understand what the word means apparently. One does not cooperate with an omniscient, omnipotent and omnipresent force or entity. One is at the mercy of the dictatorial leading of such. But if, in fact, God needs our cooperation, just how important does the individual believer become in His plans? And how important, then, is it that we obey, with understanding, His commands?

Our misperception of God's perfection is a distorted view of how we, as human beings, perceive ideals; the "ideal mate," the "ideal job," the "ideal place to live," the "ideal child," etc. Until we are willing to confess our own ignorance and prejudice and are willing to "go back to Sinai" and learn, we are doomed in vain attempts to understand and do the work.

God says for us to be "perfect." Is that a bad joke? If not, how are we to understand His ideal of perfection? We cannot as long as we deceive ourselves that we have understanding and our lives betray our ignorance. God plainly has a different view of perfection from our flawed ideals. But, since we are made in His image, we, like He, are able to dream, to plan and build, to gain wisdom and understanding, to hope in the face of hopelessness.

We dimly see, as through Paul's dark glass, the ideals of God, we dimly see the ideals of honesty, fidelity, unselfish and sacrificial love, forgiveness of wrongs against us, work that is honorable, fellowship that is not contingent on another's agreeing with us in all things, men and women obeying God and fulfilling their proper roles, and so much more.

God is not perfect by men's definitions; He is perfect by His own. It is God Himself that has set the groundwork for the hard questions that demand answers, answers that, unless we are most earnest and diligent in the quest, will forever remain paradoxes, dark anomalies thwarting half-hearted attempts at satisfaction.

Was it God or an angel in the burning bush? And how important is it that we know? Was God truly sorry He made man? He says He was. How does Satan rule in this world, and remember Jesus did not dispute the world is under Satan's dominion for now. How do we know when we pray that God hears? How did angels administer the Law? Why did God honor Naaman's seeming hypocrisy? Why did Jesus have to "learn obedience?" How are demons cast out? Are they less today than in the time of Jesus? If not, what are we supposed to do about it? If only God can be blasphemed, why did the Jews think and teach that Moses could be also? Does God engage in hyperbole? (John 21:25) Does God lose His temper, change His mind, and make mistakes?

There is a perfection in dreaming, trying, creating, loving, sacrificing that goes far beyond our hazy ideals. In Him there is light without any "shadow of turning." It is dazzling in its purity. It is a burning fire that purifies and strips away all the counterfeit "humility" and religiosity.

If we face God, as His supreme creation, in true humility and with the proper reverence due Him, He has obligated Himself to honor our questions and lead us in finding answers. But "The Pearl of Great Price" is not to be purchased with the tawdry treasures of this earth; it cannot be acquired by duplicity or hypocrisy, a half-measure of effort or a divided heart. The man, we are told, even warned, who sincerely seeks such a prize, seeks it with all his heart and when it is found, he goes and sells all that he has that he might own such a treasure. And Who has made such seeking hearts? And where are they today?

"When I was a child, I talked like a child, I thought like a child, I reasoned like a child. When I became a man, I put childish ways behind me." Children, as children, are to be loved, taught and cared for. They have the God-given privilege of rightly expecting these things.

If the children are fortunate enough to have Godly parents, they will learn that they cannot intrude at will in adult activities and conversation. It is their place to expect to feel important and loved by both affection and correction. As they grow older, if the lessons of childhood have not been met with rebelliousness, they have the social skills that equip them for acceptance on their merit, not on selfish ego.

But pity both the parents and children where such care is not given. Such children grow up to be monsters. They were denied the training that taught them to listen and learn when adults were talking, they "learned" that they had a "right" to interrupt, to demand that they be heard and be the center of attention. I have seen one such child disrupt and be "heeded" by an entire group of adults as though the child were teaching them! And, in a tragic way, the child was, in fact, teaching them; teaching them that they really did not care how the child grew into adulthood.

We have behaved like spoiled brats and demanded that God accept our selfishness and half-hearted attempts at obedience and instruction. But God has warned us repeatedly that such "childishness" will only bring on disaster, individually and as a nation.

CHAPTER ELEVEN

THE OKIE INTELLECTUAL

A HIGH-TONED PERIODICAL FOR THE DISCRIMINATING MIND

MAY, 1991

"It was a dark and stormy night!" It wasn't, really, I've just always wanted to start a story with the infamous line. In reality, it was a beautiful, balmy, summer evening; so there.

My brother, Ronnie, a friend and I were on our way up the Canyon on 178 out of Bakersfield to Bull Run Creek to get in some trout fishing. I was driving the friend's dad's truck, a '40 Studebaker. I hit the first "S" curve a tad fast and we managed a four-wheel slide through it. Fortunately, there wasn't any other traffic. It did not bode well for our journey but we were young and, hence, indestructible and laughed about it.

It was great to be young and single in the Fifties in America and, especially, in California. Tax-fattened hyenas, otherwise known as "politicians," hadn't yet perfected their methods of robbing responsible, working folks blind, teachers were still trying to educate, welfare wasn't yet an approved life-style, you could buy a house for $3,000, gas was fifteen cents (even twelve cents at times) a gallon and Jimmy Swaggart and Jim Baker were still virtual unknowns; all in all, a pretty good time to be alive in the good, old U.S. of A.

It was a beautiful night, filled with the aroma of the marvelous scents of the river and the vegetation as the road wound along its banks, climbing toward Isabella and Kernville. Mice scurried across the road in the beam of our headlights, we could hear the croaking of frogs and the occasional, soft, soggy balloon "pop" as a tire would roll over a toad, his tongue, eyeballs and sundry juices squirting out, tracing an intricate pattern over the warm asphalt. Once in awhile a hawk or owl would make an appearance as they chased their dinners of the smaller critters. We passed road-kills of snakes, mice and one skunk. Don't mind the smell as long as the little fellows keep it at a respectable distance. But, then, I'm not overly offended at the smell of the old privy either, so I'm a little weird that way (some other ways also, according to my ex-wives and women in general).

In addition to our fishing and camping gear, I had with me one of the first new-issue, Single-Action Army Colts. Beautiful work of art in .38 Special caliber. Colt hadn't yet put it out in .357. I got one of those later and kept it for years; my favorite sport shooter- 100 rounds and one Jackrabbit, fast-draw. That's fun and easy on the rabbits. But you have to be a hand loader to afford it and, fortunately, I had been one since I was 14 years old, living on the old, mining claim in Boulder Gulch.

The holster for the Colt was a professional "Hollywood" rig with steel insert. I had been taught by a real pro and thereby avoided the "Clutch and Grab" gang that was popularizing the sport of shooting themselves in the foot by trying to imitate James Arness and Hopalong Cassidy. Actually knew a kid that had managed to put four holes in his leg and thigh with one bullet trying this trick; wouldn't have believed it possible if I hadn't seen the holes in him. Fortunately, he was using a .22 and the slug missed the bones.

But to get back to the story; we arrived in Kernville about 9:00 p.m. and took off on Burlando Road. In those days, you could drive past the pavement on the dirt road clear up to the old smelter. Awful rough road even then and you had to know where you were going. A short distance in we could hear the Creek, the swift water making its own music. The stars were shining brightly, trout were waiting for us and we could smell the pines and lupine. Marvelous.

Then, disaster! There was one stretch of the road that cut into the side of a hill, was quite steep and overgrown with branches and often wet from a spring that flowed across it. Breaking brush and branches, I tried to barrel through when the rear wheels of the old Stude hit a slick spot and slipped off the side. So there we were, the right, rear wheel jammed against the brush and branches, dangling off the road and no means of getting it back on track. We couldn't go backward, forward or sidewise. Stuck.

Exchanging the appropriate expletives and good-natured pleasantries the situation demanded there was nothing to do but start hoofing it back to Kernville in the hope of finding an adventurous tow-truck driver at the local gas-up. Not wishing to leave the Colt unattended, I stuck it under my shirt in the waist of my Levis.

After an hour's hike through the darkness, we reached Kernville. It was now about eleven o'clock. The only place still doing business was the local "cuttin' 'n' shootin'" joint, the saloon. Feeling the need of some refreshment after our hike, we bellied up to the bar. I was mindful of the Colt, snug in my waist, but the place was peaceful and no one was being rowdy.

While we drank our beers, a couple of guys, feeling no pain, were intrigued by our tale of woe. They were up from L.A. and had been fishing the Kern and getting plastered, alternating pastimes. Nothing else would do but that they were going to take us up the road and get the "blankety-blank" Stude back on the trail. Sloshed as they were, common sense was a "no-go." Of course, we were in no real circumstances to argue against even a remote possibility. In a spirit of liquid camaraderie, we left the bar on our quest. And then I saw their car. It was a spanking, brand new, Plymouth station wagon.

Now you really have to see the trail up to the smelter to understand what was going on in my mind. It is a twisting, jagged path hardly deserving of the name "road." Pan-bustin' rocks jut up from its surface here and there, it's full of holes and in some places large granite boulders line both sides of the narrow path. In other places, tree limbs and brush rake the sides of any vehicle going through. An occasional muffler or pipe will be found to give mute testimony to its ruggedness. And a couple of drunks were going to take us up this "road" in their brand new vehicle! And we were going to let them!

Piling into the Plymouth, we hit the highway. Long live truth, justice and the American way! We got to the end of the pavement without incident. Fortunately, there was no traffic on Burlando at midnight as the driver took his half out of the middle and both sides going. Then we hit the dirt at the end of the pavement with a cloud of dust and a hearty "High Ho, Silver!"

A deep trough of sand in the road helped slow us down as we got to the first boulders. "Crash" as the Plymouth bounced off one and "Crash" it went against one on the other side. "Bang, crash, crash," we caromed off the rocks. "Wham" into a hole. "Clang" went a rock against the pan. By now, drunk as he was, a note of genuine doubt and concern began to creep into our driver's voice. A pine limb scraped against the windshield as another large boulder banged against the left, rear door and he hit a large hole at the same time. "I don't think she'll make it boys!" the guy said. We were sure she wouldn't make it.

To the accompaniment of loud and colorful language together with gut-wrenching impacts of the wagon against various obstacles, he managed to get the poor, hapless Plymouth turned the other direction. He was going considerably slower now. Even so, he added a few more dings in the skin of the "used to be new" vehicle going out.

There was a pronounced shimmy to the wagon as we got back onto the pavement. We could hear the roar of the exhaust where the pipe must have been dismembered and a loose shock was knocking against the back axle. There was also a scraping noise as a fender was chewing rubber off one of the tires.

We managed to get back to Kernville and I discovered I couldn't get the door of the wagon to open on my side. Ronnie and the kid got out ok but I had to roll the window down and crawl out it on my side. The poor Plymouth looked like it had been through the wars, as indeed it had. We didn't wait around to exchange pleasantries but beat a hasty retreat after quickly surveying the damage. I've often wondered how those good Samaritans felt when they sobered up and could clearly discern the carnage. Not good, I suspect.

Well, here we were with no answer to our dilemma. We trudged across the bridge in the hope of seeing something open on the other side of town. Suddenly, our luck changed. The local sheriff pulled up to us.

"What's the story, fellows?" the deputy asked somewhat guardedly. We explained our predicament and the constable, a young fellow also, was a good Joe and invited us to hop into the squad car saying he thought he knew someone in Isabella that might be able to help us out. I crawled in front with him and Ronnie and the kid got into the back seat. It was only then, sitting next to the deputy that I thought about the Colt in the waist of my Levis; an interesting situation.

I considered the reaction of this minion of the law if he knew I was sporting a loaded Hogleg under my shirt. My emotions were mixed as I tried to keep from laughing out loud at the possibilities. Fortunately, for all concerned, we got to Isabella without incident and the deputy found a fellow with a truck who was willing to help us. He was a little dubious about our telling him we had gotten the old pickup in as far as we said. He knew the "road." So, bidding a fond "Adieu" to the nice young deputy we set out into the warm night back to Kernville.

To make a long story short, he got us there and managed to get the Stude out of its predicament and, after giving him twenty bucks, a princely sum back then, went on his way. It was now about 3 a.m. and we finally crashed in our sleeping bags.

We were up early and the trout were obliging. Some of the pools at Bull Run are as much as twenty feet deep with beautiful waterfalls emptying into them. I've caught five-pounders here. Some years ago, Forestry put up a gate at the end of the paved road to keep the riff-raff out. I'm glad they did as some bums had begun to litter the place with trash. Let's face it folks, if it's easy to get to idiots will ruin it.

It was later that I found out that Ronnie had an AAA card and could have used it to pay the tow truck driver. I was not happy. But my brother has never been noted for his quick wit in a crunch. Oh well, if you are a real fisherman and know Bull Run you know that in spite of our minor set-backs the fishing made it all worthwhile. Now, many years later I have almost forgiven my brother his moral lapse, having that Triple A card that would have saved me the twenty bucks and the whole incident is a mostly pleasurable memory of simpler times and continued thankfulness that poor, unsuspecting deputy never learned of the Colt.

Speaking of idiots, in this case, our elected "leadership," have you heard about the Washington Report newsletter from U.S. Senator William Donnemeyer discussing the national debt? Seems that if we include Social Security, 16.5 trillion dollars, Medicare, 1.8 trillion, civil service and military pensions, 1 trillion, government direct loans, loan guarantees, loan insurance and deposit insurance, 5.8 trillion, crank in the S&L bail-out and a few things like farm subsidies, student loans and housing subsidies and you get a figure around 27.3 trillion dollars; over $109,000 for every American.

I don't know about you folks but that's not pocket change for me. In fact, I don't know anyone with that much money in his or her sock. I don't even know anyone who is even working on it or ever hopes to have it. I guess I just don't move in the right circles.

Most of the folks I know are not even making it on their present incomes. How in the ever-lovin'-blue-eyed-world can we ever hope to pay a debt this size? Simple, we can't! It's beyond the scope of the tax-paying public to ever pay this debt.

In an attempt to balance the State budget, Californians are going to be required to pay approximately twice as much in state taxes. It just has to make a person think about what we are being asked to pay for? Illegal aliens, deadbeats, crooks (Juvenile and otherwise), welfare mothers and kids; I know the kids don't ask to be born, and what kid in his right mind would ask to be born into such circumstances. But who holds a gun to these women's heads and says: "OK, breed!"

A recent report by Legislative Analyst Elizabeth G. Hill leads me to believe that California will soon tax such items as food, eliminate mortgage interest deductions and other deductions that will hit the property owner and small businesses the hardest. Renter credit and a host of other deductions will also be eliminated. Sales taxes on virtually everything you can name will be increased. In some cases, like food, new taxes will be added.

Government is out of control. It is so big it can't hope to keep up with the abuses, let alone straighten them out. A simple example is the problem of uninsured drivers.

I recently read of a Shafter woman, named Rodriguez, who was convicted of vehicular manslaughter hit and run. Killed in the accident was another woman, Dana Hilderbrand, 20, who was on her way to school at Cal Poly San Luis Obispo. She was scheduled to graduate in December. This Rodriguez woman was uninsured and driving with suspended license; certainly nothing new to California drivers.

The judge, North Kern Municipal Judge Gary Ingle says he "... did not believe the case justified felony charges." So he will probably let the Rodriguez woman cop a plea to misdemeanor charges and give her probation. Now Dana Hildebrand is dead at 20. The Rodriguez woman probably has nothing worth suing for and didn't even carry insurance. The surviving family would have to sue at their own expense in civil court and have no hope of even collecting burial expenses for their daughter. No doubt the Rodriguez woman will continue driving without insurance or license. I wonder if she has relatives in Mexico who are laughing about the crazy "Gringo" system of "justice?" I know the rest of the world has to wonder (I've recently learned that this Rodriquez woman is still driving. She just got a ticket. She exhibits no remorse whatever for killing Dana).

I have been the victim of similar "accidents." Once, a kid with no insurance and no license hit me. I have a permanently, crippled hand. The judge fined him $17.50; might have been $18.50 if he had killed me. Again, there was nothing worth suing for, the kid and his folks were deadbeats and I would have spent more on lawyers and court costs than I would ever have collected from these bums. This kid is still probably driving around without insurance or license.

Not long ago, an illegal alien totaled my car. I couldn't even get an address for the Mexican from the cops. As usual, I got to pay the entire cost, the loss of my own car, because government won't do anything to get these deadbeats off the road or even put them in jail if they cripple or kill you.

By now, most of you know that if you are the victim of "Juvenile" crime, you get to "eat it." I lost another vehicle, along with thousands of dollars worth of tools and personal property, to this madness. These crooks stole my car. They were arrested in Santa Cruz. The C.H.P. didn't even notify me about it until the impound fees were too much to retrieve the car. The D.A. in Merced, residence of the "Juveniles," couldn't cooperate because it was a "Juvenile" matter. Again, I was left with the "citizen's" option of suing the family, at my own expense. The crooks had the benefit of all the legal counsel they needed at my (taxpayer's) expense. I couldn't afford an attorney but my tax dollars would pay for theirs. In any event, I couldn't get sufficient information from the "authorities" to pursue the matter in court had I been able to afford to do so. The "kids," illegals, deadbeats and just plain crooks know the "system" works in their favor. And there is virtually nothing responsible working taxpayers can do about it. No wonder the middle class is "vanishing!"

The "System" stinks. The David Duke's are entirely correct in their assessment of the situation. It's too bad the "Kluxers" and "White Supremacists" are so ignorant in the leadership category as they go about their business. Like

Louis Farrakhan, speaking for Negroes, they have a lot of the right answers but for the wrong reasons.

Besides taxes and crime, another reason for working people failing is divorce. Any man who has been through a "typical" California divorce knows the "System" is stacked against him. By the time she gets the "gold" and he gets the "shaft," most men give up in disgust. In many cases, the men just give up and get "lost." In such cases, the taxpayer gets the bill by paying welfare for the woman and the kids. And, in many cases, she and the kids might be better off!

For example, I can't afford medical insurance, let alone going to a dentist. But, as a taxpayer, I will pay for welfare mothers and their children to go to a doctor and dentist. Is this a country or what? But we can trust our elected "leadership" to cozy up to "minorities," special interests and the Zionists and fight wars for the Arabs so the oil can flow. We can let perverts infect the blood supply and get "partnered" in San Francisco (a bill is pending in the Legislature to make this state-wide), we can afford to help the Kurds, folks in Bangladesh and Ethiopia but we can't do anything about crooks stealing the homes, legally, of old folks here who can't pay their property taxes! There's something terrible wrong with this picture!

I'm glad I got an education. At least the tax-fattened hyenas, clowns and blood-suckers (lawyers, politicians, judges, and real estate salesmen) can't accuse me of calling a spade a spade because of my being a simple, ignorant red-neck. I'm an educated redneck and those that know me know I ain't simple. I earned my Ph. D. the hard way, attending the university and paying my own costs without government "help."

Another case of the "Night soil" striking the electrically powered, wind turbulating device is the matter of drugs. These account for approximately one half of prison populations and have created an entirely new criminal class. But the government, in its mindless attempt to legislate "morality," would have us believe it's in our best interest to incarcerate people whose real crime is to break laws that have proven to be impossible to enforce.

Now, while alcohol and tobacco are, properly, drugs, what is the real difference between these and marijuana and coke? Taxes! If a bum gets plastered on "Who-hit-John" and goes out and kills someone with their car, the victim is just as dead and for the same reason as if the scum had been high on coke. But consider how the law treats the two. We'll let the riff-raff off with a tap on the wrist for the one but throw the book at them for the other. Madness!

If we were to spend one-tenth of the money we spend on the losing battle in the "war on drugs" on keeping drunks off the road, we could win that one. Here's another thought; how about spending the money we would save on over-hauling a failed educational system? Nah, that would be too sensible; and where would the C.I.A. find the money for its operations if we legalized drugs? And how would we provide employment for all those "civil servants" that we employ now in the "war?" Like school administrators and most teachers, they might be qualified for flipping hamburgers but McDonald's can only absorb so many such "skilled" workers.

It's a good thing the Lord has a sense of humor or we'd all be dust by now. I'm reminded of the time I was "weeding" the yard next to one of our cabins on the old mining claim.

Kids being kids weeding was not high on my list of enjoyable activities, especially when there were more important things to do like hunting quail. And, being a kid, work was a matter of interpretation; if I had to do it, it was work; if I wanted to do it, it wasn't; funny how that never changes. And, being a kid, I looked for the easiest way to get the job done. So it was that I nearly burned the cabin down.

It was summer and the weeds were really dry; a real fire threat. But, I figured, I was smart enough to keep the fire from getting too close to the cabin. And think of all the time and energy I would save in the process. So, striking a match, I lit the stuff off.

It's truly amazing how fast fire travels in dry weeds. In no time at all it had reached the tarpaper side of the cabin and took hold. It's equally amazing how fast a kid can move when inspired by the image of a grandfather with a piece of firewood in his hand, ready to administer the appropriate punishment for catastrophic, damned, lazy foolishness.

Inspired by the threat of certain death at the hands of grandad, I immediately, with my bare hands, began to throw copious amounts of sand and dirt against the flaming tarpaper. My effort would have shamed the most industrious badger going after a ground squirrel. Helped along by a legion of guardian angels, I managed to extinguish the impending holocaust. Only then did I wonder why, in my planning, I didn't have the presence of mind to have a bucket of water handy? Simple; the stupid cabin wasn't supposed to catch fire! Also, lacking the niceties of electricity and indoor plumbing I would have had to pump the water from the well by hand and you just didn't pump a bucket of water unless you really needed it. I was the innocent victim of a plan gone awry. I chopped the rest of the weeds with sore and bloody hands and, by the good Lord's grace, grandad never did discover how close we came to losing the cabin and my entire back end.

Of course, what I did in this respect as a kid trying to make a job I didn't want to do easier and more "interesting" might be forgiven. The job our "leadership" has done on us can't be forgiven. We are told we only have to work about half a year now to pay our taxes. We get to work the other half for ourselves. That means if I earn $20,000 a year, I get to spend an entire $10,000 on myself. Of course, half of that goes to rent. The rest, about $5,000, I can squander on food, clothing, transportation (largely for going back and forth to work so I can earn enough to have all this money to squander), medical expenses, insurance to cover the deadbeats who keep running into me, electric, gas, water bills and such other non-essentials.

Now, if I'm really careful, I can avoid eating dried dog food but the best I can ever hope for, in these circumstances, is to simply continue to exist. I can never hope to gain any ground. So much for the "American Dream." So much for even entertaining the thought of supporting a wife and children under such circumstances, of any hope of the children having it any better, especially if they are Caucasian males and unrelated to the "Kennedy's."

Since the churches are reduced to begging in the name of God, though He never made a beggar out of any man, since they are led by spineless "men" who let women do all the work, since such "ministers" are only looking for, as teachers and politicians, a "paycheck," there isn't much hope in "religion." If, as Will Rogers said, "This nation needs cleaner minds and dirtier fingernails!" we are indeed lost. Nothing that is happening in our society today lends itself to any hope that this is a direction we will take. On the contrary, we will, undoubtedly, have to resort to "Hitlerian solutions" that are no solutions. But they are "solutions" that the "State" will impose by force of expediency.

The mindless entity of the State will continue to grow like a cancer. It will, of necessity, eliminate property ownership except for the favored "class;" those, like those of Hitler's Germany, employed in enforcing the will of the State. It will continue to erode personal liberties such as gun ownership and freedom of speech in respect to the true Gospel of Jesus. The churches have already succeeded in making God and the Bible a laughing stock in too many cases, The Bible, a "quaint, antiquated" book, not to be taken seriously or literally in any sense.

Folks, you just can't win at the Devil's game. If you let him call the tune, you have to do his dance. One of my greatest fears is that the situation is going to get so bad we will either have "leaders" arise who will advocate anarchy or ones that will sell the country to the highest bidder. We are already a long way down that path. Look at what the Japanese and Arabs have bought already.

Just ask yourselves who sold out our industries; auto, steel, lumber, etc. Who put us in the position of a "Debtor" nation? Who created the situation that has resulted in "honesty" being for "chumps?" Where was the far-sighted "leadership" that made it more profitable for Remington and I.B.M. to ship its factories overseas? How did it "happen" that someone looking for "quality" had to specify pre '64 in that .06 or Model 94?

What ever happened to a man's pride in his work and being a skilled craftsman? When did "chastity" become a joke? What ever became of "Statesmen," those with a long view of the good for a society rather than the next election? Who decided, for you, that you were better off living and working for a welfare nation than what you could do for yourself by honest, hard work? Who decided perverts should become a "protected" species with special rights and privileges, able to flaunt their perversions among our children as an "alternate life-style?"

Much as I love those men, where do we read about D. L. Moody speaking out, as Thoreau did, against slavery, that cancer that spelled, more than any single sin, the downfall of our nation, or Billy Sunday damning perversion and heretics in the pulpits; when the honest power of the Gospel was abandoned by the nation's pulpits, the glory departed and with it along with a national conscience and soul.

What we are left with today are wimps in the pulpits, plastic-painted hussies of the Tammy Baker variety on TV with their poor imitations of MTV or "Doomsday Prophets" crying for our dollars; and the Episcopalians and Presbyterians "agonizing" over ordaining perverts and women; so much for the "consolations" of religion.

Of course, things might be worse. The Baptists might take over and they would stone me for having a cigarette or drinking a beer. Maybe the Assembly of God will get someone like Swaggart elected President of the U.S. Then he could have a "vision" ala Pat Robertson or Oral Roberts and nuke Iraq or Iran because "God told them to." Why can't we get someone to do it just because it's the right thing to do without making excuses or blaming God?

You "mature" citizens. Do you remember when it was the "patriotic" thing to send our "boys overseas" cigarettes? Now the government wants to wipe out smokers. We who enjoy our "cigareets" are fast becoming the most discriminated against minority in the country. The government has decided we have to wear seat belts and motorcycle helmets "for our own good." You bunch of sheep need Big Brother to make you do what is "best" for you because you don't have sense enough to do it on your own. And, because you don't know what is best for you, Big Brother needs to take away your right to bear arms as well just in case you get angry enough to take action against this bunch of hypocrites.

To paraphrase the words of old Ma Joad, "Some people simply need killin'." Like Alton Harris, a few bureaucrats need to fry or be gassed. But we don't read much about the "murders" these "public servants" are guilty of. Like doctors that "bury" their mistakes or a new paint job on a used car wealth and power will cover a multitude of sins.

Speaking of Alton Harris, why do you suppose we can't get the state to "do" these cold-blooded murderers? Because bleeding heart liberals and judges have no concern for the victims of crime. No matter how thin you slice it, its still baloney. They cry crocodile tears for the "poor accused's" civil rights and need of "fairness" while the victims and their families have no rights at all. Insane! If I had my way, I wouldn't settle for "lethal injection" or gas, I would make sure the murderer died in the same manner in which he killed his victim. That would be Justice with a capital "J." The flaw in the death penalty is that it is too capricious from state to state much in the manner of child molesters for their crimes.

Of course, when it comes to insanity, why are we, taxpayers, bailing out the S&Ls; why are we asked to bail out school districts when their "leadership," the boards and superintendents, spent the money without any regard to personal responsibility and accountability? Once started down this path, where does it all end? It doesn't. It just gets worse.

For instance, when the "leadership" decided that everyone would get an "equal education," they managed to cater to the lowest common denominator and we have produced a generation of illiterates as a result. "Race Norming" is the rule, giving those who are Black and Brown the edge over more qualified, but obviously "racist" people, WASPs particularly, the back seat in the bus. Now we no longer have a pool of mathematicians, engineers or scientists. Your "family" doctor probably has trouble speaking English and if you call a Federal office, or a State office in California, you will probably get an "ethnic minority" woman on the other end of the line. In many cases, she will have problems with the language as well.

Business and industry cannot hire the most qualified; they must be "fair." As a result, the nation cannot any longer compete against other nations who don't have the "scruples" we do. Germany and Japan don't have the problems of "ethnicity." Neither do Taiwan, China or Korea. Sensibly, they take care of their own and "mind the store." Small wonder we are a laughing stock among the community of nations. We are obviously, just plain "silly" when it comes to behaving in a rational way as a nation.

Just what is an "American" anymore? We got "African-Americans, Hispanic-Americans, Asian-Americans, and Native-Americans..." Why are there no "Irish-Americans, German-Americans, Italian-Americans, English-Americans, Jewish-Americans ...?" Just what is an "American" anymore?

The politicians tell us it's good for us to cater to all these nationalities, even printing our ballots in foreign languages. Who is kidding whom here? The nations that gave us the kinds of men that built this country were European. Racist? You bet; especially when you look at the rest of the world. To speak of other "civilizations" in history, like the Arab and Oriental in comparison to ours is to speak nonsense. There is no comparison in relationship to ingenuity, inventiveness, industry, personal liberty and responsibility, justice. "Old Glory" used to speak to hearts that had a right to national pride because of all these "Old-world," primarily European "values." The United States was unique in its inception and early history among all the nations of the world. No longer.

We are on the downhill slide as a nation because it no longer pays to be honest and hardworking and responsible. We must be "fair" to all. No matter that the best and brightest of our students are Caucasian; we must give every minority the same chance to excel even if it means we have to lower all the standards of excellence to comply. The Federal government will hire them in droves even if it means making D.C. the murder and crime capitol of the nation, even if it means that the "wheels" of government travel on the flat tires of "civil servants" that can't even write or speak proper English, that have no sense of personal responsibility because, like "educators" and politicians, they get a paycheck no matter how bad a job they do. The irony of all of this is the fact that by denying the truth of the matter, by not encouraging and devoting our limited resources to the best students and workers regardless of race, we are effectively cutting our own throats and making it even less likely to help minorities.

I recall the time when I was actively dealing in guns. When you are in this kind of business, you meet every kind of person, both the good and the bad. Guns naturally attract both responsible people and "kooks," just as does the job of being a policeman. The job just naturally attracts the kind of people that like to wear a gun and thump people's heads. The wonder of it is that there are so many good cops, not that there are so many bad ones.

Anyhow, I was approached by a few guys that were thinking about forming a "Posse Comitatus" and wanted me to be the leader of the group. This was over fifteen years ago. I declined the opportunity but now I wonder? If some folks saw the necessity of such "Vigilante-ism" back then, what is their thinking now? Things have certainly gotten worse since then and isn't it realistic to believe that there are many more people that have given up any hope of being able to protect themselves, that have given up any hope of seeing anything like justice for the victims of rampant crime?

You really have to have your head where the sun never shines to not recognize the fact that the "justice" system in this nation has, like the educational system, failed entirely, that taxing responsible, working people into penury to pay for failed, "social welfare services" can result in anything but anarchy and the death of our nation? When good people lose faith in our system of government, what's left? When good people can no longer afford to keep their homes, see a doctor or dentist, get their cars repaired, can no longer expect to be rewarded for honesty, industry and integrity, when you really are a "chump" because you try to work within the system, when the leeches and criminals fare better than you such a nation is doomed.

My grandparents raised me in a time when the world was a much simpler place and not nearly as threatening. Life in Little Oklahoma and Boulder Gulch was, compared to the world today, a fairy-tale existence. Way back then, we went through a "righteous" war. We knew who the enemy was and believed in our cause as a nation. We turned in rubber and metal toys and flattened tin cans for the war effort. We removed the foil from cigarette packs, saved grease and lard, bought war stamps and bonds, all because we believed in the justness of our cause. And we won that war. We haven't won one since. Don't let that little skirmish in Iraq fool you. That was necessary to keep the oil flowing but don't think for a moment that we have "won." Iraq was only the opening shot.

I well remember the rationing of gas, tires, sugar and meat. No new cars were built and most of us were restricted to travel by the ubiquitous "A" stamp. But we pulled together and folks took pride in the little flags with blue stars, sometimes gold, in their windows.

But we were just a bunch of simple, trusting, and dumb "Okies" back then. We had faith in God, in our leadership and the "American Way." We believed the government would do what was best, we trusted teachers to care for and educate our children, we never heard the word "Homosexual," dad went to work and mom took care of the house. Drunks were Drunks, not alcoholics or people with a "drinking problem" that needed "understanding" and "treatment" at the expense of the taxpayer. Dad and mom didn't risk jail for disciplining their children. No one burned a draft card or the flag. Employers could hire and fire on the basis of competence alone.

No, things were never really that simple and I know the seeds of our destruction were already being sown in that time long past; that religious and political scoundrels and charlatans were already plying their trades. And I wouldn't want to give up my indoor toilet and the convenience of flipping a switch for light and heat. But I would gladly go back to cutting wood for cooking and heat, I would gladly pull water from the old well, I would gladly put the toilet back outdoors, all this I would gladly do if it would turn this country back to what it was when I was a child.

As a boy on the mining claim in Sequoia National Forest, I would shoulder my gun and take off into the wilderness alone. There, even as a child, I had some intuition that a man was a man for such things. I enjoyed the absolute freedom of choices and decisions that men can only make in such an environment. The kind of character that results from such responsibility; like cutting wood, caring for the livestock, keeping the lamps filled and the wicks trimmed and hunting for the family "pot," together with the guidance of honest and loving "elders" cannot be gained in any other way. While I, like any normal boy, always had "better things to do," like fishing, it never occurred to me that I was being "abused" by being made to learn to work and accept responsibility. Of course, government and the schools weren't yet in the business of raising kids and telling them what their "rights" were, of giving parents the responsibility for the kids but removing all the authority of being able to discipline them.

Tragically, that kind of life is denied the vast majority of young people. The cities are evil and child-destroying, child-hating entities. And how quickly would "Child Protective Services" respond if a child was found to be made responsible for sawing and chopping wood, being made to do the dishes or sweep the floor, if dad took a belt to his son when the kid thought calling mom a nasty name was "neat?" We've come a long way folks. To where?

CHAPTER TWELVE

THE OKIE INTELLECTUAL

A HIGH-TONED PERIODICAL FOR DISCRIMINATING MINDS

JUNE, 1991

II Corinthians 11:13-15

God did not make a mistake in making the seeds so large in Avocados. But I do find fault with Him in not providing more Trout streams. To me, there is nothing closer to heaven on earth than the crystal clear waters of a pristine, wilderness stream with deep pools, waterfalls and rock-studded, short rapids, the sunlight glancing all about with the brilliance of countless diamonds from the splashing play of the cold waters rippling and spraying off the rocks. Put all this with the rugged country of huge, granite mountains, scented pines, a clear, blue sky, the call of quail and rustle of deer among the trees, trout lazing in deep, cool pools of crystal water and you have the closest thing to perfection for body, soul and spirit you can find on earth.

I have fished the ocean, lakes and rivers but these lack the gem-like perfection of the forest fastness of a wilderness trout stream, to drink in the beauty of sun-dappled pools as the rings spread toward the banks from a trout taking some insect on the surface. There is magic in the electric strike of the fish taking a hand-tied fly of your own creation or a simple bait of red worm or salmon egg.

It has been my happy lot to have enjoyed the vastness of the Mojave Desert and Death Valley. There is a peculiar beauty in the rugged, unspoiled (then) "bigness" of these "Lonesomes," particularly at night when the air is so clear that each star stands out with sapphire quality and you can tell the grains of sand in the moonlight. I have watched from sunrise to sunset, in rapturous silence, the variegated subtle changes of myriad colors reflected from the rocks and mountains of Cuddeback and Fremont Peak.

The openness of the majestic, spiked Tetons, the grandeur of Bryce, the romance of Colorado, Wyoming and the Dakotas, all these I have relished in my travels. I will never forget my taking the summer, long years ago, to tour in my '54 Chevy station wagon every national park between the Twin Cities and California. I have seldom spent my time in a better way. No crowds of people, no trash or beer cans, no traffic, only the scenic grandeur of things the way God left them. The irreplaceable memories in my night visions are beyond price. How I wish children today could have had their souls enlarged by such experiences.

Like Thoreau, I can "settle" for a special "tree" where I can sit on a granite boulder and, watching and listening, commune with The Lord in an often wishful state of mind that wishes things were different in the world. I prefer the rugged beauty of "my" trout stream where, in sacred solitude, my line in the gleaming water, I lift my soul to the granite peaks and rest in the coolness of a great, old pine and am free.

I walk the pine needle carpet and, plucking a couple from a handy branch, crush them between my fingers and drink in the perfume of them. I take a pinch of resin, the beautiful, translucent, amber, aromatic "blood" of the pine from the bark and savor its aroma, then, placing it in my mouth, relish the pungent tang of the unadulterated "taste of the forest." I will cook the fresh trout by the side of the stream and, with pinion nuts and berries, "Indian coffee and tobacco," enjoy life in a fashion that no Wall Street tycoon could buy for any amount of money and those too busy with the affairs of this world might envy but never emulate. Tom Sawyer and Huckleberry Finn would understand.

It often makes me wonder what others are striving for, what they think they really want of life that drives them to rob, cheat and steal, to work even honestly for some unidentified "something" that they think will satisfy that "itch" they can't seem to scratch. But it does seem that people do, indeed, live lives of "quiet desperation." Too busy to what purpose? No time to do what? The tragedy of lives that are too tired and busy to do anything but flick on a switch and escape into ersatz, vicarious "entertainment."

As I have said so many times, its too bad "religion" gave place to the Devil in making hell more exciting and enticing than heaven. If there is supposed to be "joy in our salvation" the churches have certainly "missed the boat." The silliness of such people like the "showmen" on TV notwithstanding, trying in the flesh to make "religion" exciting, I will take my trout stream or the "Great Empty" of the Chocolate Mountains.

The old towns of Isabella and Kernville used to be "heaven on earth." The Kern flowed unrestricted through the valley; numerous sloughs were home to abundant wildlife. Catfish and frogs made for great sport as, Indian fashion you sneaked up on them for your breakfast or dinner. The outdoor aroma of the water and vegetation, mixing into some kind of mental satisfaction and joy that "plastic" would profane.

It's no wonder I feel "trapped" in a city environment. Concrete, asphalt and plastic make a "prison" to me. It just isn't natural for people to live in cities. Like rats in a maze, I see folks trying to "get by" in circumstances animals show more sense by avoiding. In fact, only people are capable of building their own "prisons." Animals would never "build nests with no escape." But animals have the enviable attribute of instinct. They don't have to "plan." People have to think and plan. Most don't, of course, and since they don't plan for success a plan for failure is assured.

So, before you accuse me of altruism and "utopian thinking," consider the fact that if you don't want much, you don't need much. For example, if you are willing to drive my old '69 Dodge, you escape $300 to $500 plus car payments. But if your "goals" are so skewed you aren't working and putting in your time to escape the "maze," you have no one to blame but yourself.

As a teacher and administrator, I designed a class to teach "survival skills." These included such things as building houses, repairing cars, making a "still," agriculture basics, animal husbandry and alternative energy sources. I did this for one of the private schools I started since the state schools, due to bureaucratic bungling and the fact that most of these people have no idea of what the real world is all about, would never see the necessity for such learning.

And so, as I have done for years I preach a "gospel" of individual opportunity and responsibility. The answers are there but only on an individual basis. While we live in a country that is bankrupt financially and morally, we still have far more liberty than any other nation for the individual to escape being a victim of the "system."

I still preach that people must exercise responsible citizenship, they must vote and do all they can to help others less fortunate. But this should be done with planning, with educated and knowledgeable involvement and leadership. In other words, know what you are doing and quit "winging it."

Most of the bitchers and complainers out there are the very people that are doing the same things they have always done and, as I have said many times, if you are still doing what you have always done, you will never have more than you have now. This is one reason I try to shake people up. I say and do some outrageous things in order to get people's attention. I learned this tactic as a teacher. It works. But unless you get their attention, people don't listen. And if you aren't listening, you aren't learning. "Listen up, Adam; let me put it this way. If you don't take a bite I'm cuttin' you off'" said Eve.

A slanderous, vile canard, a calumny has been raised against me. I did not accuse Eve of threatening Adam with having to sleep on the couch if he did not cooperate with her and the Serpent in eating us out of house and home. I simply raised the possibility. A far greater possibility, to my mind, was a threat to Adam's "manhood." I think it far more likely that Eve appealed to Adam's ego, his sense of "superiority" as the "High Mucky Muck" of the Garden. "What kind of wimp are you, anyhow, Adam? 'Scairty Cat, Scairty Cat,' afraid of God. The Serpent and I aren't afraid. I took a bite and nothing happened. Big man, afraid to do something to stand up to The Boss. The Serpent's really got your number. If you were any kind of a 'Real Man' you wouldn't have to let a woman go first!"

Ah, gentle reader, the possibilities are really there. You men, what would you have done in Adam's place? Taken "Abiola's" advice and given Eve a punch in the mouth? Or, like Adam, possibly, let the "Real Man" in you feel threatened and "rise to the occasion?" Or, would you, as Adam should have done, as a truly Real Man would do, obey God and let Him handle the consequences?

Well, in any event the possibilities are fascinating but the bottom line is that Adam "hearkened" to Eve and we live with the results of his rebellion to God and his failure toward her. I do wonder if Adam became the first Wife-beater as a result. Perhaps this would account for their first son, Cain, becoming a murderer. Adam did try to blame God and Eve for his own failure. That was a poor beginning for a relationship. It may be the reason that God finally had to destroy the world by a flood and start over again with Noah. Unhappily, Jesus was right; things weren't going to get any better until God calls an end to this age.

Now if Eve had been smart she would have moved to California before all this took place. If poor, old Adam tried that "Rulership" nonsense here, then she would have divorced him and her lawyer would have made sure the "Mine" was "equitably divided" so she would have gotten the gold and he would have gotten the shaft. She would have wound up in Mink instead of "leaves and skins." But, alas for poor Eve, Lawyers hadn't been invented back then unless you count this as one of Satan's areas of expertise, something that comes readily to mind.

In any event, Adam could hardly have been looking for a suitable companion among the beasts of the field. So I think it possible the Serpent described as beautiful and cunning may have been in the running; and if a female we know "Hell hath no fury..." So when God came up with Eve, the Serpent may have laid plans for an ambush. She gained Eve's confidence, invited her to Tupperware parties and so on, all the while plotting revenge. The Biblical account infers Eve was used to visiting with the Serpent so there was no surprise by the creature striking up a conversation with Eve.

Jewish theologians came up with a "first wife" of Adam called Lilith in an attempt to make sense of things. But I think the Genesis account has it right with the Serpent playing the hypotenuse in the Eternal Triangle.

Whatever the truth of the matter, God's curse fell most heavily upon Eve and the Serpent. The curse of sex and the ruler ship of men over them would be most harsh on women.

Since the curse of death took quite a while to come about for Adam and Eve, it may be the Serpent didn't immediately start crawling on its belly but may have gone off to the land of Nod and waited for Cain's arrival, the two of them producing children of the Devil leading to violence filling the earth.

I recently had an interesting conversation with a fellow who was looking at a house I had to rent. He had just been through a typical "California" divorce. He had a business and was doing quite well when his ex-wife got the "itch" for "greener pastures." To make a long and sordid story short, his conclusion was, he said, that had he known what the outcome was to be, he would have simply "packed his bags and disappeared."

It is the "system" that stinks; whether we are discussing politics, religion or education, the system "stinks." The criminal, the irresponsible seem to prosper while the honest and hard working keep paying the bills for the leeches and deadbeats.

I don't believe women really set out to get a "legal club" to beat men into submission. But that is the system we have. It's satanic in its inspiration and in the way it works. When it comes to the matter of divorce, it is blatantly obvious that many men give up and run away when confronted with the impossible demands made on them via child support, alimony, property settlements, outstanding debts, etc. This is no excuse for any man, as my own father and brother did, to fail to do his best for his children. It's just that the system stacks the deck against most men to the extent that it becomes virtually impossible to comply; as a result, they "run away in droves," leaving the taxpayers to pick up the tab via welfare, etc.

It has been a long road to come to such a sorry pass. I subscribe entirely to the Biblical injunction that men should rule their families well: I Timothy 3:4,5. It is men's failure to accept God's judgment and command from the "Fall" on that has created the nightmare we live with; spineless "jellyfish" that bow to women and cop out of their responsibilities, which sell out their manhood to the rule of women. And, like Adam, blame both God and women for their failure.

How many times, over the years, have I had to witness this tragic destructiveness play itself out in numerous families. Just recently I have had to watch another "man" bite the dust as he gave in to a willful woman who has the "rule" over him. He allowed her to destroy his own children while he took care of hers. And "hers" includes a grown daughter (with an illegitimate child, purely a cultural distinctive, the children don't ask to be born) who calls him vulgar names while living off this guy. The woman also has a son that has seen a judge a few times and done the poor guy in on a number of occasions. This poor, wretched person has to live, daily, with the consequences of his failure to his own children, to God Himself, and, though this conniving and domineering woman doesn't really realize it, toward her as well. As an ex-student of mine in high school, I still love this poor kid but I sure don't like him. H.L. Mencken was right; he hated the hypocritical, so-called "fundamentalists" but could almost love them when he saw what they put up with in their wives.

But what does such a person face if he suddenly decides to obey God and try to "rule" such a "family?" He surely knows the courts and lawyers would "clean his clock." His options, because of his own, sinful choices, are pretty poor. I lost my own family because I obeyed God rather than come under the rule of a woman so I know whereof I speak. But she tried to do me in for 21 years before she ran off with a truck driver.

Unhappily for all concerned, this "kid," and he represents millions of others, never accepted the fact that he had anything to learn. He "knew better than his teacher" and despised the counsel of "gray hair." As is symptomatic with most of his generation, a phony "Macho" pervades their thinking; this to the detriment of any woman who knows better. It is tragic that most girls don't learn about this until too late. And, so, the silliness and childishness of this facade is readily apparent and the poor kid fails to be a "Man of God" and his hypocrisy is seen of all. And he will shame God every time he takes The Lord's name on his lips until, and if, he repents. But, there are plenty of "churches" out there who will gladly welcome such "families" because of the simple fact that the "ministers" are only "hirelings, false shepherds," collecting a "paycheck," telling people like this kid what they want to hear.

As an example, this poor kid has already got one "lined up" who has told him God's Word is two thousand years out of date and God doesn't really mean what He said anymore. I pity the deluded people who "buy" this heresy. They are bound to come under God's judgment. And, so, I have no choice but to "deliver such a one over to Satan." He, like so many other "just religious" people, thought he could get away with cheating and robbing God for years. He is bound to discover God won't let him get away with such a shameful thing.

"Theologues" and the "righteous," those who have been thoroughly brain-washed by listening to too many syrupy "sermons" about the "meek and lowly Jesus" are greatly offended by my plainness of speech. I respond. Jesus was the essence of Real Manhood and no one will ever make it otherwise, no matter how the "polite churched" try to make him some kind of "pantywaist." It took a Real Man to thoroughly confront those hypocrites of Jesus' day and drive the crooks out of The Temple. It took a Real Man to pay the price he did for doing what was right no matter if the whole world was against him. Now, "preacher-boys," what happened to most of you? Did you "check your manhood in" when you decided you had something to say for God; when you decided you had a "call" to stand for Him in an evil and adulterous world and let women "run the show?"

It must be freely admitted that most religious programming makes sensible people sick. Whether the "Snake-oil salesmen" of the class of a Robert Schuller, the insane antics of a Cerullo or your local "Clown," reasonable people have to wonder; "What in makes people buy this crap?" Simple answer to an honest question: "Satan."

Only the "great deceiver" has the know-how to make something like this work and pass it off as something God is doing. Only the "Master of the Counterfeit," with his experience in dealing with people, could be this successful in making large numbers of human beings act like they had taken complete leave of their minds in this fashion.

A careful reading of II Cor. 11:13-15 and II Thess. 2:1-12 gives us some insight into how Satan gets "credit" for this kind of delusion. It does not excuse people for thinking God is a fool or treating Him as such. But it does offer some explanation. After all, Satan does "reward" his followers and "ministers" and, while the "wages of sin is death," Romans 6:23, worldly success was one of the things the enemy offered Jesus if he would only follow him. Matthew 4:8,9.

For those of you who are not knowledgeable of the charismatic heresy, the "touchy-feely" and "prosperity gospel" crowd with their poor imitation of Hollywood and Broadway entertainment complete with "healings, miracles, tongues" and "visions and voices," all for a "love-gift" to their monstrous egos, I offer the following for your consideration:

The Holy Spirit according to the Bible does not call attention to Himself, but is exactly what Scripture says: The Spirit of God. Notice that the hellish doctrine of the charismatics gives the preeminence, they think, to the Holy Spirit as though divorced from and separate from God. I am at a loss for words when I call attention to this hellish, perverted doctrine that makes God and the Bible look so foolish to the entire world.

While it may have gotten President Bush's son off the hook, its too bad "stupidity" can't be prosecuted at times. Of course, when it comes to swallowing some of the trash that passes itself as the "work of God," terminal stupidity comes to mind.

An example of "terminal stupidity" is clearly found in any, metropolitan phone book. Just look under the heading: "Government Offices; Federal, State, County and City." Consider the fact that these multitudes of "Services" are being paid for by the taxes of the fast, shrinking middle class. They contribute virtually nothing financially. And ask yourself how much more you can afford. Logically, you can't afford what you are already being taxed for. And our governor is going to raise taxes even further to bail out the state budget! And lawyers (legislators) are intent on adding to the list in your phone book.

Can you believe that school districts, like Richmond's, have the guts to ask the state (that is, taxpayers) to bail them out after their idiot superintendents and boards have driven them into bankruptcy? And then they have the gall to say, as a means of extortion, that if we don't bail them out, we, the taxpayers, don't care about "quality education!" Lord have mercy, when was it that we last had anything like quality education in the state schools? I repeat like a broken record: As long as we continue to ask the same greedy idiots who created the problems, those, primarily, with worthless "doctorates in education" who have absolutely no idea of how the real world operates, never having had to work for an honest living, for answers there can be no hope of improvement.

Religious charlatans and equally greedy politicians, together with a tax-fattened "educational and welfare" system have doomed us financially. The responsible working class feeds all these "angels of light". It is no wonder that people are dropping out of the struggle and giving up. You can't seem to get ahead, let alone win. Who held a gun to the heads of the irresponsible and insisted they have children they could never hope to support without a husband and honest work? It's hard to feel sorry for such people when I look at what people are suffering in other parts of the world. One look at Ethiopia and, recently, the Kurds, is enough to make you wonder where people's priorities are. As a parent, an educator with many years of experience and a Ph. D. in Human Behavior, I am well qualified to tell you: "It's all madness!" And you don't need a terminal degree to figure that out.

It's a good thing I have, by God's grace, the time and means to enjoy the beauty of His creation before men have totally ruined it all. The momma, gray tree squirrel that now comes into the house demanding pecans will scratch at the door and "cuss" until she gets what she wants. The quail and other birds gather in the yard and eat the seed I throw out to them.

But I wonder at the foolishness that tries to pass itself off as "teaching" among the "religious." Where is the practical value of a Copernicus or Newton among them? Where is the beauty of practical value in my trout stream that enables me to commune with God in the truth of His wisdom and knowledge? Where do charlatans like Oral Roberts, Schuller and others place the distinctives of God's gifts to men in their creative abilities?

"Yankee Ingenuity" is religious in its purest form of practical expression. The genius of men and women as expressed in the greatest nation the world has ever seen is, preeminently, Christian and God fearing in its very essence. It was the values of a people that placed such importance on the individual's God-given right and responsibility to do work, to create, to govern in such a manner that reflected the mind and wishes of The Creator that blessed this nation so. But when the generation of those men passed, when such things as slavery were countenanced and even "blessed" by ungodly leaders, the seeds of our own destruction were sown to bring forth the crop of hedonistic materialism with every man "doing what was right in his own sight." A nation of hypocrites that pays lip service to "rugged individualism" has, by the insanity of its laws to protect the "privileged" and give the poor "bread and circuses" has reaped the whirlwind. "Who will show us any good?" The godly man ceaseth."

There was a time in this nation's past when to worship God meant a person had practical sense. Who can make any sense of what tries to pass as worship of God today? When God told men to "subdue" the earth, He clearly meant that we were to learn, to work, and to teach our children and build; all this to prepare a people for eternity where we are to enter into the plans of a God who wants our help in His on-going work of creation.

I do not think it improbable that Satan and the fallen angels were responsible for the so-called "Prehistoric" drama that displays itself in the fossil records; that God may have intervened with His own creation and that the *Adam*, placed in special circumstances in a special place, the Garden, was to become the envy and object of hatred by an implacable enemy, Satan, as a consequence. It is a curious fact that the theory of evolution was doomed at the outset by a lack of evidence for the scientific demarcation between sexes. They were male and female from the very beginning and no "missing link" anywhere in sight. But where, in all that passes for "religion" today, do we fare any better than the ignorant, superstitions of those that practice occult arts, believe in evolution, reincarnation or a host of other means used as an excuse to try to escape personal accountability to God?

It is God who is reasonable and imminently sensible. He gives the genius of ability and appreciation of beauty that is evidenced in a Botticelli and the esthetic value of the Doors in Venice and a genuine reflection of God in us. The melding of these things in exceptional people like DaVinci or Michelangelo, no matter the personal, even corrupt and disgusting sinfulness of many such gifted geniuses, the stamp of the Creator is plainly seen in their works just as surely as the brilliance of heaven, resplendent in its vast array of stellar beauty declares Him. Faulkner, Hemingway and Steinbeck, in their genius, remain faithful in their witness to God no matter how they might vilify Him in their personal lives. Wagner and Rembrandt "testify" in spite of themselves.

I have recently passed through the "Canyon," the "Grapevine" and Holiday Valley. The "March Miracle" has resulted in turning the fields and hills into brilliance of colors DeMeer would envy. Against a carpet of emerald green, God has painted fiery beds of glorious orange with poppies, the shimmering, subtle purples of Lupine and the wild, yellow sulfur of mustard blossoms. When mixed together, the effect is breathtaking! While it is, at times, difficult to make the transition between the lyrics of "There's a tear in my beer when I cry over you," the "genius" that produces noise from hard rock guitars that sterilizes frogs at 300 yards and such mentally uplifting "literature" like Playboy and such "lesser" works like Shakespeare, it is still incumbent on us to make the distinction between trash and treasure.

But a society that teaches its young that sex is a commodity to be bartered, of value only as a "trade" item, as long as women popularize pornography by deeming themselves as "pieces of meat" to be exchanged for money to satisfy the ungodly lust of men, such a society is doomed. What value can men place on something women treat as of no real value, as they go from one man after another and divorce no longer carries the stigma of failure to commit, faithfully, to a "life partner?" It is tragic that such people openly lie to God and society as they take "vows" to be faithful to one another. What a laugh in today's culture. But God doesn't think it's funny. And there are the idiotic religious "professionals" still talking about "praying mothers" and "Dad" is made to look ridiculous. No wonder women are giving up in disgust when real men are so hard to find!

Mom and my grandparents were of incalculable value to me in giving me a broad background that could "make do," could appreciate the value of even the most transitory things, could take joy in such varied circumstances as Las Vegas or Little Oklahoma. I can, in my imagination, enjoy such "magic" as to be the envy of the most skilled "sorcerer" or "conjuror." To be able to appreciate the forming of metal by lathe or mill, to turn walnut and ash into something of beauty and practical value, to wire or plumb a house, to get an engine humming and teach these things to others; these are things that fulfill a man, that tells him "It has meaning" and is "worthwhile," these are the whispered promises of "immortality."

A mother teaching the little one to "do dishes," sweep the floor or do laundry might not speak as loudly for the present, but when that little one learns she is contributing something of value to the family, it has eternal potential. When that boy is taught to take on the obligation for disposing of the trash, cutting the lawn or washing the car, he is learning lessons for living a productive life.

Pity the child that learns not to obey until the pitch of his mother's or father's voice reaches the correct crescendo that is confused by orders that result in threats of bodily harm or death unless followed. Such children do not dream of the joy of fulfilled expectations while marveling at the industry of ants or the transient, glinting beauty of a butterfly. They, too often, are shoved in front of the "tube" and treated as the unwanted liability they, in actuality, are, to such "parents."

"I hope the ACLU sues me for depriving these people of their right to be ignorant. ... You're going to be judged in this country, like it or not, on how you write and speak. I want to send a message to every youthful offender that we take their education seriously and so should they."—California Youth Authority Director B.T. Collins, saying he will reject improperly written complaints. My congratulations to Mr. Collins. I have written to him and encouraged him in his stand in this. But, I fear, the bleeding heart liberals will do him in. Just wait until the NEA gets to him. He has more to fear from the "educational establishment" than from the ACLU. I wonder how long he will be able to stand against the economic and political clout of the adversary and his perverted cohorts?

My brother recently made the comment that someone should edit these letters before I send them out. But he chaffs under my "Okie" appellation and, like others, thinks that just because I have the alphabet after my name; I should assume a more "appropriate" pose of decorum. He has forgotten to have fun. For example, I'm sure he does not approve of my toy company: MACABRE TOYS INC. The home embalming kits are real winners. These range in size and complexity to satisfy ages six through adult. The smallest kit, for the budding young scientist and biologist, is suitable for the family goldfish when he is found swimming upside down. The intermediate kit is designed for the family cat or pooch when they give up the ghost. The largest kit, the "Mother-in-law Special," is available only by approval of the local officials in your city.

Another big seller is "Freddie the Frog." Freddie is a very life-like, soft, plastic model that pees when squeezed lightly. A little stronger squeeze causes his eyes and tongue to pop out with a very satisfying grunt and a number of small pores in his realistic skin exude a mucus-like substance. Freddie can be fed real flies. He is very popular with small boys who quickly learn how teachers, little girls and their mothers react to this fun item.

My companion company, ROMANTIC GIFTS INC., offers a wide array of things for those that still cherish the blush of young love in their breasts, for those in whom the soul of the poet flourishes. The rubber rolling pin, inspired by Maggie, of "Maggie and Jiggs," is selling well to women and men are enjoying the Calendar Flower arrangement. This is a quality, plastic, floral beauty with built-in calendar that can be set to remind the forgetful of important dates like anniversaries. The fact that it can be used year after year is a big selling point. For those husbands whose wives might be "picky" about getting the same gift every year, an exchange program is offered by the company. Our catalog lists other items like the recyclable five-pound box of chocolates and entrancing "Beer Can jewelry." Details upon request.

If you do ask for the catalog you will be amazed at the variety of gifts, each one exhibiting the good taste and sensitivity these few, artistic samples exemplify. The gallon jug of "Eau de Kitchen" is still available for the astounding price of $2.98 plus shipping and handling. Don't delay as quantities are limited and we are having problems with the still.

The publishing arm of my company, GET BUCKS BY BOOKS INC., has a few copies of that best seller, "How To Pay More Taxes," but supplies are limited so don't delay. Still left in quantity are copies of a hot number, "Getting To Know Your Favorite Legislator." We still have a number of "How To Eat Less Day By Day." This is on its way to becoming a cult classic among those that are homeless and jobless. Included are a variety of recipes for often-neglected dishes like.... No, I won't spoil the anticipation for gourmets who have a taste for the exotic. But if you order five copies or more, you will also receive a copy of the children's books "Our Friend, The Beaver," and "Vultures, Friends Or Relatives?" This offering should make nifty Christmas gifts for those special "someone's."

It reminds me: my daughter, Karen, is raising four little possums. She rebelled at my suggestion of serving them with sweet taters, persimmons or parsnips. And just who was the idiot that thought of putting an "O" in front of possum? How many of us, raised with Walt Kelly and Pogo, would have stood for such foolishness? For orders of $20 or more, you will receive a gift copy of "101 Uses For Unmatched Socks," or, if you want, the companion volume, "Handy Hints For The Relatives Of Winos," a "must" book for people who live too far from Rescue Missions. "Adopt A Derelict" is, sadly, out of print at this time.

My "religious" books have not been doing well. "Having Fun With The Baptist's And Moonies" did not sell. The cans of Mormon and J.W. repellent gather dust on the factory shelves. The "Smaller Catechism of Episcopalian Jokes" was a disaster as was my "A Dozen Ways To Disguise Ham." Jews stayed away in droves. No, not all of my efforts have been successful but I keep trying. There have been some successes. Arabs seem to like my commentary on the Koran, which explains, in Mohammad's own words, why whisky is a religious experience and sand is a "gift." There is some dispute over my research that proves the Dome of the Rock used to be the site of a Hebrew brothel.

By now my conservative "brethren" have consigned me to the outer reaches. But life is far too short not to have some fun out of it; and when I can't reach the trout stream, my fancy takes wing in other, less reputable, directions. But really folks; is my poking fun at those that treat the most somber issues of life as "fairy tales," those like the charismatics who make The Lord look foolish, such a bad thing? I think not.

And, while I would never accuse Peter of giving John a "hotfoot," I'm sure there must have been times when The Lord and the Apostles had a good laugh together. And, make no mistake that was real "Kick-a-poo joy juice" he made at the party in Cana no matter what "Blue-nosed Baptists" try to make of it. The greatest humorist of all, God, must surely get a chuckle out of a few of my jokes on myself. As has often been mentioned in respect to God's humor; He made the squirrel, the monkey, and some of you. Not theologically correct, of course, but you get the point.

A word of consent to some of my detractors: I am quite willing to admit to fallibility and a lack of propriety in certain areas. But, honestly now, what can you expect from someone who thinks Ballet is a grim and grotesque distortion of the human body, twisting it into shapes it was never intended to be bent, from someone who can spell "licorice" four different ways? Far from being an esthetic delight, I find ballet about as "graceful" and "natural" for the body as a bib on a hog. See, there's no hope for me.

Which reminds me of a recipe I read about many years ago for chewing tobacco; you bore a hole in a sugar maple during the winter before the sap begins to run. Then, you pack it with alternate layers of tobacco and licorice and plug it up. When you remove the "plug" the following autumn you have something you can chew at the opera.

It is a sense of humor that brings us through so many trials, grief and tribulation. "Life's hard; then you die!" Who can fail to see the humor in that statement? To be able to laugh at yourself is great medicine for the soul. In the ageless words of Porkypine: "Don't take life so serious son, it ain't no wise permanent." A real "Pilgrim" of God's Word and promises certainly has no reason for failing to see the point of that comment. In the words of James: "For what is your life? It is even a vapor, that appeareth for a little time, and then vanisheth away." James 4:14b. We should never fail to apply the words of Moses in this regard: "So teach us to number our days, that we may apply our hearts unto wisdom." Psalm 90:12.

In all that he does, the child of God should always keep in mind that we are called to "Strive to enter in through the strait gate..." Luke 13:24a. Certainly perseverance and work are involved in our pursuit of God's Kingdom, but don't lose your sense of perspective, priorities and humor in the process. God expects us to maintain a "balanced diet."

Because of the constant stream of grim news that, daily, bombards us, I often advise folks to think in terms of a "worst case scenario." I say: So what's the worst thing that can happen; you lose your job, your home and starve to death. Come to think of it, maybe that's not such good advice after all. It reminds me too much of the situation where a guy was contemplating suicide and called a friend to come over and talk to him. By the time this guy got through telling his tale of woe, the friend said: "Put another bullet in that thing for me!"

Well, its time once more to find my "tree and boulder." I'm enjoying the heritage of my mother as I listen to 40's music and type. I miss the simple joys of Abbott and Costello, Red Skelton and Spike Jones, the "Silver Screen" simplicity of "Bogie" and Cagney, of being able to tell who the good guys were without a program or a graduate course.

Few men could be as monstrous as women and their lawyers paint them in their divorce complaints. As with "education" in America, it's always the children who are the "forgotten victims" of the greed, egos and vindictiveness of small-minded people. When I was a kid, building model airplanes, I loved the smell of the "dope" and glue. It never occurred to us kids, then, that, someday kids would do this to get "high." We just enjoyed the smell of the stuff. Just as I can still, in my memory, enjoy the cold, crispness of a first snowfall, of tracking rabbits and quail in the beatific silence of the fresh whiteness. Few things are so indelibly imprinted on my mind as my breath, exhaling smoky in the fresh, cold air; the acrid but enjoyable smell of burned powder as I hunted for the family "pot." Long ago and far away. Oh, the magic children today have been cheated of.

CHAPTER THIRTEEN

THE WEEDPATCHER

MAY, 1991

Over the years, I've noticed some differences between men and women. Now some will applaud the sagacity and profundity of that statement while others, those without a sense of humor or lacking Attic Wit, will say, "It's about time!"

Even someone like me needs the guidance of the "Little Woman" in matters like dress. For instance, when I think my outfit of chartreuse shirt, brown, plaid pants and two-toned, perforated shoes with argyle socks appropriate for dinner at Burger King, it takes the little woman to notice the possible clash in my sartorial choices.

It's true that men and women have many, different priorities and notice different things. That's often a good thing. If only they could cooperate rather than making such things a chip on the shoulder or a line in the dirt where each dares the other one to cross.

Y' ever notice that mothers spend a lot of time worrying and warning their sons about girls? It's what they know about themselves, as women, that causes their concern. Think about that one.

I've also noticed that when it comes to fishing, men and women simply don't communicate on the same level. The real importance of fishing is lost to women but is obvious to men. That's why no amount of explanation to a woman will suffice. Now I know some women who like to fish. But they don't comprehend the religious significance, the true "worship" of the devout angler. The "ritual" of adorning one's self with the liturgical vestments and equipment of Holy Office is, mostly, nonsense to a woman.

I have asked women if they have something as peculiar to their sex as fishing is to men. So far, none have been able to come up with anything. If you have any ideas on the subject, please let me know. It seems quite a conundrum at the present. I believe we could all profit from a thorough research of the question. If women do have something of a like nature that speaks to their souls as fishing does to men, it seems an elusive thing for the time being.

Remember one thing; if such a thing exists only women, as with men and fishing will be able to understand it. If it does not, I have to wonder why?

In conversation with women it is admitted that fear of predatory men is a legitimate concern that deprives women of the "wilderness experience." It may be, that, while the peculiar distinction between men and women that results in men being the real romantics, explorers, artists, inventors, risk-takers, etc. exists, it cannot be denied that women have every reason to be afraid to wander in the wild. Imagine what must go through a woman's mind if she finds herself alone at some distant stream and three, strange men approach.

While in today's evil society even men must be on guard against one another, it is women who bear the brunt of having to be constantly vigilant against the depredations of two-legged "creatures." And this has been the case throughout history. It goes a long way toward explaining the resentment, animosity and need that women have toward, and for, men. And it certainly doesn't help, on the religious side, to have women represented by the likes of a Marilyn Hickey. I know it's unkind but I can't help but be reminded of that old saw: "Beauty may only be skin deep but ugly goes clear to the bone!" Old brother McGee was right. In reference to the use of cosmetics among the "saints" he said: "Some women need all the help they can get." My personal objection to such use is warranted by the plastic, painted look of the likes of women T.V. "evangelists." They look like they have been "done up" by a Geisha school dropout. Since this whole, dangerous subject should be the focus of a much larger work, I return to the much safer theme of fishing.

Now a man seems to have an instinct for what is acceptable "worship" when embarking on "Pilgrimage" to the trout stream. He knows that to enter the "Holy of Holies," the "Cathedral" of the wilderness, requires the proper "sacrifices" and attitude of worship or God will not bless his quest.

The first and most important sacrifice is time. It takes real grit and determination, real honesty and integrity to make the time available from his busy schedule, for the true "believer" to "go to church." He must do this at the possible risk of incurring the wrath of those less devout, like the little woman. She may think it more important to clean the garage or cut the grass. Heresy! But the true believer will not let such inconsequential things stay him from his course.

It's unfortunate that women don't seem to understand the significance of having a man who loves to fish. If they knew that the time he spends at the lake, river or stream might be the one thing that makes him different from a man who would punch her lights out, she might be properly grateful.

If you are a woman with a man who loves to fish, it would help you to accept the fact that, like a woman with PMS, he will suffer the same symptoms when deprived of his soul's need of the supply of a pool of trout or catfish. When that "time" comes upon him, you'd better let him go or be prepared to suffer the "headaches, bitchiness, lethargy" and other complaints common to the malady. And, of course, nothing you say or do, during such a time, will be "right."

Keep in mind the fact, that, if a man denies the "spirit" and does not go fishing when it is his clear duty to do so, it will only create a "situation" at home. His inner battle will result in all kinds of inharmonious behavior; he will wander aimlessly and listlessly, he will seem to be distant and not hear when spoken to (Some women will say I have just described their man whether he loves to fish or not). In some of the worst cases, he may resort to watching football or basketball on TV. If he takes up golf or watching bowling on TV, the situation is irreversible- terminal. You have lost him. A word to the wise.

Now we all know that there is a difference between the true believer and the fanatic. When I first received the "call" to fish, I was a small boy equipped with cane pole, string and rusty hook. A hapless angleworm dangled from the end. But the "Damascus light" struck with my first fish off the muddy bank of the old, Kern River. I say the "old" Kern because that sacred spot is now under the waters of Lake Isabella. Sacrilege!

It was a marvelously sunny, warm summer day. My granddad and grandmother had taken me to the river soon after we moved to the old mining claim in Boulder Gulch. The river, its surface mirror-like between the rapids, glistening in the sunlight, moving slowly around large, granite boulders, its banks shaded by rows of leafy, old Cottonwoods, looked and smelled like heaven on earth; the good, warm, honest mud and grasses of the riverbank squirmed up between my toes; heavenly. The water was crystal clear, the bottoms of the pools with their rock-strewn and sandy terrain easily visible. Fish could be seen moving about. Electric excitement!

I don't recall that grandad had given me any specific instruction in the art of angling but being an Okie; he probably knew it was in my "genes." His own equipment and dress were little different than my own.

That first fish and I were both "hooked" irretrievably. Even though my "tackle" was the most rudimentary imaginable, even though I was barefoot, shirtless and had on bib overalls, I was doing the best I could with the "light" I had and The Lord rewarded me accordingly. Even though that first fish was the "lowliest of the low," a seemingly, worthless mud-sucker, it had done its task; the dew of "The Chosen" sprinkled my feverish brow. It remained for time to do its work in establishing a "systematic theology," a "doctrine" of belief and acceptable "Worship" and "Service" of "Devotion."

But, for the sacred moment, holding aloft my "wriggling treasure of the deep," the sun sparkling, glistening from its iridescent scales, Isaac Walton, split-bamboo rods and Royal Coachmen, hand-tied, were yet future unknowns. I had much to learn, was ignorant of so much, but I had entered upon the "Pilgrimage" and my "calling and election" were sure.

Time has passed and, while the "spring" has long gone from my steps and my "pilgrimages to Mecca" (the trout streams) are, now, less frequent, my memories serve to take me there whenever I choose. Pity those who know nothing about such things.

A note to the "non-cognizanti" about Poets: In the Greek, the word "Poet" means a "Maker." These were the men who "made" stories. They created characters, some of heroic proportion, and wove tales to relate history, to make moral points, to uplift the spirits of those in need. I try to do the same thing. The "Okie" designation harks to my use of the simple, honest verities, the work and sincere, religious ethic that so distinguishes such people and my early, character formation which was so passionately ingrained by my birthplace (Weedpatch) and tenure in Little Oklahoma (Southeast Bakersfield) and Boulder Gulch. The most important thing in my life was my early acquaintance with the King James Bible. The early reading in this literary masterpiece contributed the most helpful thing to my education and appreciation of the English language. And, to beat my detractors to the punch, I had never heard of Edward George Bulwer-Lytton. But I was thoroughly imbued with the spirit of Steinbeck and Faulkner.

A poet does not always have a popular following. If he is true to the craft, he deals with the truth and the truth is not always a pleasant thing. Recent Russian poets are more readily attuned to that than those of the West. They, correctly, recognize the fact that America is a nation without a "soul." And, while the line between prose and poetry is often merged and, at times, indistinguishable, both are vehicles of the expressions of the soul.

It is a tragic thing that the souls of so many men are so shrunken and mean in our society; so many are afraid of the truth and lack the backbone of conviction of truth. It is a "truth" that the division among people along ethnic lines in our nation is a most hurtful thing. I mentioned this in a previous publication and recently, in "Parade Magazine," a popular columnist, Marilyn Savant, was asked: "What internal situation do you feel poses the largest threat to the well-being of the United States?" She answered: "Over the decades to come, I believe one of the greatest threats to the stability of the United States may well be the declining number of people who call themselves Americans. I wonder how long the hyphenation of nationalities can continue without bringing the hyphenation of loyalties. Whenever people ask me whether I'm a French-American, for example, because of my name, it irritates me, and I tell them, 'No. I was born in this country, I'm a citizen and I'm an American!'"

If an intelligent woman like Savant sees the danger to our nation in this "hyphenation" of ethnicity, it is clearly not a matter of "prejudice" when responsible people address the issue. But it is a truth that most find unpalatable and one that we would rather keep "in the closet" and not talk about.

One of these "truths" is the fact that our nation has disgraced itself by countenancing homosexuality, even to the point of making it legally "respectable." No nation in history has ever survived this abomination of perversion.

When people like California State Senator, Ed Davis and Supreme Court Justice, Harry Blackmun, say the "Courts should protect homosexual activity!" that is a direct challenge and an affront to God Himself and He will not let such a nation go unpunished.

Blackmun, of course, wrote the 1973 Roe vs. Wade decision legalizing abortion, therefore, it is not surprising that he would come out on the side of perverts. Ed Davis and others like him are simply responding to the "politics of expediency." This dictates allaying yourself with every "minority" in the hope of keeping your office and paycheck. It all appears very "liberal" and "open-minded." No matter that you offend God and punish those that disagree with your position; God doesn't sign your paycheck and His "vote" doesn't seem to count for much.

Of course, when such people like Blackmun and Davis look at what the churches have to say about the issue, one can hardly blame them for thinking God doesn't much care about it one way or another. Confusion reigns among the Episcopalian, Catholic, Presbyterian, Lutheran, Methodist, and Baptist churches on the theme of "sexuality." But the confusion is on the part of men, not God. He is very plainspoken about it. He destroyed the world by a flood because of sexual perversion and, later, the cities of Sodom and Gomorrah.

I applaud the courage of L.A. Judge Sally Disco in ruling a pervert, Timothy Curran, did not have the right to be a Scoutmaster, that The Boy Scouts of America had the right to determine perverts were not acceptable role models for young men; to think that we live in an age and society when such a thing would even be questioned. The satanic A.C.L.U. is, of course, contesting the Judge's ruling. Its attorney, one Jon Davidson said: "It is a sad day when a judge concludes that the Constitution gives such an organization a right to model hatred and intolerance to the youth of our country." I've often contended Satan is the role model for lawyers and of a certainty Davidson worships his master that was a murderer and liar from the beginning as Jesus made clear.

Attorney Davidson, it is an infamous day when you and your fellow satanic perverts think your perverted "values" should be the "models" for the youth of America. The very fact that you are able to peddle such abominations in the name of "rights" is an indictment of our whole society and its "legal" system, beginning with the likes of Blackmun and Davis.

A certain Tori Osborn, executive director of the Los Angeles Gay (there's a misnomer if there ever was one) and Lesbian Community Services Center says: "It's just irrational. This is true homophobia at its worst. This judge is saying prejudice is a constitutional right." Given the character of the framers of our Constitution, the perverted view of Osborn is laughable. But leave it to the perverts of Satan to try to legitimize their perversion in any way they can, even trying to make noble men and women seem to be the "irrational" ones. And, of course, anyone who calls this perversion and its practitioners for what it is, a stench in the nostrils of God and an abomination to, and a blight upon our nation, will invariably be called "Homophobic" regardless of the truth and the facts of our position.

One Donna Douglas speaking for Satan displays this irrationality of perverts in a letter to the Editor of The Californian. She says: "We are just regular folks." If perverts are just "regular folks" I'm a black-striped bandicoot. This perverted person claims in her letter that Gays are not destructive of family values! Given the perverted activity of how perverts "recruit" to their ranks, this only illustrates the utter blindness of such abominable fools. I know, personally, of one case where just one young man infected three different families with his perversion. This involved EIGHTEEN children from just this one individual! By the time it was discovered and he was tried and convicted, many of these children were well on their way to practicing the same abominable behavior they had learned from him.

While I applaud the stand the Scouts have taken, I do fear for the organization when I consider how low such others, like the Y.M.C.A., the Y.W.C.A., the Salvation Army and Youth For Christ have fallen. They bear little resemblance today to the time of their founders, who would be the first to disavow any connection with them in their present form.

If I appear to some to be "fixated" on the subject of perverts it is simply because of the preeminence God Himself gives it. It is an abomination of such magnitude, like abortion as contraception, that I fear how God will deal with it in our nation and I feel a great responsibility to warn others.

Let me disabuse anyone, right now, that this is a subject I want to deal with. It isn't. It grieves me deeply that my educated colleagues, both religious and secular, haven't the stomach for the battle, that they, largely, remain silent leaving me largely alone in saying what needs to be said and in language everyone can understand.

Also, I am fully aware of the fact that many have been involved, to a greater or lesser extent, in at least one homosexual encounter. No one is a homosexual because of such an experience; many of these happen as a result of circumstances beyond the control or understanding of children, the result of low self-esteem, a searching for love and acceptance, of broken homes or a host of other things.

A part of God's judgment against this nation can readily be discerned through the recent "war" in the Middle East. If it were not for the tragedies involved, it would be laughable to watch the procession of "instant heroes" paraded before us. The "Knighting" of "Sir Norman." What a farce! His "victory" leaving U.S. troops bogged down in Iraq, 500 oil wells still burning, Saddam still in power, 2,000,000 Kurdish refugees, no democratic reform in Kuwait, no closer to an Israeli-Arab resolution, Syria obtaining Scud missiles, etc. But, if a Western-European "presence" in the area was the goal, as I suspect, of the industrialized nations, with their own agenda, they may very well celebrate a "victory." But, Oh! The end of such a "victory!"

It is a mind-numbing task to wrench myself from my trout stream to deal with such things. How much more desirable to my soul to meditate in the forest or desert, far removed from such affairs of this evil, world system. But it is not enough to discern evil- action is required; but what action?

Thoreau, in his excellent and thought-provoking work on Civil Disobedience, would, doubtless, have much to say on the subject. I am, presently, at work at emulating his Walden experience in the hope that it will grant me some of his insight. Though much of this was gained during my childhood while living on the mining claim in Sequoia National Forest, I am much older now and in need of a "refresher course" in the "simplicity of living." In the process, it may be that I, like he, will have the "opportunity" to spend some time in "gaol" as I confront the local "bureaucracy" which is not disposed to the independence of kerosene lamps, woodstove and privies as a lifestyle.

But I feel, keenly, the need to, once more, wield hammer and saw. There is nothing that takes the place of a man doing for himself. My "cabin" will be of the simplest design and construction. But, surrounded by the large Pines and boulders, the quail, squirrels, and other "critters," the wind making its distinctive, soul-stirring music through the trees, I hope to recapture some of the "magic" of the independence of spirit and soul that is so vital to maintaining a correct perspective of what is important and what is not. Essential to this is, of course, the proximity of the trout stream.

I plan to construct a small pond on the property, certainly nothing of the magnitude of Walden, but it will suffice to satisfy the deer, quail and squirrels, without which, the place would certainly be lacking in the proper "companions" suitable to a gray-bearded "curmudgeon." I'll keep you all informed on the progress of this "experiment" in "If you don't want much, you don't need much" and "A wise man lives simply." It should prove to be most interesting.

Since "The price of liberty is eternal vigilance!" we can no longer depend on our "leadership" to pay the price. For most, their only "vigilance" is the next election and lining their own pockets as they lie to get elected and lie to stay elected.

Even the "experts" are in agreement that government, at virtually every level, is out of control. Crime is rampant, people are being taxed beyond the ability to pay and the "fixes" are proving worse than the "disease" in too many cases. I mourn for those, trapped by their circumstances, unable to even dream any longer, unable to entertain any thought that things will be any better for their children. These people never thought about "planning" for their lives; they must have thought that "somehow," everything would "work out." But life is not like that. The world is a rewarder of results, not wishful thinking.

As I travel the open highways of the San Joaquin, passing through Weedpatch, Arvin, Lamont, Pumpkin Center, Taft, Shafter, I wonder? The open fields of cotton, beans, onions, the orchards of almonds, oranges and grapefruit, the vast vineyards filled with the promise of "plenty," I wonder? I'm sure Steinbeck and Saroyan wondered as well.

People in California are awakening to the harsh reality of the scarcity of water. Jobs are being lost in Silicon Valley clear down to San Diego, companies are revising their plans for expansion, and builders are having to contend with agriculture, much in jeopardy.

I skirt the East side of Bakersfield, now a teeming metropolis, the air discolored and heat waves wriggling up from the asphalt, concrete and arid, alkali soil, distorting the view. I travel through the oil fields and watch the "Iron Birds," heads bobbing rhythmically as they sip black "nectar" through "steel straws." I drive up the canyon, marveling at the rugged, granite monuments and the Kern, beckoning the fisherman, cutting through the magnificent solid rock formations, unchanged since childhood. I delight in the grass-carpeted foothills, smooth, rounded, undulating and appearing as soft as a woman's breasts, inviting the gentle, tender caress of caring love.

How very horrible that human beings must live like rats in a cage in places like Los Angeles, deprived of fresh air or a view of the stars, where young people have no hope of anything better and join gangs in search of "something" that they think will make their lives "relevant" and "purposeful." And what of a society that seems unable to offer them any better hope?

As I sit by a campfire of Juniper, stirring the coals and watching the coffee boil, absorbed in the aroma of its richness and enjoying a cigarette I can't help but think about the skewed priorities of men. The black silhouettes of the mountains outlined against a star-bright night speak peace to my soul. The hoot of an owl, the bark of a coyote, the scratch of some other "night creature" nearby all tell me that people were never meant to pass their time in this "vale of tears" in a constant attempt to "have," at the expense of their own souls. I'm sure David got to the point where he would have gladly traded the palace for the peace and tranquility of the sheepfold bears and lions notwithstanding.

Just had an interruption in my writing; "Missy," one of the resident, gray tree squirrels, was at the door demanding nuts. She prefers pecans but had to settle for walnuts. She now takes them from my fingers. She is fun to spoil. A momma and papa Valley quail spend most of their time in the yard now. Something to do with the ready availability of fresh seed I'm sure.

I used to be an avid pilot and have my share of "war stories" as all pilots do. I even owned a couple of birds at various times, an Alon, a real "kiddie-car" to fly, very simple, and a venerable Stinson, not as simple as a "taildragger" but built like the proverbial brick outhouse. I only mention this as an aside to the real story of life at Minter Field outside of Bakersfield shortly after WWII.

The barracks on the old, Army Air corps base had been opened to veteran housing. The only "authority" in residence was the base fire department. This meant that all us kids had the entire facility to explore and explore we did. Many stories to tell about our tenure there like discovering the mortuary-what our imaginations found to entertain there!

One of our favorite "toys" was the parachute, training rig. A facsimile of a fighter had been placed at the top of a high scaffold. A tall derrick with parachute harness attached was alongside. The idea was to climb into the "cockpit" of the fighter, put on the harness and, swinging out of the "plane," pretend to be jumping from a disabled aircraft; really great fun. It's a wonder none of us were killed.

One day, a biplane landed at the base. I don't know why the pilot landed there but he had left the plane and wandered off somewhere. We kids had watched the plane come in and, with the aircraft unattended, it acted as a magnet drawing us to its wondrous, mysterious and magnificent presence. What a sight! It sat gleaming in the middle of the vast, empty airstrip, its siren call beckoning our attention.

Now we were all avid model builders but, apart from the "mock fighter," none of had actually ever touched a real plane. And here was the "real thing" just begging us to examine its mysteries. Off we ran toward it.

There were only four of us and, when we reached the plane, we circled it in rapturous awe at its magnificent closeness. Tentatively, fearfully, we touched the smoothness of its fabric wings and fuselage. Somewhere, I found the courage to climb up on a wing and stared, entranced, into the open cockpit. My eyes consumed the intricate array of inscrutable instruments, the rudder pedals, the actual seat where the pilot sat, and the "joy stick" that gave him control of this "magic carpet."

In my mind's eye, I was transported far above the mundane, earthbound cares and concerns of earth, I was free as an eagle, carving paths through the ether, dodging clouds and enemy aircraft; I was "Pappy" Boyington, the Red Baron and Eddie Rickenbacker, I was John Wayne of The Flying Leathernecks and Flying Tigers.

And then, disaster! As I stood on the wing of the plane, enraptured, the "stick" began to oscillate side to side. Now I hadn't touched anything in the plane but, since I knew, intuitively, I had no business being on that plane or even touching it, when that stick began to move of its own accord I just knew I had done something terrible. I had somehow incurred the wrath of the "Genie" of the machine. Those of you that grew up with the knowledge of "Gremlins" know what I am talking about. I was terrified!

I jumped from the wing like a turpentined cat and hit the asphalt at a full run, never looking back. It took a while for me to later to deduce the obvious; one of the other kids had to have been moving one of the ailerons, causing the stick to move. But don't bother trying to explain that to a kid who believes in Gremlins or has enough conscience to know when he has been doing something he shouldn't.

It's a curious fact that most people think "God" and "Jesus" are four letter words. I've counted the letters several times and can't quite get four out of either. Now, while even a good Baptist might not settle for "Golly, Gee Whiz! " when he pounds his thumb with a 24 ounce framing hammer, he will usually go for an honest, heartfelt and enthusiastic "Hot-Damn Sombitch!" (Under the circumstances this becomes a trifle garbled among the brethren). But it's a curious fact that even some professing Christians treat the name of God and Jesus as epithets. I strongly believe such people have no real fear or knowledge of either person.

Reasonable and intelligent people understand the purely therapeutic efficacy of a truly well needed curse, relieving the anguish of all forms of torments, anguish and pain. But it must also be pointed out that most cursing in the English language is really lacking in imagination. Other cultures, particularly the Arabic, far surpass us in this art. For them, it really is an art; with us, it's often simply crude and utterly lacking in style.

Perhaps those of us with roots in the Southern tradition are more adept at truly "artistic" cussing. Try to improve on the expression: "That boy's so slow y' gotta make a mark t' see if he's moved" and "Lower than White Trash in a Snake hole."

The English language is marvelously expressive; I won't sell it short. But we simply don't apply ourselves to its potential in pronouncing curses, calumnies, and epithets. Too bad. This is a rich and most over-looked area deserving of much examination. Someone should really do doctoral research in the subject.

I'm sure it would be much appreciated (and certainly more deserving and useful than many of which I have personal knowledge). Imagine the market for a "Thesaurus of English Curses." It would sell millions. But the A.C.L.U. (All Consciences Left Unused) would probably sue to have it banned. They might even find common cause among the Baptists on this issue.

Given the "genius" of music today, its no wonder kids are confused. They have a choice of "music" that treats guitars like loaded weapons and lyrics that make truck driving equal to becoming rocket scientists and "noise" that makes salamanders impotent and scrambles the brains of amoebas.

And today's "dancing?" It reminds me of the time a visiting idiot was trying to pry a jammed .22 out of a rifle with a screwdriver in a flood-damaged house my daughter Karen and son Michael and I were rebuilding. A nine-year-old girl who was visiting happened to cross the line of fire when the round exploded and the slug punched a hole through her leg. Talk about timing! She put on a dance that would have shamed a Hottentot or Comanche warrior, all accompanied with the appropriate "music" of howls, squirting blood and screams together with the urging encouragement of general, good-natured, shouted curses.

But it wasn't all fun and games working on that house. We worked our backsides off and I helped the kids learn that nothing is impossible if you know what you are doing and are willing to "sweat."

Thursday, May 30. I have just returned from starting work on the "cabin" up at Erskine Creek. Muscles I haven't used in too long a time ache. I got the floor joists in and spent the night in the old, Dodge wagon; cold, but it was a beautiful, moonlit night, the wind soughing through the pines lulling me to sleep.

Make no mistake; building without water and power on site is nothing to write home about. Breakfast consisted of boiled coffee, eggs and hotdogs scrambled together in the cast-iron frying pan. But that is the price of some degree of solitude among the rocks, pines and critters. I will have to condescend to getting a portable generator eventually.

The sun really warmed up toward noon. Knocked off and took a drive over to Boulder Gulch before heading back down the Canyon. We have to contend with the roadwork and I had to wait until 4:00 to get through.

As I sipped coffee from my "disreputable" and omnipresent cup and mused of my childhood on the old claim, my mind was flooded with the memories of the simple life I had enjoyed here with grandad, grandma and great-grandma. Grandma and great-grandma died in their own beds here in the old cabin. I miss all of them sorely.

Sadly, the campground was littered with trash. The "Styrofoam Generation" with its uncaring and selfish attitude was well represented. Incongruously, a gray tree squirrel scampered about and a Valley quail perched on the limb of an old pine calling lustily to the covey. But the noise of the traffic on the highway and the litter profaned the moment.

At some distance, I noticed a young woman and a small boy going about looking through the trash. It became obvious that they were looking for aluminum cans. The young woman was clearly handicapped; she walked with a difficult, wrenching stride from some kind of hip problem. Their clothes were dirty and they needed a bath.

Since I was going to return to Frazier Park in a little while, I called them over to me. I asked if I could give them some of the food I had left in my ice chest. They gratefully accepted a loaf of bread, some hotdogs and a large blueberry muffin. The little boy's eyes really lit up over that treat. Grandad, grandma and great-grandma would have helped and I honored their memory.

As I walked about the place, I could see a young man with the boy and young woman. It seems that they were staying at the camp and trying to stick together in extreme circumstances. Homeless and jobless; depending on the warm weather and the cast-offs of campers.

Here was a young couple in their twenties with a boy about five. I thought of the growing number of signs, held in the hands of young people, "Will work for food!" Bangladesh, Kurdistan and Ethiopia may be far away but these things are here at "home," in the "Land of Plenty;" the shame and disgrace of it all!

People, as I have said many times, do not "plan" to be destitute, uneducated, drunkards and drug addicts, jobless, welfare mothers and wards of the courts and jailbirds. But, as I have also said many times, without a plan for success, a plan for failure is already assured.

But what can people plan on anymore? Jesus said: "Because of the increase of wickedness, the love of most will grow cold, but he who stands firm to the end will be saved." Matthew 24:12,13. And how are folks to "stand" when faced with the breakdown of authority, when the cops are "thumping heads" and stealing, when judges are more concerned for the "rights" of criminals than those of victims, when our President echoes Hitler's "New World Order," when the honest, hard-working and responsible tax-paying people are made increasingly aware that they are "chumps!" What are people to do when faced with choices, not between good and bad, but between bad and worse?

I will continue to build my cabin and write. Not because I particularly want to, but because I must. There are still souls that can be "scratched" by the poet's pen, no matter how humble the words, that will have hope because of these things I am doing. In following in the footsteps of Jesus, of Thoreau and those Russian poets, hope is constantly renewed in the hearts of those with an ear to hear.

It has always been thus that "only a few will be saved." Man, created in the image of God, has always been given the privilege or curse of choice- to "stand firm" or acquiesce to the forces of evil.

Some years ago and shortly before his death, I took grandad with me on excursions into the "outback" of the Mojave. That was in the days before the "off-roaders" and riff-raff ruined things. Many of the artifacts of long-gone mining operations were still intact- old cabins and shacks, some over a hundred years old. In only a brief span of time, I witnessed the destruction of all these relics by a process of plain, vicious vandalism. I will always be grateful I took grandad (and my children) with me to visit these places before they were ruined.

When I call from the store of "precious memories," I continue to wonder what it will be that will make life a "wonderful experience" for the young people of today as they grow older; how tragically poor in spirit any nation that robs its children of dreams. And its children, left confused, knowing they have been cheated and too ignorant and selfish to do anything about it.

CHAPTER FOURTEEN

THE WEEDPATCHER

JULY, 1991

James 1:22

Where is Sam Clemens when we need him, the man who could so colorfully describe "Judicial rottenness" and "Congressional corruption" in such vivid terms; the man who called Judas Iscariot a "Low, mean, premature Congressman," who described "New legislators" as men who had "... not enough time to sell out?"

His advice to would-be writers is unexcelled: "Write without pay until someone offers pay!" As a successful author, he was constantly bombarded with requests to examine some budding writer's work. His comment on one young fellow that believed himself blessed of the Muse: "Well, sir, there was a young fellow who believed he was a poet; but the main difficulty with him was to get anybody else to believe it." Reminds me of several people I know.

I am grateful God gave us Sam Clemens. The world would be the poorer for the lack of his genius. Like Will Rogers later on, Sam had a quick eye and ready wit to puncture the balloons of pompous asses and keelhaul political and religious charlatans.

It is a tragedy that the United States has become an illiterate nation; that reading has reached such a nadir that "Classic" literature is considered a two-year old edition of Rolling Stones magazine. We are paying a heavy price for our ignorance.

When I was doing undergraduate work back in the 60's in one of my majors, English Literature, it was expected that we read at least 30 books per class per semester. Now, almost thirty years later, I find myself re-reading many of these books with new insight that only age and experience can bring. A new appreciation for Sam Clemens has aroused me by reading the excellent anthology of his work entitled: "Life As I Find It."

Over a hundred years have passed since Clemens wrote these articles; yet, there is a "timeliness" to many of them that fits our present situation to a "T." It is most unfortunate that he received such a bad "rap" from religionists because he exhibited more Christian understanding than most of his religious contemporaries. But, like Sinclair Lewis, he was too outspoken in his criticism of hypocrisy in both religion and politics.

It is most ironic that, while few remember anything of T. Dewitt Talmage, Clemens' name still shines bright. Yet, a hundred years ago, Talmage was at the forefront of "Evangelical" action. I use the word evangelical in quotes in respect to Talmage because of an observation of him made by Clemens.

I quote the offending statement of Talmage: "I have a good Christian friend who, if he sat in the front pew in church, and a working man should enter the door at the other end, would smell him instantly. My friend is not to blame for the sensitiveness of his nose, any more than you would flog a pointer for being keener on the scent than a stupid watchdog. The fact is, if you had all the churches free, by reason of the mixing up of the common people with the uncommon, you would keep one-half of Christendom sick at their stomach. If you are going to kill the church thus with bad smells, I will have nothing to do with this work of evangelization."

I now summarize Clemens' remarks: "Dr. T. has had advantages which Paul and Peter and the others could not and did not have. There was a lack of polish about them, and a looseness of etiquette, and a want of exclusiveness, which one cannot help noticing. They healed the very beggars, and held intercourse with people of villainous odors every day. If the subject of these remarks had been chosen among the original Twelve Apostles, he would not have associated with the rest, because he could not have stood the fishy smell of some of his comrades who came from around the Sea of Galilee. ... Now, can it be possible that in a handful of centuries the Christian character has fallen away from an imposing heroism that scorned even the stake, the cross, and the axe, to a poor little effeminacy that withers and wilts under an unsavory smell? We are not prepared to believe so, the Reverend Doctor and his friend to the contrary notwithstanding."

Fortunately, while I have an imposing background in the history and literature of "Fundamentalism," I am not blind to the effete snobbery of T. Dewitt Talmage. Though he ranks among the "giants" of the "faith," though his sermons are still carried, reprinted in fundamentalist periodicals such as "Sword of The Lord" (And, while I do not always agree with some of the things Sword of The Lord says, particularly under the guidance of its present editor, Curtis Hutson, I am a faithful subscriber and applaud most of what The Sword stands for and recommend it to others), I am not ignorant of the fact that, by his looking down his nose at "common, working people," he gives the lie to his flowery sermons. And I am not ignorant of the great harm done by him and his followers by their hypocrisy.

One cannot, like Clemens, fail to see the assininity of the posturing of this "soldier of the cross," who claims to have any interest in real evangelization and is put off by the odor of "common, working people." The real stench, to God as well as to Clemens and me, is men like Talmage.

If you are one of those ignorant people that are drawn to flowery speech utterly lacking in any real depth of practical value, you will love the writing of men like Talmage and Spurgeon. But if you are a lover of getting to the "nut" of a problem, if you want reality and no mincing of words instead of "feel good" nonsense, you want to read Clemens.

It will come as a great surprise to my fundamentalist "brethren" that Clemens made the remark: "All that is just and good in our particular civilization came straight from the hand of Jesus Christ." Clemens made this statement in the process of taking to task another "man of the cloth," a certain Reverend Sabine of Episcopal persuasion.

It seems the Reverend Mr. Sabine refused to perform the ceremony for the burial of an actor, a Mr. George Holland, contending the theater and actors "... taught no moral lessons." Clemens, in a portion of his rebuttal, made the excellent observation: "Where was ever a sermon preached that could make filial ingratitude so hateful to men as the sinful play of King Lear? ... But to cease teaching and go back to the beginning again, was it not pitiable, that spectacle? Honored and honorable old George Holland, whose theatrical ministry had for fifty years softened hard hearts, bred generosity in cold ones, kindled emotion in dead ones, uplifted base ones, broadened bigoted ones, and made many and many a stricken one glad and filled it brim full of gratitude, figuratively spit upon in his unoffending coffin by this crawling, slimy, sanctimonious, self-righteous reptile!" I couldn't have said it better Sam. And I wonder how the "Reverend" Mr. Sabine would respond to a recent headline: "Episcopal bishop ordains lesbian to priesthood!" Would he recognize his own hypocrisy as a factor in hastening the demise of this august denomination? No more than Talmage would recognize his duplicity in segregating "common people" from "uncommon." Of course, it has always been thus that the "Pharisees" make clean the outside of the cup but remain "Whited sepulchers."

Reminds me of the time, long ago, when, as a young fellow, I went to the beach. I was visiting a cousin who lived nearby and, taking advantage of the warm weather and the proximity of the ocean we decided to go swimming and look at girls (that was a long time ago). I had brought with me, for the occasion, beautiful, brand new, white swimming trunks. The vision of my lean, bronzed, young body in those white trunks had to catch the eyes of the fair sex. More, the trunks were made of some gleaming, new, synthetic material- quite dazzling. We spread out our blankets and went running into the surf. A beautiful day, girls everywhere, clean beach and water (this was indeed a long time ago). Terrific!

We swam for a while and my cousin finally decided to get back to the beach and check out the "action." I was a while longer getting up my nerve. Finally, girding my mental loins, I swam back toward the beach and, reaching the surf, stood up only to discover that my marvelous, new, synthetic trunks, when wet, turned to the transparency of cellophane.

Now, gentle reader, you must remember that there was still a good deal of modesty left among young people of those years long past. Teenage girls were still around that could honestly blush and there were a few teenage boys (me among them) that still believed sex was for marriage only (my, it has been a long time).

So there I was. What to do? I rapidly backtracked to deeper water and hollered as decorously as I could for my cousin. The cold water was beginning to get to my bones. But my cousin was distracted by the pulchritudinous display of attractions on the beach. After about twenty minutes of my absence, it finally occurred to him to look my direction. Flailing my arms and hollering, he managed to discern something amiss. It was all totally embarrassing. He came out to me and, splitting a gut at my predicament, was kind enough to go get a beach blanket for me. There was much curiosity on the beach at my strange behavior as I wrapped the towel around me before coming out of the water. But modesty commands that I draw the curtain on this miserable scene without further elaboration.

Suffice it to say that there are many politicians, judges and religious "professionals" that don't dare come out of the water without a "blanket" less they expose their own nakedness. But as long as they stay in their "cesspools," they have profound faith in their "dazzling, white trunks." Nonetheless, they remain, "Whited sepulchers."

While Clemens had a finely honed edge for religious charlatans, he was equally eloquent when it came to politicians, calling Congress "Organized imbecility." Anyone who reads a newspaper would agree that the phrase is, if anything, charitable. One can only wonder in awe at what Sam would call the present Congress.

It was, undoubtedly, the very ugliness of the world, its politics, its religious and ethnic hatred that drove Sam, as Mark Twain, to escape into Tom Sawyer and Huckleberry Finn every bit as much as Thoreau and I escape into the simplicity of the wilderness and stories about squirrels. The world is too real to bear without some surcease from its multitudinous sorrows.

And, while we can be grateful for the humor of a Dave Berry and his "exploding cows," together with the humor of Congress spending thousands of dollars on a study of cow flatulence and the danger this poses to the ozone layer and contributing to the "Greenhouse Effect," we still need the humor of a Clemens to get us through the really tough spots in life.

Now if Sam had had his way, the electorate would have been composed of educated and landed taxpayers, not "... ignorant and non-tax-paying classes" ala Gandour. And, of course, women would not have the vote because, as he said: "That would debase women to the level of Negroes and men." (One must remember, that, given the era of Clemens, as with Currier and Ives, his comments about Negroes were without prejudice) You ladies take due note. Your enfranchisement, as with that of Negroes and "non-taxpayers," has not bettered your lot and has worked a great deal of mischief. You now have the looming possibility of finding yourselves in the trenches with men in hand-to-hand combat on the basis of "equality." Naturally, in the interest of such "equality," we must require the legislature remove all rape laws from the books as well. "Common sense" must prevail.

How very "nice and pretty" sound the words of "liberal" thought today. I quote Louis Sullivan, secretary of the Department of Health and Human Services: "I am afraid that we have lost our frustration and anger, our natural aversion to racism. Many of us no longer feel disdain or revulsion when we read of racism or see the results of discrimination."

Poor, benighted and naive Mr. Sullivan, to believe that racism was ever in the category of "natural aversion." I wonder how such "pretty words" would play in China, Japan, Iraq, Ethiopia, etc. A recent show of Sally Jessy Raphael had, as its guests, a number of K.K.K. women. These were pitted against an audience of, primarily, "minorities," to use the present and "politically correct" euphemism. It made for excellent "gonzo" T.V. and ably depicted the intense, racial hatred inherent in our society on all sides.

People, historically and in general, remain "Hitleric" in their ethnic thinking and while the advocates of "Black is beautiful" and "White supremacy" beat each others heads in, God remains faithful in looking at hearts rather than colors. The "pretty words" of nice "liberals" may play in Peoria but they fall on the deaf ears of a Farrakhan, Saddam or David Duke. It is "nice" to talk of a "pluralistic" and "democratic" society as long as someone else is made to pay the price for such fine sentiments. "Forty acres and a mule" is still the purview of the present crop of "Carpetbaggers" in Washington.

The ugly truth concerning "racism" is that a certain "elite" have always, like the Nazis, been attracted to a basic fact; if you can inculcate race hatred to your advantage, you can get the "great unwashed" to do your bidding, killing off "undesirables" and giving you the power to "inherit" the "Darwinian" right to rule.

Intelligent and educated people know the truth of this chilling statement. Though the "leadership" is, in fact, a seeming bunch of "imbeciles," or, ala Grace, a "Bunch of Clowns," they are not really stupid. Many are more than willing to foment race riots if they think it will serve their purpose. Willing or not, that is exactly the end they are striving for and, the way things are going, that is exactly what will happen!

Fortunately for my readers, I have not fallen prey to the use of extensive lists of statistical information (This in spite of the fact that advanced statistics was one of my graduate courses of study). I long ago discovered the curious fact that not all the statistics in the world can take the place of holding a starving baby in your own arms or burying your own child, of being the object of racial hatred, of being the relative of a victim of murder or having your own home violated by thieves.

"Uncle Tom's Cabin" was the catalyst for one of the bloodiest civil wars in history. The preaching of Billy Sunday gave us the Volstead Act and Prohibition. People are emotional by nature. You can't change that. But, you can use this fact to your advantage as any successful religious or political "Con" can testify. It was certainly the basis of Hitler's success.

Most of you have heard, by now, responsible newscasters finally making forecasts about the demise of the United States and the looming bankruptcy of California. As incredible as it seems, the United States is so dependent upon foreign investment that with the threat of it being siphoned off to Eastern Europe, we face becoming a second-rate power. What do you suppose the "Leadership" is cooking up in an attempt to stop this from happening? I anticipate more talk of a "New World Order" and the "borrowing" of many pages from Hitler's "How To" book.

California cannot possibly make up its deficit in the face of increasing "Social Welfare" programs, the growing number of government-services dependent and non-taxpaying drones in our society coupled with extraordinary increases in federal and state taxes. The stage is being set for catastrophic "Solutions" that hark back to the dark ages and "Hitlerian" tactics.

The schools continue to spend themselves into bankruptcy without any concern for "accountability" as with the S&Ls, Banks and insurance companies. I had to wonder, back in 1975, when I did my doctoral dissertation on Accountability in Education why no publisher would touch it? I have since learned why. No one wanted to believe things were as bad as my study proved. As one publisher told me, the issue was "too hot to handle."

As taxpayers, we are expected to pay for all the corruption, greed and incompetence of the "leadership" in all these fields. But when these "leaders" look at the fact that people are still keeping the likes of Oral Roberts, Swaggart, Cerullo and Schuller in business, why shouldn't they believe the public will swallow anything they dish out?

I have to make a comment on "Tithing" at this point. Few things I have written have caused so much animosity among the "saints." I suppose it is largely because there are so few that really have any real belief in, or fear of,

God. That is the only plausible explanation because no one can truly believe the Bible to be The Word of God and miss the clear command that Christians are to tithe. Many I know personally have written me off on this point and found some other "minister" who will comfort their pocketbook by leading them to believe what they want to believe, that God doesn't really mean what He says on this subject. Of course, how do they then determine what He means on any subject? Ah, that is, indeed, a conundrum. But those who have no real desire to obey God will always find a satisfactory "loophole" and continue to delude themselves that they are "good Christians." Their first three seconds in Hell will quickly dispel this myth. He is Lord of all or He isn't Lord at all!

But this command of God concerning tithing is far deeper in its significance than most realize, otherwise, professing Christians wouldn't treat it so lightly. It was clearly God's intention to place responsibility where it belongs in the order and ministry of the Church. No sane individual is going to throw away ten percent of his hard earned income. He is going to make sure the money is spent for all the right reasons. Strict accountability is a most responsible thing. A person who earns $2,000 a month is most assuredly going to want an accounting of where and how his $200 tithe is spent. And it is that person's responsibility to know!

One has to wonder how Jim and Tammy could have been so successful at fleecing the "flock." The answer: No accountability. And that accountability began with those that fattened these religious sharks. I have no sympathy for any of those that got taken. If they had believed anything God says, if they had had any sense of the honor and integrity of The Lord, any real love for Him and His Word, they could not have believed such outrageous liars and con artists.

Sadly, my emphasis on Scripture memorization and tithing are among other things that has left me without a congregation. Too many times people have had their consciences stirred and made great promises only to turn away when the going got rough. Despite the wisdom of "Thy word have I hid in my heart that I might not sin against thee" the excuses are endless. In regard to memorization, "There just isn't enough time," or, "It's so inconvenient!" Can such people really love God; can such people really be believers? The testimony of God is against them along with both, seeming, extremes of Bunyan and Hitler.

And, of course, there are those men who, spinelessly and shamefully, let women rule over them rather than accepting God's command that they are to be responsible for ruling their families. These "men" obviously have no real faith in God or any desire to obey Him.

So, "churchless" once more, I continue to write and work on the cabin. There is something so very contenting in laboring with my hands. To take the raw lumber and transform it into a dwelling is joy. The walls are now going up and it's thrilling to my soul. The pines and rocks, the mountains all around, the critters keeping me company. Unlike my work among the "saints," lo, these many years, there is no hypocrisy or betrayal here; only honest work and sweat. And, furthermore, if anyone I know offered to help me, I would probably turn them down. The price of too many "friends" over the years has exacted its toll, leaving me far too disillusioned to accept their "help" even if they offered (No one has, by the way. Thoreau would understand). But the "Little Red Hen" must have entertained some, possibly, perverse enjoyment in reaping the benefit of "doing it all herself." To owe no man anything but to love him is still good advice. It is well to heed the solemn admonition that no one be given any justification to say they "made Abraham rich!"

I have bought a generator. I use it sparingly as the noise is detestable. Now I have to acquire a pump for the well so "Walden Puddle" can become a reality. It will also beat carrying water to the site.

I realize, as I gaze at God's starry canopy that this poor, old world cannot much longer stand the strain we have put upon it. Our society cannot much longer hold itself together against the onslaught of disasters and the greed and monstrous villainy of unscrupulous men and women. Something has to give. The "Band-aid fixes" are running their course and the bills are coming due. "Pay Day Someday" is here now.

It was early afternoon on a mild, summer day years ago. The forest was quiet. I had been outside doing some chore and came into the cabin through the door to my grandparent's bedroom. My grandmother had become bed-ridden and grandad was out front doing laundry with scrub board and washtub by the well. There were only the three of us now since great-grandma had passed away.

As soon as I entered the room I sensed something was wrong. Looking down at the face of my grandmother, I knew, instantly, she was dead. She looked still and peaceful; a thin line of foam had formed at her lips.

I walked slowly, trance-like, out to where grandad was rubbing sheets against the washboard. He had an apron tied around his waist and his shirtsleeves were rolled up above his elbows. All I could do was say quietly "Grandad." He turned and one look at my face together with that one, softly uttered word was all that was needed. We stood looking at each other and, slowly, he dried his hands on the apron and, with reluctant, halting steps, he began to walk toward the door of the cabin, knowing and not wanting to know, what awaited him. I followed. I was sixteen years old.

Samuel D. G. Heath, Ph. D.

He was crying softly by the time we reached my grandmother. Bending over her, he used the corner of the apron to wipe the foam from her lips, his tears dropping down on her.

We do not attain any sum of years without confronting the finality of death. Nor do we reach much age without some moment crashing down on us that so indelibly impacts our senses as to imprint itself beyond any forgetting. Some are so dreadful as to render the victim incapable of any further attempt to cope with life in any sense of normality. Insanity is often an escape to an unreachable world, far removed from the impossible dread of things, which are too horrible to bear by mere rationality.

And, some others, like walking into that cabin on that day in summer, or watching my eldest daughter die and my son trying to deal with it, forcing yourself to live after an adulterous "wife" has, without any conscience, hurt and twisted your children, will forever be there, intruding and insistent, making a difference that works itself out in countless ways, decisions and actions throughout your life.

My grandparents loved each other. Grandad had cared for grandma like a baby throughout her invalid, bed-ridden, short remainder of life. He washed her, he did the laundry; he cooked and did all he could to make her comfortable. Here was the proof that fidelity and commitment were not just grand words.

God says that love covers a multitude of sins. My grandad was far from a perfect human being. He had a violent temper, so much so, that my mother, with a temper to match his, married early to escape it and my grandparents had had some terrible fights over the years. Theirs was not a storybook marriage. But among my store of precious memories there will always be the sight of grandad, bending over grandma, wiping her lips and his tears falling on her. There was love in its rawest, mind searing, most redeeming and priceless form and truth.

I suppose most people realize that "families," as such, are no longer the mainstay of America for, in truth, there aren't that many left. Marriages and "vows" are a meaningless form, the parties generally entering the relationship without the slightest intention of fidelity or genuine commitment. Perverts are "partnered" with the state's "blessing." Children are a liability more often than a blessing and treated as such.

And, so, I retreat with Mark Twain and Thoreau. I write, travel and build. Knowing what I know, how can I do differently? "To him that knoweth to do right and doeth it not, to him it is sin." And I know, as I sink "sixteens" in those two-by-fours and wipe the sweat from my eyes, this is right!

This Saturday I must go to Bakersfield and try to "cure" a "sick" Datsun 4 by 4 so I can get it up the Canyon where I hope it will do service in reaching the silver mine; more about that later. There are times when ignorance is bliss and its folly to be wise. Being a mechanic, more often than not, it seems, lends truth to the statement. If I didn't know how to fix cars I could, in good, ignorant conscience, hire somebody else to do it.

Isn't it tragic that Detroit was so smug and greedy that the driving public was forced into buying "Rice-grinders?" But I foresee a time in the near future where people will be, literally, throwing rocks at Japanese cars. It was for this reason that I caution some against buying one. When you couple racism with economics, you have an unbeatable combination, as Hitler so well proved, and, I strongly believe, we will shortly see in this country.

For thirty years, I have made it a practice to write letters to legislators and the editors of metropolitan newspapers. For the first time in my life, I have failed to have a letter to the editor published or have legislators refuse to answer my communications. And this on one, single subject: Homosexuality. Government leaders and editors are so afraid of the power and influence of this "special interest group" that they are fearful of acknowledging my comments. This should tell us all something of the truth of my warnings about Satan's influence through perversion. Small wonder he is trying to class perverts with "suppressed minorities" and ram it down our throats through "legally protected status." Even Hitler "looked the other way" when the perversion was in the "family" of his cohorts. This in spite of the fact that he had many arrested and murdered.

At least Clemens didn't have to deal with perversion on a national scale. He and Bret Harte could do battle with the more "seemly" sins of their day like political corruption and religious and "scientific" chicanery. Henry James could content himself with innocuous and wordy novels. Sam could, safely, take to task, the Boston Girl with her ungrammatical attack on his misuse of the adverb and tautological tendencies. Some things, as Sam pointed out, are simply "unlearnable" such as his use of "Rose up." "I have a friend," he says, "who has kept his razors in the top drawer and his strop in the bottom drawer for years; when he wants his razors, he always pulls out the bottom drawer - and swears. Change? Could one imagine he never thought of that? He did change; he has changed a dozen times. It didn't do any good; his afflicted mind was able to keep up with the changes and make the proper mistake every time!" And so it is that we are, in some ways, doomed by bent of mental curiosity to make some of the "proper mistakes" every time; some things are, simply, unlearnable.

But I did learn, early, not to gamble on games of chance. Though I agree with Sam and Bret that the scholarly pursuit of poker and a thorough knowledge of the refinements of the game are at least equal to the pretentiousness of chess, and, I further agree with them that: "... for the instruction of the young, we have introduced a game of poker. There are few things that are so unpardonably neglected in our country as poker. The upper class knows very little about it. Now and then you find ambassadors who have a sort of general knowledge of the game, but the ignorance of the people is fearful. Why, I have known clergymen, good men, kind-hearted, liberal, sincere and all that, who did not know the meaning of a 'flush.' It is enough to make one ashamed of one's species."

It never crossed my mind, throughout my entire childhood, to ever steal anything from my mother or grandparents. Purses could be left open and in plain sight with impunity; never a stirring of larceny in my thoughts. It was, in my case, simply unthinkable. Until "Poker!"

Now my brother and I could, and did, draw blood over games like Canasta and Monopoly in our childhood. But we did not learn to play poker. If we had, the nefarious incident may not have taken place and sullied an otherwise perfect and pure conscience in this regard.

An older child, much wiser in the affairs of this world (and not so "pure" when it came to theft) was visiting. He knew how to play poker and, deeming me deficient in knowledge of such things and being ever so solicitous for my education, was more than willing to introduce me to this worldly refinement. After a few hands, it was determined by my mentor that I was ready for the "real thing." Of course, this meant using real money.

Needless to say, my "teacher" soon exhausted my small supply of pennies and nickels. But my brain was hooked by the possibility of "easy" riches by the simple mechanism of the turn of a card. It was an intoxicating thought. And I just knew "my luck had to change."

Beats there a heart, anywhere in the land, no matter how seemingly pure, that does not shelter, in the darkest recesses of its innermost closet, some shameful thing, the common knowledge of which would cause the perpetrator of the dreadful act to die of terminal mortification? NO! We are all of the same, common clay.

And so it was, that, I betook myself to my grandparent's bedroom and stole the "thirty pieces of silver" (a couple of half dollars, some quarters, dimes and nickels) from their supply of change they kept on a shelf.

It didn't take my tormentor, nie "teacher," long to clean me out of my ill-gotten coins. The shame of my cowardly and greedy act began to burn into my mind and soul. But the dastardly deed was done and was not to be undone.

I never confessed my crime. The shame and betrayal of trust were too much for me to do so. But neither was I ever tempted to repeat it. Between that experience and my short tenure in Las Vegas not long after, I was forever "cured" of any propensity for gambling and, I do believe The Lord is opposed to it as well. Whisky was another thing entirely. I liked it.

Strong drink and tobacco (and gambling) were an absolute taboo of my grandparents. Not so with my mother. She both smoked and drank. Between the popularizing of such "sports" via "silver screen," the license of society because of WWII and rebellion to her parent's mores, Mom heartily engaged in both of the fascinating and sinfully attractive practices. Then, as now, one of my favorite odors is acquired by sticking my nose into a pack of cigarettes or pouch of pipe tobacco. I even enjoy an occasional cigar.

It was while living at Minter Field (remember that place?) with my mother and Stepdad #3 that so many things of great interest occurred, among them, my introduction to drunken debauchery at the tender age of nine or ten. My brother and I had discovered the "wine cellar," a stash of booze Mom and the Stepdad thought they had well hidden. A bottle of whisky was among the "forbidden fruit." There are some things that just have a natural attraction for kids; along with blood, guts, guns, explosive devices and sundry items of mayhem and destruction, there is booze.

Now no child with any self-respect can deny a righteous dare. And when one's younger brother advances the dare, well, you can imagine for yourself the humility of not meeting the challenge. And I was up to the mark.

My brother: "Bet you can't drink any of this stuff!" Me: "Of course I can!" I did. In fact, I liked it. No challenge at all. It was so good and impressed my brother so much that there was nothing to do but have another snort. I felt good. I felt real good. I was thoroughly drunk.

I recall, basking in the "hero" admiration of my little brother, going into the bedroom and, getting up on the bed, beginning to jump up and down like crazy. What great fun! But, suddenly, I was lying on my back staring at the ceiling, watching it swirl in a hazy circle above me. "This is not right," my mind was saying. My stomach knew it was not right; in fact, my stomach was plumbing new dimensions of never before felt uneasiness. No, not uneasiness; my stomach knew I had purposely tried to assassinate it! Well, my stomach was not going to take that lying down you can bet. It didn't.

You've heard the one about the passenger found bending over the rail of the ship who, when told that no one had ever died of seasickness replied: "Please don't tell me that. It's only the hope of dying that's keeping me alive!" I discovered the absolute truth of that statement. I had never known such sickness, never believed anyone could live through such living death.

But, I lived. It wouldn't be until some fifteen years later that I could even endure the smell of whisky. But once overcome, but I leave the sordid details of that stage of my youth for another time.

I must conclude with a much more mundane and matter of fact business venture- my sortie into the exotic field of Iguana ranching. It is a little known fact, largely because those "in the know" keep it a cherished and, sacred secret, that there are millions to be made in Iguanas.

In my forays to the "outback" when I was dealing in desert properties, it seemed that there must be some way of utilizing these vast tracts of seemingly, worthless lands (I utterly disdained the "commercial cons" of Lake L.A., Salton Sea and Hesperia). It was quite easy to sell property which, with some small water source, lent itself to a promotion of "Raise Bullfrogs For Fun And Profit" and my bronzed Bullfrogs had sold very well, but demand was beginning to taper off and, being an inveterate entrepreneur, I was casting about in my mind for another, equally successful enterprise.

My gold mine and precious metals reclamation project ... but I'm getting off the track. I needed something worthy of my industry and genius. It came to me in a kind of "revelation," a "vision" if you will that the great Mojave would be ideal for Iguana ranching. If only I knew anything about them. But there was the challenge. I'm a good student and always ready to learn new things- especially for fun and profit.

Now while I was somewhat familiar with Iguanas and was quite "up to snuff" on the nomenclature via National Geographic and other worthy periodicals, I was, admittedly, somewhat ignorant of the beasts in respect to the actual raising of same. And, so, I set out with a will to do the necessary research in order to determine whether my scheme was realistic and practical. But I quickly discovered what seemed to be a "conspiracy" of silence concerning the lizards. Not only was there, to my profound consternation, no available literature about Iguana ranches in America, the few people I gained any leads were very secretive, even downright rude, whenever the subject was brought up. I knew they were hiding something.

During a stint of "Pastoral" duties, I had performed the wedding ceremony for an ex-brother-in-law. He had decided on a Mexican bride and, being an Anglo, his family (my, then, in-laws) had refused to even attend the wedding. I did not endear myself to the, then, in-laws, by my participation in the "ugly" affair. But the bride and her family were most appreciative. It was thus, through the "Mexican Connection," that I began to make progress in the venture. To be continued.

CHAPTER FIFTEEN

THE WEEDPATCHER

AUGUST, 1991

Psalm 50

I would like to begin this issue with thanks to State Senator Don Rogers for his candid remarks in response to some of the things I have been writing about. Not all politicians are "Imbeciles and Clowns." But it will take a great many good men, pulling together to give us any hope that things will get any better in this country. All of you have a responsibility to communicate with those legislators that you feel warrant your support. If good men fail because of, as the Senator said, "Apathy and shortsightedness," not only on the part of Congress but the electorate as well, we have only ourselves to blame. After all, if Congress is really "Organized Imbecility" as Clemens called it, who elected the imbeciles and keeps them in office? Emerson, the greatest intellect America ever produced in my opinion had pointed out no one would choose to be a politician if they had any choice of a noble occupation.

I would also like to applaud Representative William Dannemeyer, R-California. for echoing my own statements concerning AIDS and being the chief sponsor of a bill to require regular AIDS testing of health care workers and some patients. The bill is named for Kim Bergalis, a Florida woman who is dying of AIDS that she contracted from her dentist. "We have waited long enough," said Dannemeyer, "Politicians and doctors have been treating the AIDS epidemic as a civil rights issue, not a public health issue." Watch how the perverts will attack this, common sense, legislation.

By now, everyone is fully aware of the truth that our President's "Shiny Victory" in Kuwait is a mockery. Nothing can detract from the heroism of those that really fought and died for the "cause;" but what, exactly, was that cause and, what exactly, was accomplished by their sacrifice? It seems to me that Bush, having "blown" it, will have to go back and try to do the job over again. Won't that be something?

It is really difficult, at times, for me to try to "Aw Shucks" my way through some of the shenanigans Foggy Bottom pulls. So building my cabin and trying to provide water for the "critters" and me becomes increasingly important.

And, as if there weren't enough problems, what about the recent article in The New Republic where author Henry Fairlie tags "Oldsters" with the title: "Greedy Geezers!" With 20 percent of America's children living in poverty, how can we, in good conscience, spend so much on health care for the elderly? And, pitting "Pre-natal" care against "Intensive" care (Sen. John Rockefeller IV), the Gray Panthers against Americans for Generational Equity, what will politicians do?

The "generational war" will be solved one way or another. Remember the article I wrote a long while back in respect to a candidate for Governor's honest comment about "The old should get on with the business of dying and let us balance the budget!"? People like Ken Dychtwald (Age Wave) calls it "A battle that threatens to divide the nation and set generation against generation for decades to come."

Having recently come of age to receive my Burger King discount, but, yet, having enough teeth to get the job done and still being able to swing a framing hammer with a degree of effectiveness, I am filled with curiosity as to how, in its "infinite wisdom," the Congress will deal with this one? Given the facts, I still believe the "Hitlerian Solutions" such as euthanasia will be the result. As with the absolute necessity of containing Welfare costs, the enormous, government "bail-outs" etc., we do not have choices between good and bad, only between bad and worse as per Plato. At least Dychtwald is honest enough to say it out loud: "The American family has been sold into financial slavery." I hear an echo of my voice long ago. But, who listens?

Are you a "Pale Greener" or "Deep Greener?" Another conundrum; It is popular to be "Ecologically" minded these days. As I have written extensively on this subject I won't belabor it here. Suffice it to say, again with Platonic reason, it depends, as always, on whose ox is being gored. The truth of human nature is always exposed when the choice is doing with a little less, as in the case of water, or trying to do without entirely.

So-called "Third World Nations" want "theirs" also. I will only say, we are going to have to find "solutions" whether we choose to do so or not and the choices are not between good and bad, but between bad and worse. Genocide and slavery are the historical "solutions" and are, even now, being discussed behind the "closed doors" of those that realize what actions are going to be required to "save" the world.

These past few days, I managed to get the roof trusses built and get the roof sheathed and covered on the cabin; hard work but a welcome respite from the cares of this poor old world's sorrows. But, how I longed to be able to take a righteous shower! While there is nothing wrong with honest toil and dirt, there is nothing wrong with wanting to be clean either. Hopefully, "Walden Puddle" will come about in the near future. Then, at least, I can immerse myself in the pool until I figure out shower facilities.

While the sun was beating my brains out as I was nailing CDX sheets to the trusses, I recalled the "Quilting Parties." These are a fond memory of my childhood when we lived on the corner of Cottonwood and Padre in Little Oklahoma (Southeast Bakersfield) during the late 30's and early 40's.

As an aside, my mother tells me that they found Amelia Earhart's kidnapped husband in this house while it was under construction. I need to check this out. Maybe the archives of the Bakersfield Californian have the story. She also corrected me on a couple of other things. She says my second stepdad was in the Army, not the Marines. In fact, she said, she would never go out with a Marine or Bartender. Curious. The stepdad in question, she told me, was not only in the Army; he was in the Messenger Pigeon Corps. Now how about that?

Another curiosity- my grandparents, due to circumstances I have described in my book, were married by telephone; an extremely rare occurrence during that era and, reputedly, the first done, with the governor's blessing, in Louisiana. These were inventive people.

My grandparents had a quilting frame that hung from the ceiling of the living room. At times, the neighbor ladies, mostly members of my grandad's little congregation of Faith Tabernacle (which he built himself and stood on the same property as the house) would get together and make quilts.

It was something my brother, Dee Dee, and I always enjoyed. Bakersfield, as you may know, is noted for its "balmy" summers and pungent odors. My earliest memories of the smells of the packing plant down the road, mingled with the oil wells and holding ponds, the various flora of our little neighborhood, are deeply imprinted in my mind.

But the thing that made the quilting parties so much fun was the fact that, as the ladies all gathered around the apparatus Dee Dee and I could crawl under the thing and, in the coolness of our shadowed "sanctuary," listen to the "genteel gossip." We were far too young to understand much of what the ladies said but it was pleasant to hear their lulling voices and share the enjoyment they obviously were having as they sewed the various pieces of fabric into fascinating mosaics of a quilt.

Quilting was a communal thing. Grandma and great-grandma were precious to my brother and me. It made us feel good whenever they and all the neighbor ladies got together and had fun. Like crawling into our private "preserve" of the Cannas in the yard, there was some kind of "magic" in the warmth and security of just being around good people and a shaded place during the hot, summer days, of listening to Jack Armstrong; the All

American Boy, Captain Midnight, Amos and Andy, Duffey's Tavern and so many more that kept our imaginations alive and made us laugh. The "old" Saturday Evening Post, Colliers and National Geographic; Great-grandma would read to us by kerosene lamp and make "Tugboat Annie" come alive.

You know, women and children have lost a lot to "equality." When women were responsible for the home and little ones, when they gathered in "community," as for quilting and washday, they shared the work, they talked, and children felt secure. It was hard work but by working and sharing together, they and their families gained a great deal. Women and men had clearly defined roles.

But now it takes two paychecks to make ends meet. Children, in droves, suffer the consequences. All our "modern conveniences" have left us with less and less time for the really important things in life. Thanks to pornography like Playboy, Hustler, and Penthouse, men think they are being "cheated" when they look at their wives or girlfriends. And, because sex is no longer a sacred trust, because women have devalued themselves so much, men are always "looking" for something, "someone" else. And concerning trust, women are just as bad or worse.

You women ought to read "The Beauty Myth: How Images of Beauty Are Used Against Women" by Naomi Wolf. The author makes the telling point, as I do myself, that women are "sold" a bill of goods when it comes to beauty. Wolf says beauty discrimination has replaced gender discrimination as the nation's most serious social problem. The objectivity of the author is questionable to that degree but the fact remains that men chase pretty women, not ugly ones. The tragedy of it is, that, lacking a spiritual dimension appearances become everything. Materialism is an adjunct of this pernicious truth.

Quoting from an article by Connie Keeler she quotes Janet Pierucci, a therapist at Westchester Counseling Center: "... too much value is placed on youth and beauty. There are very few role models for women over 50. ... In our society there is a strong prejudice against women who are not young, thin and beautiful. ... As men get older they are said to be seasoned; but women retain less value. ... It's a double standard and will remain as long as women continue to buy into it. Why is it men have the right to get bald and pot-bellied, while women are expected not to get gray hair and wrinkles."

While I deal with this issue extensively in my writings, I will add here, women "sold their birthright" for a mess of pottage in the mistaken notion of "equality." Satan has always been most successful in duping women. And it will never be any better for women until they put The Lord first in their lives. And I certainly don't mean that they become fakes of the Tammy Baker variety. Ladies, you are never going to win the battle by trying to dance the

Devil's tune. A good man, one who fears God and believes His Word will not be chasing skirts as he gets older. But God requires you to accept such a man as your master, one whom you will obey. This is not a "partnership." And it sure ain't "equal." But such a man will never abuse such rulership knowing he must answer, personally, to God for the responsibility of ruling well.

"Remove not the ancient landmark, which thy fathers have set!" Proverbs 22:28. We desperately need those "ancient landmarks." They are the sheet anchor that enables us to wander, to explore, to try, to dream and imagine. But those ancient landmarks give the stability, the fixed point that should keep us from losing our way.

Jesus said: "... Therefore every scribe which is instructed unto the kingdom of heaven is like unto a man that is an householder, which bringeth forth out of his treasure things new and old." Matt. 13:52.

We cannot hope to offer a future to our children unless we provide for it. The ancient landmarks of family, integrity, honor, fidelity, truthfulness, honesty, hard work, justice, they are all gone. Who stands on the horizon as our Paul, Luther, or Washington?

I was spoiled as a child. I knew and believed in the ancient landmarks. But I was too young to realize that my generation would see the last of them, that with the end of WWII, a "new world order," grimmer than that of Hitler's had established itself. You so-called "Christians" and "Theologians" why don't you apply yourselves to the question of why God seems to be looking the other way while countless children are suffering and dying, and the industrialized nations look the other way? Is it because, as I contend, you really don't believe in Him, you really don't know anything about Him, because there is really no fear of Him in your corrupt souls?

But this "way" is too hard. I'm too old to long maintain such anger. It depletes my strength. I would far rather look back to that time of simple verities, to, in my imagination, live again the magic that used to be childhood. Like the magic of "digging holes."

Now children are naturally born with some Badger blood. There is nothing more natural to a child than digging holes. Throw away the "Nintendo" and give a kid a shovel. He doesn't need any "instructions" with this implement. He knows, intuitively, what that thing is for. And, unless you say he has to dig a hole for some real purpose, like planting a tree, thus making a "fun" thing "work," he will set to with a will and make holes. And what do you do with the hill of earth removed during the project? Well, naturally, you play on it. You roll down it; you play "King of the Hill" and, in general, make productive use of the material. Honestly! Adults just have to have these things explained.

My brother and I, and some of the neighbor children, were prodigious diggers. The rich, yielding, rock-free soil of our neighborhood was designed of God for just such a purpose. We didn't just dig, we "excavated." A truly marvelous "hole" was made in the side yard next to the church once.

We had a "Victory" garden there. Acting on instinct alone, we must have realized the church and garden would shield our efforts from the prying eyes of the resident and misunderstanding adults.

Like Topsy, the thing just "grew." What started out as just your ordinary hole soon became two large holes with a connecting tunnel. Somewhere, a couple of pieces of plywood came to us and, covering the project with them and a thin layer of soil gave us an underground "house" safely concealed from the prying eyes of adults. With a candle for light, we had a marvelously mysterious hide-a-way of our very own.

Sadly, the enterprise came to an end due to the common occurrence of a fire. A storage shed caught fire and the fire truck, in an attempt to get close to it decided to use the side yard. There was some consternation among the adults, particularly the firemen when the truck's wheels disappeared up to the axle in our secret "house." Fortunately for us, no one was "home" at the time.

In retrospect, it is a wonder that none of us kids died as a result of such activities. Small wonder, as we get older and have children of our own, that we live in fear. I have a profound belief in Guardian Angels. If it were not for these Beings, how would most children live long enough to grow up?

Negro folks played an important role in my childhood while living in Little Oklahoma. The Dust Bowl migrants of our neighborhood not only brought their simple, generally honest, viewpoints with them, there was also the prejudices and bigotry so common to ignorance and superstition.

The railroad tracks separated Little Oklahoma from "Nigger Town." Grandad, in spite of his Southern background, and because of his "calling" as a Pentecostal preacher, was one of the few white men acceptable to the inhabitants of Nigger Town and we frequently traveled in the area. As with all human relationships, you can generally expect to be treated as you treat others, regardless of color. This stood me in good stead during my tenure as a high school teacher in Watts. Has it really been a quarter of a century since the riots and the burning and looting of this area? And what has really changed for the better for these people since that time?

Cicely Tyson of Jane Pittman reminded me of this early association in Little Oklahoma with black folks after watching the excellent portrayal. What a cruel hoax has been perpetrated on black people in this country.

Louis Farrakhan, Tom Metzger and white trash are not the problem. Jim Crow laws were not the problem. The K.K.K. was, and is not, the problem. Those who are willing to recognize the ugly truth realize that prejudice is inherent in human nature. Real education coupled with the lack of being "taught" prejudice, enables us to deal with that fact and accept it. Its roots are deep and have the same source as those "monsters of the Id" that frighten in their insistent reality.

The "Cruel Hoax" consists of the promises, by unscrupulous politicians, religious charlatans, fuzzy-minded "do-gooders" (usually called "liberals") and "teachers" that have tried, in their greed and, sometimes, in their naiveté, to attempt to legislate and preach some kind of "equality" that, somehow, always seems to elude their efforts.

But a country that was settled by Europeans is not ever going to accommodate itself to cultures as diverse as those of African, Mexican, Asian or Indian. Color simply amplifies the problems and conflicts. The unscrupulous will continue to take advantage of this fact. Negroes and Hispanics are doomed, by dent of cultural distinctives and color, to a subservient role in a European dominated society. The cries of "equality" for a so-called "pluralistic" society fall on the deaf ear of reality.

Slavery has always been a cruel, God-shaming injustice. But nowhere in the history of the world has the "experiment" of "forced equality" been successful. It flies in the face of logic to expect people to accept the "liberal" legislating of morality. The festering sores of resentment such laws brew will eventually, of necessity, demand action.

It does no good to stick our heads in the sand and pretend that this country can survive "legal equality." As I have said before, neither Negroes nor women are any better off with the franchise. There is far more at work here than people realize. But, I fear, there are, out there in the shadowy darkness, like Blake's "Tiger," those with influence and power, waiting, waiting.

And, while the battle rages as Satan walks to and fro seeking whom he may devour, the two so-called "evangelists," Swaggart and Gorman square off in court. They are both adulterers and, if they really knew anything about The Bible and believed it, would never be appearing in the courts of men against each other. God says that such "dirty laundry" is to be settled in the church. But, alas, the churches long ago lost any backbone to confront real wickedness let alone deal with charlatans like these two "soldiers of the cross."

Of course, things are no better among those that make no pretense of being "born again." In regard to the Rodney King case, a Hispanic activist, one Al Belmontez, president of the Mexican American Political Association sent a threatening letter to the appellate court considering a change of venue in the case. He states: "If this case isn't dealt with justice and equality, it's going to get very hot in Los Angeles and the youth have demonstrated they're not going to destroy the barrios and the ghettos!"

Belmontez says he can easily see the Negro and Hispanic communities going on a rampage equal to the 1965 Watts riots. But he transparently implies the "rampaging" will occur in white neighborhoods this time. Rhetoric like this reminds me of recent events in Germany. The neo-nazis are gaining ground; and for all the same reasons Hitler was so successful. While teaching at Gavilan Community College some years ago, I warned a Jewish colleague, "It can happen here!" All we need are a few more like Belmontez and Farrakhan together with Tom Metzger et al.

It is tragic that human nature is so imbued with prejudice but "legal equality" is not the answer. It's just that apart from God it's the best that men can seem to come up with. And it is doomed to failure. "Forced equality" will only breed more fanaticism of the Hitlerian variety and when the economic circumstances are bad enough, even "good Germans" will look the other way. The fact that virtually half of our teens are not prepared to hold a job (a recent Bush administration estimate) bodes nothing but evil as young people become increasingly aware that they are living in a bankrupt society that has little sympathy with their plight and no resources with which to respond to it. Who even remembers Paul Copperman or Damerell, let alone Rushdoony?

Because we feel so helpless to change the things that, obviously, need changing, we often have to escape to the world of humor for release. And for that reason, I take up the Iguana story where I left off last issue.

Before I continue to share my experience with Iguana ranching, I must warn you that my "bona-fides" have, on occasion, come into question concerning the whole affair. Let me assure you that the entire incident is just the way I am describing it. Some of my detractors are still smarting from having lost out on a ground-floor opportunity (as some did with the gold mine) and, feeling foolish, have resorted to the common strategy of trying to sully the name of an upright citizen, an honest and truthful businessman without a single bone of guile in his body (yours truly).

I know that you, the objective reader, will most surely agree that if a man's name does not stand for honesty, integrity, veracity, the keeping of an oath even to his own hurt, he has nothing of value for nothing is of the value of a good name! That good name is gold, to be passed on to a man's heirs. I know that, you, an honest and objective reader, will not fail to understand why, baseless as they are, these charges demand an answer even at the risk of some few misunderstanding my honorable intentions.

But let them whine and grouse, the taste of "sour grapes" setting their teeth on edge; my record for veracity speaks for itself and I have no need of a champion coming to the aid of my good name no matter how many libelous, villainous terms and phrases of "Lying Swindler, Cheat, Cutpurse, Poor Box John, Loathsome Reptile, Insect, Conscienceless Con Artist, Excretory Sediment of a Duck's Bladder" and, even some downright bad, unsavory appellations with which they try to damage my good name and fair reputation.

It is only because of these shameless few, who with distortions, lies and miscellaneous innuendo have attempted, in vain I might add, to bring discredit upon me and, hence, upon my innocent children, that I take pen in hand to answer their contemptible allegations. I will rest content with the objective verdict of you, the reader, once you have determined the facts of the matter for yourself and seen for yourself, how baseless the charges against me.

More, if the facts of the matter should cause you to judge me (inconceivably) guilty of any wrong-doing in the whole affair, I will most assuredly, joining myself with that other most truthful and upright citizen of Greece, Socrates, take the "cup" to my own lips, in mortal shame, welcoming the sweet release of the Hemlock from such an ungrateful and callous society. So certain I am that you will not fail to find in my favor and silence, forever, those that seek to bring me down by their disgraceful accusations and calumny.

Having cast the gauntlet, I continue. Another point requires some clarification. At the time I began this venture, I was employed as a high school teacher in Antelope Valley. Now anyone who knows anything about teachers knows they are an incredibly ignorant, lazy and gullible lot. A large part of this naiveté is easily attributable to their having never had to work for a living. Consequently, they are very "sheltered" and have little knowledge of the real world and, coupled with their natural greed and laziness, are quite easy to take advantage of by the unscrupulous.

It did not help matters that, when I first started teaching for this district, some "shark" had successfully promoted a scheme for reclaiming precious metals from mine tailings by some exotic and never before known, "secret" process. This nefarious liar and con had cleaned up just before I got there; a pox on the scheming miscreant, his unconscionable "fleecing of the flock" undoubtedly accounted for some of the distrust and skepticism I encountered while trying to promote my own righteous enterprise. Ah, well, "A prophet..." and all that. It certainly did not help matters that some implied they had knowledge of the "fact" that I, in some manner, had a mining background and might have known the scoundrel that had taken such outrageous advantage of them. Admittedly, I was some hurt by such thoughts.

Now I am a "Desert Rat." I love the vastness of the great "Lonesome," the rugged beauty of that wide-open "Empty." It is hard for me to accept the fact that there are those that do not share my enthusiasm for such of "God's Country" and do not envision the many opportunities and chances for wealth the desert supplies. I am truly saddened by such sheer prejudice and shortsightedness. It makes me, as Sam Clemens would say, "Ashamed of my species!"

Well sir, to go on. I had learned through my "Mexican Connection" that there was indeed a huge market for Iguanas but breeding stock was very scarce and expensive. Further, while breed stock might be gotten, breeders were a tight-lipped bunch and not amenable to some "Gringo" butting in on the action. But my Mexican friends were, for a small "donation" to their favorite charity, T.P.F.F.E.&T.A.O.H.L.I.N.A. (The People For Free Elections and The Advancement Of Hispanic Legislators In Norte America) able to get me in touch with a reputable supplier.

I am sorry to burden the reader with such details but it is necessary for a complete understanding and vindication of what was to transpire when I was finally able to make this astounding, investment opportunity available to my learned colleagues in the school district. Only by giving the reader all the facts will I rest comfortably in his verdict that I have surely been the innocent victim of simply offering them something that was too good to be true.

Before another word: Yes, I know; "If it sounds too good to be true, it probably is!" But this was an honest exception to that sage statement. You will discover for yourself, to your frank and honest amazement, upon honest and quiet deliberation of all the facts, that, in an attempt to give good people a chance for wealth involving virtually no effort on their part, for only the surprisingly modest sum of an, initial, $5,000, there would be a few ungrateful wretches that would try to discredit my good name! And those those that didn't even invest would look me upon in suspicion! (I hasten further, to add, the District Attorney never did actually prosecute me. The entire affair never even came to trial! That, if nothing else, any reasonable person would think, should silence my carping critics).

I know that you, as I, will wonder at my forbearance and forgive my coming close to tears when all the facts are finally before you. No sensitive soul will fail to be touched as I, unashamedly, bare my own soul, nor fail to feel the outrage that an honest and truthful man should be the target of such vile accusations as I have had to endure. The slings and arrows ... but I must continue before I give vent to embarrassingly, seeming, self pity. Far be that from me. The bare facts of the matter will speak for themselves.

If you, gentle reader, are a person like myself, honest, truthful, modest, self-effacing, seeking no great wealth or fame, doing no man injury, abhorring lies and deceit, a daily practitioner of that great and noble "Golden Rule," you will, doubtless, upon consideration of all the facts of the case, chaff under the restraint to keep from shouting: "How could they even think such things of such a noble man who sought only their welfare! Who sought only to make them rich at such paltry expense and with literally no effort on their part!"

But calm yourself. Bear, as I have done, the ignoble curses, crass canards and cant of the coarse crowd of critical, caviling, crowing censurers of my cynosure, with your own natural goodness and grace. "Blessed are ye, when men shall say, etc."

Now most people have an altogether wrong perception of the Mojave Desert. As I have said, they miss the possibilities, the potential for wealth the desert offers to those with the vision to take advantage of its great generosity and ability to reward the earnest industry of honest men.

While it is true there are some parts that are somewhat inhospitable and a trifle uncomfortable to living creatures, most of the desert is quite congenial. I once looked at some lakeshore property in Death Valley and when I saw the coyotes, badgers and roadrunners carrying canteens, when a horny toad tried to lick water from my radiator I said, "Now I am certainly not going to try to sell such property to people who trust my word concerning investments! No sir!" Such is my integrity that such a thought as promoting lakeshore properties where.... but no matter. I passed up the opportunity and simply took some photos for future ... but I digress.

It does remind me of the time when torrential rains had filled all the dry lakes in the Cuddeback area. An unscrupulous associate actually wanted to bring out some boats and, with a few companions, take pictures of folks frolicking on the lakes, fishing and water skiing and promote these arid places as "Lakeshore" properties. Of course I soon set him straight about any such thing.

It grieves me that there are such people that would even think about taking advantage of such a subterfuge. Why, if we couldn't at least tell people that the lakes weren't always that full, I wasn't going to have anything to do with the enterprise. I know you have trouble accepting such honesty about anyone, but such is the fact. I even refused to have anything to do with the mailing of the brochures with the deceptive pictures and contented myself with only that part of the business that had to do with the actual sales.

Ah, yes, where was I? Oh- The Mexican Connection. Well sir, it seems that in order to acquire my breeding stock, the breeder, a fine gentleman named Jose, required the hefty sum of $100 for a matched pair of the lizards. Not only that, but, he also required me to participate in an elaborate ceremony wherein I had to write out an oath not to reveal the source of the animals upon pain of certain horrible consequences and verbally repeat it while burning the paper in my bare hands (well, since I was a "visitor" to the country, I was permitted to wear gloves but Jose assured me that natives must do this bare-handed).

It can easily be seen that, having to endure such pain, together with a large investment of my own money, it would only be reasonable to expect a modest profit from the enterprise. I know any sensible person would agree with this. And, it is only good business practice that all my travel expenses should be tax deductible. And, I further say, that anyone who says different couldn't give you a nickel at the end of the day if you offered them a penny for each of their thoughts during that whole course of time!

Well, I was able, with the help of some of my Mexican friends, to get across the border with my Iguanas. It seems there was some legal technicality about taking the beasts out of Mexico without an expensive ($3,000) export license. But my friends knew of a border policeman who, understanding gentleman that he was, for a much smaller fee (ten percent of the "legal" fee, $300) was able to accommodate me.

Mexico has a very ill deserved reputation for corruption in government. I know better; I have seldom found any people who are so understanding of realities and so willing to cooperate when the enterprise is truly worthy. And talk about being able to cut through bureaucratic red tape? We North Americans have a lot to learn from our brothers in the South. We would do well to take a page from their book on government before casting stones.

Anyhow, I arrived back in the Antelope Valley with my lizards in good health. Being forewarned of their eating habits, I was well prepared with the necessary food items and soon had them comfortably nesting in their cage.

An associate had been busy in my absence. Having an "in" with the Audio Visual and Graphic Arts departments, he had some truly marvelous brochures ready for my approval for the cost of only a few beers and a nebulous promise of future "reward." In a customary moment of largess, I even allowed the department heads that had supplied all the school materials for the brochures a "cut-rate" price of only $4,000 each to "buy in" to the project; a nifty saving to both of them of $1,000 over the cost to others. They were most understandably grateful.

Now my accusers, base cowards all, would have you to believe the Iguanas were only "Window dressing," that my real "scheme" (dastardly accusation) was to sell "worthless" desert real estate at a grotesquely inflated price. Can you believe such effrontery? After all this time, I still smart over such a vile charge! Well, they have certainly had sufficient time and suffered sufficient loss by not taking advantage of my extreme generosity, to shamefully realize their errors. I shouldn't be too hard on them nor should you, deserving as they are of the scorn and the contempt of honest men.

In any event, with the lizards available for viewing, multi-colored brochures of the properties and a prospectus of the potential wealth to be derived from such a modest sum ($5,000), it didn't take long for the most astute among the faculties to "leap on the band-wagon."

Now my own return for all my labors, and I'm sure you will agree they had been nothing less than "heroic," and expenses (about $432 plus a cage and food for the animals), was about $250,000. But I had worked hard for almost an entire month putting this whole investment together and don't forget the "pain" and having to go through all the trouble of actually acquiring the little beasts (This had cost me three whole days. I even had to make it a weekend trip and take a paid "sick day" to do it). And what of the real value of my "Mexican Connection" together with the cost of travel and finding and taking pictures of suitable properties?

I tell you, it was a lot of work and I'm sure you will agree that the remuneration to me was, if anything, not really worth all the trouble. But such is the sheer ingratitude of people that some actually accused me of an "exorbitant" profit in the venture. Even my trusted associate seemed to express an attitude of being ill-used after my paying him the magnificent sum of $50 for his slight effort.

There was some confusion among investors when they discovered that their contracts required monthly payments of $200 for the "upkeep" of the ranches. That they did not really "own" the properties was a minor point of dissension as was the fact that I had only taken out government grazing leases ($1 per thousand acres) and, thereby, could, clearly, not give them deeds to property that belonged to their government. But most people are not "business-minded" and it was only to be expected that some would be unsettled by the fact that the only thing they were "buying" was the expected progeny of the initial breed stock (the two lizards in my cage).

I had made it very clear to investors that, at $5,000 each, in order to maintain tight control over the operation, we could only sell fifty shares in the enterprise. This modest amount of $250,000 would be all the "start-up" capital needed so it was "first come, first served." Many, unfortunately, were left out as a consequence. But I am nothing if not a man of my word. When those fifty shares were sold, I shut the door (naturally, I had to allow a few extra among those close friends and relatives which, kind-natured that I am, I simply could not, in good conscience, leave out of the venture).

It can readily be seen that the additional $10,000 a month that investors were obligated for in order to "maintain" the ranches was a reasonable sum. I would have to make regular trips to the ranches, at least once every six months, to keep an eye on the operation (once my breed stock started producing and the need for the ranches became a reality). To be continued.

An afterthought: What do you do with the "Clowns" and "Crooks" (Congress) that vote themselves a $23,000 pay raise in a recession and many families are trying to survive on less money than the "raise" of these "public servants"? Answer to the enigma of less traffic on L.A. freeways: People can't afford to drive their cars!

CHAPTER SIXTEEN

THE WEEDPATCHER

SEPTEMBER, 1991

Psalm 73

Well, there is certainly enough going on these days to exhaust any writer with a proclivity for gloom and doom. The topics of Education, Politics and Religion continue to be grist for our mills with no improvements on any front in sight. The blind still lead the blind in education (for a real "laugh," read Lamar Alexander's, our new Secretary of Education's "plan," to reverse the course of national illiteracy. He should have stuck to playing the piano), politicians continue to lie to us and feather their own nests at our expense and the charlatans continue to ply their trade in religion. In short, little has changed. The rich get richer and the poor get poorer. The only change is that it is happening at an accelerated rate.

I could easily exhaust myself reporting on the significance of lowering S.A.T. scores, "Big Brotherism," charismatic "fruitcakes," Russia in turmoil and so much more. But, since change in all these things for the better depends on honoring God and following His precepts, I have little hope for anything getting better. That and the fact that change for the better depends on an educated, aroused, and enlightened electorate dooms us.

There is no comfort for me in seeing my own "prophecies" come to pass as with the great popularity of books like "Final Exit" and "Medicide," as the world trembles at events in Russia and politicians and religious "leaders" scramble to make "hay" of it all. Given the circumstances and the "theology" of "The End Justifies the Means," Hitler was right. And, I repeat: "Yes, It can happen here!"

My own source of contentment is in feeding the "critters" and working on my cabin in the "wilderness." I have it roofed and will be putting the finishing touches on the screen porch soon. Total capital outlay will be only about two thousand dollars plus the cost of the land. Not bad for a roof over your head these days.

Raccoons have become a favorite source of entertainment for me lately. There has been a family of them- Papa, momma and four babies. Papa is a bit "pushy," momma watchful but the babies a pure delight. They seem to thrive on dog food but the babies will eat Cheez-its out of my hand. I still count my fingers afterward. The little "bandits" will get into anything. They are not "ideal" house pets unless you want the house continually rearranged.

The squirrels still get their nuts and the quail wander through the property, but they make few demands. Not so the raccoons! These little stinkers are prone to nocturnal carousings and will not be denied. If I opened the screen door, I would soon be up to my neck in ring-tailed, masked critters. It makes me wonder how we will get along come winter? Will they insist on coming in and warming up at the fire? Interesting prospect.

It continues to amaze me that so many, after all these years, still think God has a "magic wand" that He is going to wave on their behalf and make things "all better." There ain't no free lunch with this world system and there sure isn't one with God. We reap what we sow and He says He will not be mocked. "If any not work, neither shall he eat" is still part of God's Word.

I got off on this tangent when I think of how very many who ought to know better aren't doing better. They continue to "whistle through the graveyard" holding to some hazy concept that "somehow" things are going to get better for them without either honoring God or planning for success. Lots of luck!

As I told my students for years, "There are answers but only on an individual basis. Learn to plan and do for yourselves or you will be lost to a system that will grind you up and spit you out."

I recently received a letter from my old friend Gary North. I haven't yet answered him personally (may not, in fact since, he like most others, doesn't listen to what I have to say anyhow) but I do want to thank him publicly for his remarks about my book "Confessions and Reflections of an Okie Intellectual."

Gary picked up on the one thing in the whole book for which he knew the majority of readers would be on his side, page 241 where I say that God has made mistakes. In choosing this one statement, Gary, intelligent as he is, knew it was the one thing that even the non-religious would be on his side about. Even those that make no pretense of religious convictions are quick to condemn such a thing. "God make a mistake! Never!"

Admittedly, it is a scary prospect. If, in fact, God has made mistakes and is capable of doing so in the future, where does that leave us? A most interesting thought, one few would want to entertain; certainly not someone like Gary.

But the justification for such a statement is clearly stated in God's Own Word, the Bible. No matter how people, religious or not, wish to distort what the Bible says God Himself admits to having made errors and wishing He had done some things differently. How very "human."

Now Gary has "warned" me as a "friend" that I will "... roast in the Lake of Fire forever" if I do not publicly recant my statement. It reminds me somewhat of the relationship Luther faced against the Pope. But, unlike Luther, I am sincerely appreciative of Gary's comments and concern for my soul. But my old friend is too good an example of "blind orthodoxy" to pass up. He, like so many others I know personally, cannot seem to distinguish between what is knowledge and what is belief. There really is a difference no matter how religious "professionals" try to obscure the fact.

If I were to ask Gary, as I have so many others: "What do you really know about God?" I would, undoubtedly, get the same, pat "answers." The plain fact is that what anyone "knows" about God is, as the philosophers would say, "Known in the bones." I "know" of God when I see the expanse of the stars at night, I "know" when I see love expressed between people, I "know" as I read His Word, I "know" in a thousand ways as people dream, plan, build, create beauty but only within my "bones" and my thoughts. And it is enough for me, that, as I pray and meditate on all that I believe God is and has done, that I "know in my bones." And it is within that context together with His Word that I "know" God makes mistakes and, like His creatures, loves, hopes, learns, dreams, plans, works, and creates.

The "knowledge" of God exists in the belief system of the one who makes the claim of such knowledge. It is simply not open to empirical demonstration. So, when anyone says they "know" this or that about God, they are basing such "knowledge" on their particular belief system, not demonstrably empirical fact.

The phrase "God told me" should cause reasonable and rational people to avoid the speaker like the plague. Such a one is either an outright, bald-faced liar or in need of time in some well-guarded institution devoid of sharp instruments. It has been over eighteen hundred years since any, to me; certifiable instance of God's actually speaking audibly to anyone has occurred. Admittedly, and I have to wonder why, this is a long time. I can only conclude He has remarkable patience with us.

If someone like Gary or myself says they know something about God, they are using the Bible, primarily, as the source of such "knowing." Unhappily, such "knowing" can be so disparate as providing cause for such distinctives as justification for the most inhuman actions like the inquisitions, crusades or our own Civil War; a most dangerous condition of "knowing."

The failure to distinguish between belief and knowledge is a damning indictment of most of what passes for "truth" in theology. While we are not presently experiencing "The Iron Heel of Rome" in this present age, people like Gary still pose a threat to the extent they see themselves as the sole arbiters of "truth." It is really my refusal to accept Gary as such that has him in an uproar about my own writings. He feels a debt, rightly, for my being the human instrument of his own religious "successes." My refusal to be his convert is most disconcerting to him and, no doubt, galling. But, though he curse me and consign me to the "outer reaches," I continue to love him nonetheless. And, I will continue to pray that his own eyes will be opened to the truth of his own egotistical blindness.

As a "self-excommunicated heretic" (Gary's words for me) I will plunge a littler deeper by calling attention to another curious fact of the Bible- the fact that believers are called "sons of God" and Jesus' favorite title for himself: "Son of Man." Unlike Gary and others who have tried to move me to political and religious "correctness," I won't pontificate on these things. I present them as seed-thoughts in the hope that legitimate scholars will give them the attention they deserve.

Since we are told that God has made man in His image that is worthy of much study. It cannot be denied that all people have an inner yearning for the knowledge of God, that they feel that death is not the end of meaningful existence; that all this has to have more meaning than religion usually accords it.

Jesus himself makes the statement that he considers believers to be "born" into the family of God. Now, I ask you, if we are indeed his brothers and sisters, what is the difference between him and us? He uses the term "adopted" as well as the phrase "spiritual re-birth" to explain the relationship and distinguish between himself as the "only begotten of the Father" and us.

Scripturally, Man is so god-like that we are commanded to have the "mind of Christ" in us. We are supposed to have the authority to forgive or retain sin in others. We are to act as his "Ambassadors," speaking for God Himself. Now that is profound.

In Jesus' use of the phrase "Son of Man," I believe he used it as a badge of distinction; that he used it to underline the extreme importance of our relationship to God as His supreme creation, that of His "children." If so, he was trying to make the relationship plain in a way that has been successfully obfuscated and obscured by religious "professionals."

I have made the statement that we are desperately in need of an army of scholars to undertake a study of a "new" systematic theology that will not ignore the plain Word of God, that will not try to ignore, gloss or "dance" around the really hard questions that legitimately arise from a reading of the Bible and life itself. Unhappily, unless there is a willingness to set aside "blind orthodoxy," such is not likely to happen. Too few even have the God-given intellectual honesty to admit of their own ignorance and admit the questions even exist. The world is poorer for the fact.

People need leadership in how to make a living and keep a roof over their heads. No, it simply won't do to try to "sell" euphemistic nonsense about God when people desperately need realities in order to cope with this evil system that threatens them at every turn in their lives. And, as long as those that continue to obscure the nature of God for the sake of their own egos and, not incidentally, to make a buck, there is little hope of meaningful help from that quarter. Folks need help and the encouragement of seeing examples of what they can, in reality, do to find their way out of the mess. To this end, I return to the cabin.

Now I purposely designed the cabin, called a "Sourdough" in the West because of the '49ers and a "Saltbox" on the East coast, to be a true "do it yourself" proposition. One person, working by him or herself, can do the job of construction. It can even be accomplished using only the most rudimentary hand tools. Power or a generator does ease and hasten the project but are not essential. I have experienced real joy in having a few people, folks who have never done any building, look at the cabin and say: "Hey, I could do this myself!" Now that is real success to me, being an inveterate teacher.

We are told that California is to grow at an alarming rate and will nearly double in population in the next twenty years to over 50 million. The only alternatives are to lower the birthrate or reduce the number of people moving into the state. Neither is likely for several reasons. The larger birthrates are due to minority growth and that is not going to change. Further, as California becomes, increasingly, a "Mecca" for welfare, nothing short of seceding from the Union will change that situation. Politicians, in general, will cater to those that will keep their paychecks coming so there is not likely any help from that source.

So, for those that will do for themselves, those not afraid of honest perspiration and sacrifice, building a cabin is part of the alternative. It's not only smart; it's fun as well. You will always have a roof over your head and, hopefully, in a place like the Kern River Valley where a good water source and clean air are available.

Most folks entertain the notion of that "someplace" where they can drink clean water, breathe clean air; a place where they can hear the wind in the pines and watch a spectacular sunrise and savor the haunting enchantment of the mountains, rocks and trees bathed in silver moonlight. Far from the smog and noise of traffic, the "view" of row after row of rooftops and the daily grind of simply trying to exist.

Believe it or not, it can happen. But, as I have said, it takes planning and sacrifice. You cannot do it with an average income and a $100,000 mortgage, a "maxed out" Master card and $400 a month car payments. Unless you extricate yourself from this dismal situation, you are doomed.

I dreamed for years of doing just this kind of construction. I have been a builder and developer and know how to design and build the kind of houses that are ruinously expensive. Few have any hope of ever paying off such mortgages. But people cannot live without hope and that is where a "cabin in the wilderness" comes in.

Virtually everyone dreams of "owning a little piece of land" where peace and quiet pervade the atmosphere, where they can escape the rat race and find some surcease from this old world's sorrows. You can. It isn't necessary to quit your job and move; you only need the actual cabin and land to, in your mind's eye, be there at the same time you are "punching that clock." The hope and dream are real when you actually own such a place.

As I listen to friends say "I could do that!" when they see my little cabin, it came to me that I might be able to help them do it. Why not? I'm free to do such a thing (one of the prerogatives of being, essentially, retired and a writer). And so, I am going to look for land for a few of these friends who have no time to do so and I will help them build and plan and I'm going to enjoy myself doing it.

But, I will only do so if they demonstrate to me that they are willing to make the necessary sacrifices of planning to get their budgets in order. I'm too old to waste time on those that do not demonstrate sincere resolve. And what better way to spend weekends with the children than being in a place where they can learn to drive nails and saw lumber and watch the critters?

Most of my life I have had to work with no help from anyone. It's a lonely proposition. But, fortunately, I have the skills to do the work; I was raised to be self-reliant and I tried to raise my own children in such a fashion. And, while they have "blown" it in many ways, they are far beyond the average in being able to do for themselves.

There have been countless times when I would have liked to have looked over my shoulder and be able to see a "helper." But such has not been the case. I suppose that is why the cabin is a truly "do it yourself" project. As with the roof that needs repair on one of my rentals, the bathroom I am installing in my office and the cabin, repairs on the vehicles, setting the pump in the well, I "do it myself" and thank God I have both the skills and strength to do so. I have what I have only because of the fact that I learned to "do for myself." Pity those that lack these necessary "survival" skills.

Nothing is more common than for people to complain that they just don't know what to do to change their dismal circumstances. And then, they will despise the counsel, like children, of "gray hair." There is no substitute for experience, planning, commitment and perseverance. Neither is there any escape from the consequences of foolish choices.

For example, if a young couple decides to marry and have children, and they lack the necessary education and skills to provide for a family, they will have years to repent of the fact. The children are a lifetime proposition. They don't simply "go away" when the times are rough. And, without the necessary education and skills, the times will, most assuredly, get rough. Too often, in our society, the young woman is left alone with the children wondering: "What happened?" Having despised the counsel of elders, she faces a dismal future with the prospect of penury and welfare, dead-beat men and delinquent children. Nor do the young men have any better prospects.

Thoreau's dictum that "A wise man lives simply" is a truth impossible of improvement. There must be a "place" where people can dream and hope, where they can "clean out their minds" and gain a fresh perspective of what is really meaningful in life. You simply cannot do it while drowning in smog and staring at the asphalt jungle.

For those of you that can, get that "place" and teach your children how to do for themselves. It simply cannot be beat as a family exercise and an invaluable investment in theirs and your future. Like the title of a recent and popular book: "Do It!"

There were many times, as a child, that my grandad let me "just do it." The "It" didn't always work out but in no instance did I fail to learn something of value, even from the failures.

Now Grandad was the idol of my childhood. He could "do things." He could build a house, do wiring and plumbing, in short, he was a "jack of all trades" as many of his generation were. But the automobile remained a mystery to him all his life. Grandad was never a mechanic.

Some time after moving to the mining claim in Sequoia National Forest, I came of age to have my own car. From somewhere in that mysterious gene pool, there lay the genius of the mechanic and machinist in my own make-up. The one essential missing ingredient was experience.

I cut my teeth driving the family pick-up, a venerable old Ford and a '28 Buick. Grandad, being a firm believer in that maxim of "hard work never killed anyone" had me earning money digging septic holes by hand and every other job requiring a strong back. I was a mean kid with a pick and shovel (not to mention the fact that I supplied all the fuel for our stove and fireplace). But a "regular" job came my way when I became the "Junior Custodian" for old Kernville Elementary.

For once, I had a "real" job and a steady income- the magnificent sum of $35 a month for cleaning classrooms every day after school. I was ready to commit to the "American Dream," going into debt on the installment plan.

And so it was that Grandad and I took off to the "Big City," Bakersfield, where I bought a '39 Pontiac for $100 payable at $10 a month; I think it was the amber fog lights that attracted me to this particular car. The fact that it had a pronounced knock from the bowels of the engine didn't seem to perturb Grandad. I drove the old car, slowly, all the way up the canyon with the engine knocking the whole time.

An acquaintance, Gus Suhre, who was a mechanic, upon hearing the knock in the engine pronounced it a loose rod. Now neither Grandad nor I had any ideas about the mysteries of the internal combustion engine. But I was determined to learn. And we all know a little knowledge is a dangerous thing.

Gus explained the procedure for curing the Pontiac's illness. It was utterly incomprehensible to me. What was a "crank," a "micrometer" a "rod bearing?" I was going to find out.

With the tools available, I was able to pull the head and pan on the car. With its "innards" exposed, I was finally face to face with the complexities of the engine. There were things called "valves, pistons, rods" and I began to "operate." With Gus' explanation I was able to locate the loose rod and pull the cap off and remove the rod and piston. But what to do with this "micrometer" thing-a-ma-jig; Gus had uttered some mysterious words about something like "Miking" the crank. I was supposed to use this glorified C-clamp to find out if the crank was "out of round," whatever that meant.

Following his mysterious instructions, I dutifully screwed the thing to fit the crank journal and moved it around like he said to do. The problem was that I simply did not know what the purpose of this maneuver was supposed to accomplish. Somehow, the "fit" of the contraption was supposed to tell me if there was anything wrong with the journal. It didn't. Mainly because I didn't know how to read a micrometer or what, exactly, I was looking for.

But I manfully checked to see if the device moved around the crank at a certain setting and called the case closed. Looked all right to me; it was smooth and there wasn't any "burning" or "galling" as Gus had warned me to look for. And I had the rod and piston out. I was ready for the "fix."

Now, as Gus had said, I was supposed to get another rod and piston. This necessitated another trip to Bakersfield where I was soon to be introduced to the exciting world of "Junk Yards" (they weren't called wrecking or salvage yards back then).

At the earliest opportunity, Grandad and I took off and I was soon examining bins of pistons and rods at one of the yards. All I knew was that I was to get a replacement for the offending '39 engine rod. But the bins had mysterious markings designating the assemblies with hieroglyphic markings like .010, .020 and .030.

Now I have already said automobiles were a mystery to Grandad. It never seemed to occur to him or me to ask what these mysterious markings meant. As a result, I simply took the one that looked the best from a bin marked with the hieroglyph .020 and off we went.

On arriving back at the claim, I inserted the "new" rod and piston in the cylinder. Seemed a tad tight; what to do. Of course! Get a bigger hammer; which I proceeded to do. Knowing nothing about "taper" in a cylinder, with a little persuasion from the hammer handle I managed to "persuade" the recalcitrant piston down into the cylinder and the rod down over the crank. Replacing all the parts in the order in which I removed them (no new gaskets, why "waste money?") I was finally ready to "crank the sucker up!"

Now for those of us that were raised with the old six-volt systems, we know how difficult it can be to get an engine started, particularly if it has had major surgery, with those old, six-volt batteries. With great foresight, I had parked the car on the convenient hill at the side of our cabin.

Getting in the car, I performed the maneuver all us oldsters were familiar with back then; I put the car in second gear, put in the clutch, let off the parking brake and "let her roll." At a fairly good clip downhill I popped the clutch and the engine fired; once; with a horrendous *bang*!

Rolling to a stop at the bottom of the hill, I quickly exited the Pontiac to find out what happened. From the place the engine had fired, there was a long trail of oil in the dirt. Looking under the car I saw a truly magnificent, jagged hole in the pan. At the place where the trail of oil started, I found what remained of the rod cap. Interesting.

And so, my early introduction to auto mechanics was an explosive success. Knowing how to read helped. I discovered what "oversize" meant in regard to pistons and that engines were actually bored at times when "majored." The experience was of incalculable value to me in latter years when I taught auto shop to high schoolers. If I could be so dumb, why couldn't they?

I latter acquired a junk '38 with a reasonably good engine and, with true grit, a convenient pine tree and chain-fall, managed the Herculean task of "swapping" out the engines. I was fourteen years old and didn't even have a driver's license. Few of us "mountain kids" and not a few adults bothered with such "niceties" in those days. Besides, there were no "Chippies" or other minions of the law to contend with. And very little traffic.

While the trans and engine bolted together nicely, the clutch linkage was not as cooperative between the '38 and '39. A short length of chain took care of this minor problem. I actually drove this car to L.A. when I left the claim in '53 and subsequently traded it in on a magnificent '41 DeSoto convertible.

A great deal of learning took place in my life on the mining claim. But it took the proper environment for such opportunities. And, while the episode of the Pontiac is fraught ("freighted" to use Sam's favorite word) with all kinds of morals, points etc., the fact that I had such gumption, ignorance and all, was due to the fact of that environment and the support of loving elders who would encourage such a task.

As I think of all the things and people that contributed so much to my own ability to dream, to do, to plan and build and teach others, I have a debt to pass things on to others, young people especially. How I wish I could give them the same opportunities to learn, plan, dream and do that it was my blessed good fortune to experience; and after all these years, with all the disappointments and failures, still strive to do.

It is a tragedy of our times that children are cheated, robbed, of the opportunities I enjoyed as a child, that even the most caring parents seem unable to grasp the eternal significance of teaching the kinds of things that can only be learned in such an environment as that which I enjoyed can supply. Young people especially need examples of "can do." They are losing hope in droves because of the mind-set that the future holds nothing for them.

But put that child in an environment, with caring elders, where he or she can do, and watch them blossom into individuals with values, self-esteem and real-world skills that will serve them a lifetime. Somehow, I suspect people like Gary never had a chance at this kind of learning. If so, he is ill equipped to understand someone like myself and is all the poorer for trying to work up in the flesh what can only be acquired by the experience.

When I visit the old claim (now Boulder Gulch Campground), when I survey the old, familiar mountains and travel Bull Run, Fay Canyon and so many other places of my childhood, I sometimes talk things over with Grandad, Grandma and Great-grandma. Do they hear me? I have no idea. But I find comfort in the conversations. I think they are proud of me and the fact that I am still "doing." They most assuredly know what really counts in life by now. Somehow I think they are still the same things they thought really counted when they taught me as a child.

It is too easy, at my age, to slip back into that time of simple verities long past, to escape the ugliness all around by dwelling with those gone on whose love and support are all too lacking for children today. So, I close by concluding the lurid and sordid saga of the Iguana Ranch:

There was a clause (actually several clauses; the contracts were approximately one hundred pages of fine, legal print) that made the investors responsible for the purchase of materials such as fence wire, buildings for the "Iguanaboys," the lizard equivalent of cowboys, generators for incubation of eggs, breeding pens and such like.

But, as I pointed out, the tax benefits alone made the entire operation foolproof; you simply couldn't help but take a loss on such a venture and any businessman worth his salt knows it doesn't matter if you make any money, all that counts is avoiding paying taxes! A good businessman knows that if you show a profit, horrible word, the government is only going to take it from you and you will wind up working harder to keep less and less. It's truly amazing how many people, astute in so many other walks of life, fail to grasp this fundamental law of operating a business.

Why, as any fool can plainly see, if you are interested in "profit," you will wind up laying awake nights worrying about how to make more money so you can pay the government more. Sheer stupidity! The most drunken, welfare sot knows better than to do such a thing. Tarnation! (Not being a man given to coarse language, strong drink or games of chance, that's as close as I come to actually "cussing") It does take all how muddy the thinking becomes among some people when it comes to such matters. They were very fortunate to have me available, and at no extra charge I might add, to help them see the wisdom of this course of action.

Another very valuable point concerning the tax picture: Since Iguanas are, admittedly, built some closer to the ground than cows, wisdom dictated that the "Iguanaboys" be midgets or dwarfs. This would be a pronounced benefit as the Affirmative Action part of any business is most important. By employing people from this class of citizens, the venture had State and Federal assistance of a not inconsiderable amount of "free money."

An instance of where this money was justified was the fencing and living quarters. I had to explain to the minions of government that, since the "Little People" required structures of a different design from the ordinary, these, while considerable smaller and requiring less materials to build, required, actually, a greater expense due entirely to the fact that they had to be "different." Fortunately, the man who had to be convinced of this was an ex-S&L executive and he, immediately, grasped the validity of my argument.

As to things like the fencing, and a few thousand acres of desert requires a lot of fencing, the fact that the fences only had to be about a foot and a half high, and requiring much less material than ordinary fencing, the same argument prevailed. They had to be "different" and, as such, must surely cost more. Common sense- as any fool (the ex-S&L executive) could plainly see.

I admit that the actual construction plans indicated there would be a considerable amount of government money left over but, not wanting to embarrass our government agencies and, with the cooperation of the ex-S&L executive, a way was found to cover the situation. Such is the wisdom of some of our government servants when offered an opportunity to really do their job. Such was the kindness and gentlemanly reserve of this individual that I actually had to force some modest gratuity upon him.

As with the Judge who refused to countenance the District Attorney's malicious allegations, it may have helped (my enemies tried to make something of this, by the way) that this particular public servant was a relative, though some removed, of a few of my "Mexican Connection" friends. It never ceases to amaze me how, when you do a good deed, the rewards are sure to come; "Bread cast upon the waters ... etc." But leave it to some vindictive people to find "evil" where none exists except in their own, malevolent minds. Oh, the tragedy of the human condition! But to continue:

My "gold mine" enterprise together with some other business activities had brought me into close association with some powerful people over the years. The venture now had grown to a size that warranted my approaching some of these past acquaintances.

For example, there was, now, the actual need of spending some of the "free" government money on the project. This amount now totaled about $500,000 dollars. By the judicious and thrifty use of some of this largess, about $10,000, I was able to actually fence about 3,000 acres of my "leased" land and build some of the structures. Through political connections, for a modest "contribution," prison labor was employed. It still warms my heart when I think of how some, at least, of our tax dollars were put to productive use in this way. Not to mention the undoubted salutary and salubrious effect on the workers of doing all this in the clean, desert air of the great outdoors.

I found county inspectors and other government officials equally cooperative and responsive when taken aside privately and the situation carefully explained to them. The necessary paperwork burden this caused many of them deserved, as with my Mexican friends, some sort of reciprocal "proof" of "good faith." Again, those that do not understand this principle of "reciprocity," should listen to Pat Robertson and other moral leaders: "If you do good to others and give, (especially to Pat) good will surely come to you."

Some money had to be spent at the E.D.D. trying to recruit dwarves and midgets. Again, I found great understanding, even compassion, when the situation was "properly" explained and gratuities distributed in a reasonable manner. But, just when everything seemed to be on track, disaster!

The State Board of Equalization needed some kind of accounting of the activity. Not understanding the voluminous documentation sent, the Board decided to send a representative to investigate. But, over a quiet dinner at a prestigious restaurant, this fellow (a real prince) was able to grasp the whole affair and, for a very modest "contribution" for his extra efforts on my behalf, was able to settle the thing satisfactorily.

To this day, I don't understand how a Congressional committee member, answerable only to the President, came upon the enterprise. All I knew was this committee had something to do with the use of government lands and, particularly, their flora and fauna.

So interested was this particular gentleman that he actually made an appointment with me to personally inspect the project. You begin to understand, I'm sure, why you must be so ruthlessly honest in anything you do that has to do with the government.

It just so happened that this particular gentleman had some knowledge of Iguanas. When he arrived, I proudly displayed my "matched pair." To my dumbfounded amazement and utter chagrin, he pointed out that "Ozzie and Harriet" (my own names for the lizards) were both males! No wonder there hadn't been any eggs yet! My mind reeled under the blow. Jose was to be cursed! I had been flim-flamed; an honest man, taken cruel advantage of!

But all was not lost. This fine gentleman, having a good background in entrepreneurial pursuits, after perusing all the facts, the contracts, the brochures, the "potential" for the enterprise together with my bank account, came up with a solution. And so it was, that, *The American Iguana Institute* came into being.

Now while the President himself never offered anything more than the most casual interest in the project, and, while false accusations of C.I.A. involvement continue to flitter around the edges of some "conspiracy" fanatics, it is certifiably false, as I latter explained to a congressional committee, that either the President or the Veep ever had anything to do with the Institute or had any personal knowledge of the source of some questionable "campaign contributions." The "money-laundering" charge together with the charges of dealings with foreign banks was, understandably, hardly worthy of a reply. And so far as the association with a world-renowned arms dealer, simply ludicrous on the face of it!

It has been a soul-wrenching feat to write all this. Many a tissue has absorbed the flow of tears at times during the telling. I can only hope that you, the reader, as I said early on, will take all I have said at face value and come to the only right conclusion that an honorable man (me) has been vilified by those who, for their own nefarious reasons, have attempted to cast doubt on my integrity and tried, in their vituperative efforts, to sully my good name. The writing has, at least, proved cathartic and I bless you for taking the time to hear me out. For those of you that take the further trouble to correspond, I may be able to offer you tangible proof of my sincerity. You will scarcely be able to believe your good fortune at such an opportunity!

CHAPTER SEVENTEEN

THE WEEDPATCHER

NOVEMBER, 1991

Psalm 12:8

It might not have been "... a dark and stormy night," but it sure as hell was black as the ace of Spades.

A friend and I had not known each other very long when we took that trip to the outback of the Black Hills area of the El Paso Mountains Northeast of Mojave. We were in my shiny, new, 1968 VW. I had bought the vehicle to deceive the CHP. Sure enough, I never got a speeding ticket in the bug so the concept proved sound.

We were "loaded for bear" (actually we were after Jackrabbits but were prepared for anything from a native uprising to attacking "Roosians"). We had, between us, my Colt Single Action Army in .357, a 12ga shotgun, a Ruger .22 semi auto, a Ruger Single Six in .357 and a .22 Remington pump. We also had enough ammo to justify the hardware.

It is a well-known fact among people that know me that the wives of my friends are not friendly to me for long. I'll explain.

Now, as I said, this friend and I had not known each other long when we made this "Safari." Therefore, his wife did not suspect that this might be the last time she would see her husband alive (or, at the least, back home within a reasonable span of time, say, sometime within the year).

It was dark by the time we took the Randsburg road out of Mojave to the Mesquite Canyon turnoff near Garlock and pointed the VWs nose North on the dirt road into the boonies. I knew the area well, having traveled it many times, but it was new to this fellow. An owl landed in the middle of the road, staring into our headlights. We stopped and stared at each other until the critter decided to take off. We continued winding our way deeper into the outback. Up jumped a Jack and the war was on. We bailed out and cut loose with the artillery, dust, dirt and rocks showering about the hapless varmint. He escaped the hail of bullets and assorted shrapnel, a wiser bunny, acquainted now with the baser instincts of perverse humans.

We had driven for some time, ever deeper into the "Big Lonesome" and had a good time rapping off rounds. It must have been close to 10:00 p.m. when we crested a steep hill, the headlights piercing out into the blackness. With no moon and far off the beaten track, the night was as dark as any I have ever been in, I knew, approximately, where we were and which direction we were heading; in the darkness, with many dirt tracks leading all over the place, I wasn't absolutely certain of our exact position. Suffice it to say, we eventually made it home.

Some headlines are funnier than others. Imagine, "Dinosaur dung points to ancient global warming!" This surely belongs in the category of the government-sponsored study of cow flatulence (this is called, in the trade, "Comic Relief").

"We the People..." somehow have gotten "lost in the shuffle of government." I don't believe those poor politicians did us in on purpose, it just seems to have "happened." Of course, it didn't "just" happen; it followed the natural course of human nature that is, inherently, egotistical, greedy and selfish.

What a month it has been! Thank God I have had the cabin and the critters to retire to and get my mind purged of all the ugliness and hypocrisy about us. I now have a cot, desk, woodstove and kerosene lamp to enable me to enjoy the solitude with the wind through the pines and chirp of the birds, the bats flitting about in the twilight and the panorama of the rugged mountains and the star-studded nights. I sit a "King" on my screen porch and enjoy the quiet, away from a telephone and traffic.

The only thing that mars the joy is someone with whom to share all this bounty. Somehow, most of my friends have become so trapped in their circumstances they not only do not have "time" to become rich, they do not have time to come and get their own priorities straightened out. Consequently, they continue to live lives of "quiet desperation" not even understanding that they have passed a "death sentence" on themselves.

When Karrie was a little girl she asked me "What did God make us out of?" Karrie knew that the Bible says God made man of the dust of the earth. But that is a somewhat unsatisfactory answer for a child. Being well experienced in the ways of childhood, not having ever grown up myself according to my ex-wives and other base detractors of my "maturity" I answered: "Sweetheart, God made us out of the stuff of the stars! And that makes you my own special little star. Karrie accepted my answer with alacrity and, since it made perfect sense to her, she was well satisfied as her imagination took my answer from there and expanded on it as only a child knows how.

The human body is composed of the "Elements," not "Dirt," that in our physiognomy is, in fact, the "stuff" of the stars. It is, I'm sure, one of the reasons that we gaze at them with such longing and wonder. Our soul and spirit knows we were never intended to be "Earth-bound."

No, much as I admire Emerson, Carlyle and Thoreau, I am not a very good metaphysician or transcendentalist. I have far too wide a streak of pragmatism for that. But that part of me that communes with The Lord as I go to sleep at night "knows" that man, though he most often fails to come up to the mark, was never intended to be egotistical, greedy and selfish. There is, in our hearts, a "something" that wants to be better, to do better. It is that "something" that has its reasons of which Reason knows nothing.

It is that better part of us that responds with such feeling to Moby Dick and Billy Budd, that can, unfortunately, be debased to a lynch mentality when the circumstances become too hard for us. And, tragically, we are living in "Hard Times." The specter of a Depression looms before millions here and in other countries. The circumstances are fast becoming those that brought Hitler to power and, yes, it can "happen here!"

I was visiting my old friends in Bakersfield. He had picked up an album of the Harmonicats and another of the Big Bands. We luxuriated in the music of that time long ago when life was so much simpler and we were young. How much our children have been defrauded of, beginning with their right to be children. I shudder to think of what our children face as the "inheritors" of the unchecked, evil future that awaits them. They won't know the strains of Saber Dance or Begin the Beguine, of Twilight Time or Blue Velvet. They will not know of the wisdom of Thoreau or the beauty of Tennyson, the adventure of Harte or the mystery of Poe. They will be unable to relate to the subtleties or profundities of Bacon or Locke.

It is an abysmal fact that my generation was the last of readers, writers, and real scholarship. Not the scholarship that produces fantastic weapons, computers, or technology in general, but the kind of scholarship that results in the dialogue of the finest flowers of our soul, that relates in kindness to the needs of another, that has a sense of wonder when looking about at God's Creation.

Lest you take exception to this, consider the fact that mine was as I said the last generation of "Readers," and, thanks to WWII and the "movies," the vast migration to the cities, we were a dwindling breed by that time. With the advent of TV, the death-knell was sounded for the scholarship of philosophers, and poets.

In reference to politics, and how these scoundrels are running around like the proverbial chickens without heads, we are the beneficiaries of the wisdom of great statesmen of times past, of the insights of Emerson and Thoreau, of the satirical wit of Sam Clemens and Will Rogers. But none of these could have foreseen the circumstances we face in today's world. However, they did recognize the propensity of human nature to evil; they were studied in the historical evidence of the ability of power to corrupt even the best-intentioned men.

The meetings in Madrid clearly show the magnitude of the problems that involve prejudice and religious hatred and bigotry. In our own country we are beginning to seriously consider the matters of euthanasia, of scapegoating the poor, the elderly, minorities, in short, the same agenda Hitler followed.

Recently, the media has turned its attention, in a very forceful manner, to the fact that keeping people alive, particularly the elderly is the real "culprit" guilty of such enormous health care costs. It has also been put forth that Retards are living much longer, thanks to better, but expensive, medical care. An ominous observation I'm sure you will agree. "Final Exit" and the vote in Washington are the opening guns to the "realistic solutions" to this problem of health care. Ellen Goodman makes some excellent observations on Initiative 119. It is, indeed, "slippery slope" time. When a large segment of society countenances making it a law for doctors, and half the doctors agreeing, to participate in the extinction of life, just how far off are "Final Solutions?"

Kavorkian makes the point that Nuremberg laid the groundwork for his approach to helping people commit suicide. And, if we are to avoid the stigma of hypocrisy, he is right. "We" couldn't have sentenced all those war criminals to death for their actions and look history in the face and take another course. What the "good" doctor has succeeded in doing is rubbing our faces in our own hypocrisy even as David Duke is doing. Kavorkian has underscored the only solutions possible to a world that has lived for its own selfish interests and denied all personal responsibility for the disasters that must surely follow such immoral action.

I recently sent a copy of my book "Confessions and Reflections of an Okie Intellectual" to David Duke. I hope he will read it. He has announced that he has become a Christian. If he has, it will be most interesting to see what happens when the commands of God come into conflict with the "politics" of office. Much as I wish to credit Mr. Duke with a real conversion, only time will tell. And, history reminds us that many, including Hitler, Himmler and Goebbels with their Catholic upbringing, made much of their "Christian" motivation as they followed the Devil.

I sympathize with the folks in Louisiana as the "leaders" in Congress ridicule them for voting for a "Nazi!" Really, Mr. Bush, who are you, with your track record, to call anyone an "Insincere charlatan!" you who so proudly display your Bible as you walk into your opulent church? And who, may I ask, is trying to "paint" Mr. Duke a "Nazi?" Tom Foley? Look at his antics and rhetoric in Washington State in leading the defeat of the term limitation initiative. If Duke's conversion is real, he will soon make that clear. If he is a

"Nazi," that too will be made clear. But talk about the pot calling the kettle black!

As though more were needed to underscore the political need for "Final Solutions," we are told that Magic Johnson has the AIDS virus. We are further told he acquired it through "heterosexual" activity. Now you all know my position on "Sports is King and Entertainment is Queen" in our society. No matter, no one would wish this terrible disease on anyone. It is a sad commentary on our society that the public reaction to this one man getting the disease has brought it to the forefront of attention far more than the disease killing innocent babies. It certainly underscores where our priorities are in relationship to our true "concerns."

One of the most recent articles on the Scrolls mentions the fact that a "dying Messiah figure" is part of the hitherto unpublished material. What an impact that is going to have on "orthodox" rabbinic Judaism. It remains to be seen what else Strugnel and the Pope tried to hide this past forty years. I repeat: it might prove to be devastating to both the churches and Jews and may separate the "sheep" from the "wolves."

"Traditional" Judaism and Christianity, what I call "Blind Orthodoxy," may take a real beating. Just how long, really, does it take to establish a "Tradition?" Not long. The so-called "Lord's Supper," and "Baptism" (Jewish and Christian), are cases in point. My point is the same Jesus made in condemning the religious prejudice during the time he made the statement: "You have set aside God's Word in favor of your own traditions!"

Jews and "professing Christians" will be left in the position of a Hitler or a Jim Lefferts, trying to find consolation in the fairy tale of "Candles and liturgy," in the childhood impressions of the solemnity and "worship" of hoary ritual. The "Noble Lies" and fairy tales are what most people want in any event. What honest Mormon really believes the fairy tales of Joseph Smith? How different, really, the stories of the Koran, a Veda or Sastra? At least Arabian Nights and Gulliver are entertaining and make no attempt to deceive.

In my last letter I talked about the urgent need to address the needs of shelter and bringing taxes under control. It is ludicrous to watch the antics of Congress trying to "sell" a so-called "tax break" by pretending to "soak" the rich. The Democrats are touting a "whopping" $200 "tax break" for a single person making less than $85,000. My, my, whatever will the great unwashed do with such largess? A whole $200! Just imagine what I can buy with such a magnificent sum the government will let me keep of my own money? It might help me pay the property taxes that are surely going to go up to compensate the state for what the "Fed" is going to chop from it. Give with one hand and take with the other is the only thing our "leadership" seems to be able to come up with. And there is no free lunch. Real tax relief can only be accomplished with less government. And that, tragically, is unlikely to happen.

In regard to housing, an absolute that must be dealt with, it is my intention to carry this to the extreme conclusion. If the Lord wills it so, I face the prospect of actually confronting Satan on this issue. For example: If I choose to buy two and one-half acres and build a non-permitted cabin on the property, I will surely be cited by the local bureaucracy. My choice, then, will literally be, to make a "Federal Case" out of it. Since I have no one dependent on my staying out of jail, I can choose to be incarcerated for the "crime" of choosing to do what I want with my own property.

With the full weight of the "Law" crashing down on a "usurper," a "flagrant criminal," the "Law" will be forced to deal with me. As with Nuremberg, those that will be forced to judge me will have to deal with the historical imperative of the situation. On the one hand, I can easily be condemned for disregarding the "Law." On the other hand, the right of the individual, as guaranteed by our Constitution, for life, liberty and the pursuit of happiness, will be on trial as well.

If I can be denied the right to deal with my own land as I choose, if the Law can condemn me for building my own shelter, no matter how humble, if the Law can prevent me from planting my own beans and cabbages, if, in spite of the fact that all this is done without any detriment to the "State" or my neighbors, such "Law" is clearly unjust and I have a Constitutional right to rebel; I have a historical, moral imperative to confront such evil and try to overcome it. It is something that has a noble history summed up in the phrase: "The Rights Of Man," that ante-dates the insanity of laws that would have prevented the founding of this nation, would have prevented Westward expansion, that even now, dooms millions who would, otherwise, be productive citizens, keeping families together, giving them hope of a future, enabling children to learn those skills that made this the greatest nation in history.

I want to make it patently clear that I am not talking about operating a business which, of necessity, must be regulated as it impinges on the rights of others, I am not talking about common-sense regulations which would have to apply on a fifty by one-hundred lot in a city, I am talking about the most fundamental right of a man to provide food and shelter for himself and his family in circumstances that are not detrimental to anyone else.

We, the great unwashed, most surely understand that it is in the interest of the "privileged" class, those with wealth and power, to "subjugate" the "masses," to turn them into "serfs" who are forced to do the bidding of their "masters," those who are "fit" to "rule." The "system" that has evolved in this country has produced serfs aplenty, those on the "dole" that must perform, like trained seals, according to the dictates of the masters who know, that in order to create a society that will make them the "feudal Lords" must crush all hopes and aspirations, must produce "laws" that will "keep those people in their place!"

It's not that I do not appreciate the enormity of the problems that confront even those of our leadership that are sincerely trying to do the job. But I ask these good men to consider whether allowing a man to build on his own property, at least an acre of land, without unjust laws condemning him, whether it might also help resolve our dependency on fossil fuels and the concomitant fouling of our environment? Allow me to explain that "quantum jump."

We have been forced to rely on the automobile to survive under the present system. Suppose, by allowing a man to build his own family shelter on two and one-half acres, encumbered by a mortgage of no more than $15,000 and grow some of his own food, you were able to make it possible for the mother to stay home and care for the children, you were able to make it possible for this mother and father to teach their children to grow vegetables and raise chickens, to build and learn the responsibility and have the feeling of self worth that such activity always produces? Other nations do this, why can't we? We used to and we produced a nation of self-reliant and industrious giants. "Go West young man!" How hollow that sounds now. But, what it meant for our nation at one time!

It hardly needs to be pointed out that such families are the ones driving "junkers," those autos that are the most polluting and fuel inefficient. They certainly don't drive them because they want to; they do so because they have no choice. Given the opportunity I have outlined, they might be able to afford to keep the old cars in better repair and, even, get something better. Mom, in such circumstances, could give up the "second" car.

But, this may be a moot point if the politicians and wealthy have their way. There is a determined effort on the part of these people to get rid of the old cars in any event; and this in the name of "Environmentalism!" Like euthanasia, it seems an imminently sensible thing to do. But what becomes of those that have no choice but to drive the junkers? More "serfs!" Unable to drive either to a job or look for one go on Welfare and "bow when the music plays and the image passes by!"

By giving folks the chance to do for herself, without intrusive and abusive bureaucracy, mom could stay home. Just think of the number of jobs that would become available if this happy event should take place? The second car and second income would be unnecessary. In the happy event that children could learn the responsibility of caring for animals and crops, devoid of the trappings of "civilization" such as nothing better to do than watch TV or get into trouble, what a re-vitalization of our nation might be possible!

It is not "Utopian" dreaming. This could be done! A man is fulfilled in providing for his family. A woman is fulfilled in caring for a husband and children, the children find fulfillment in doing and learning those things that give them hope of a future. But it cannot be done for the vast majority of people by adhering to the senseless, evil system that now makes virtual prisoners of them, that stifles and prohibits all attempts to rise above mean conditions; that, with a $100,000 mortgage and rising taxes, rob them of any hope of anything getting better.

Just to prove the point, I am willing to put my money where my mouth is. I will make a deal with the politicians and bureaucrats that if they will keep their hands off the project, I can take a welfare family and place them in just such an environment and the result will be a family that will contribute to society, not have to live off the taxes of others. Is there one, single politician out there that will take me up on this?

Mr. Bush has just made the profound statement that he is still not convinced that we are in a recession! The blindness of "privilege!" Talk about selling out to a Fairy tale! Does he possibly imagine that he can make the bad news go away simply by mystical fiat of jargon? As with his statement that he would vote for Duke's Democrat opponent, as with his obvious lack of genuine concern for the poor and unemployed, as with his getting his own son off the hook for his involvement in the S&L debacle at the cost of letting the other perpetrators off, Mr. Bush has clearly demonstrated that he subscribes to the "public be damned" philosophy of those that would "rule" a nation of "serfs."

I could easily be written off as the flea that imagines he has the attention of the elephant except for an irritating fact; I am being "investigated" and a handful of politicians do write or call me personally. But, unlike some so threatened I don't "hide" my phone number, address or refuse to have my picture taken as a ploy to exaggerate my importance. But it is a truism that, as with the educational establishment, the "leadership" has a profound fear of those people that have a real education and are proficient in doing for themselves without having such "leaders" do their thinking or doing for them.

Now consider these two items: One, the Foggy Bottom scoundrels are "blackmailing" the poor with the threat of cutting the food stamp program. Second, a grampa, one Victor Henry Salgado, was caught after robbing three golf shops of about $5,000. His defense; his disability payments of $710 didn't stretch far enough to provide his grandchildren with necessities! In spite of the fact that this "disabled" man used a gun in the robberies, he will get out of jail in about 20 months.

No matter how we try to twist and turn these two things, it is apparent that if "grampa's" feel the "system" isn't paying off like it should so the grandkids can go to the dentist or get a new pair of glasses (Salgado's "defense"), just how many other "grampa's" are going to feel justified in grabbing their guns and taking what they feel they have a right to? Now, if you further "rob" them of their "rights" to food stamps? The implications are mind-boggling!

Since we "oldsters" are becoming the targets of so much attention from draining the budget because of soaring health costs to "cheating" the young through social security, maybe it's time for "grampa's" and "gramma's" to start their own gangs? Why should the kids have all the "fun?" We could call ourselves the "Gramps" or "Grams." Our "colors" should be gray and black. Not a few of us are well experienced in the use of firearms, explosives and motorcycles. Some of us could actually teach the kids a few tricks if we put our minds to it.

Experts are afraid of Third World nuclear arms proliferation. A legitimate fear, as I have often pointed out in past years. But just imagine how scared they would be if a bunch of "gray-hairs" really wanted to resort to terrorism? Why the possibilities are staggering! What do you do, really, if some Octogenarian pulled the trigger on Bush or Willie Brown? Now if I were recruiting for revolution, I would be calling on the WWII Vets. They have the know-how and they have lived with the betrayal of our nation long enough to have a real "mad on."

They are also the generation that knows what their grandchildren have been robbed of. There are, doubtless, at least five-million "Salgados" out there, grandparents, that would love to "pull the switch" on the traitors that have sold out the birthright of our little ones and are trying to blame us for the crime.

As we watch those poor folks in Russia trying to come to grips with the job their own politicians did on them, as we watch old people stand in seemingly endless lines for hours to get a couple of cabbages, you have to ask yourself, if we, as an armed populace, will tolerate such conditions? I think not. And, will some hard-line leader in Russia call the people back to the "Leeks and Garlic of Egypt?" I think it entirely likely.

Mr. Hussein, Mr. Khadafy, if you really want to hurt America, quit trying to get to us through the means you have vainly attempted. Send a few of your "emissaries" over here surreptitiously with a few millions of your ill-gotten blood money and hire a few "Salgados." You will find them lined up a mile long to take advantage of the "opportunity" to rid the earth of the scoundrels that are ruining us for their own advantage. And, most important, they can be bought cheap! I'm also sure they will kiss your hands and your Koran for giving them the opportunity.

Mein Kampf is not exactly a "page-turner." Hitler wasn't much as a writer but boy could he hold an audience! All that is lacking in our present circumstances is such a "spell-binder" to turn this nation on its ear.

Unhappily, Goethe and Scott were dead when Emerson went "visiting" abroad. Nevertheless, he made the excellent observation, after speaking with Coleridge, Wordsworth, Landor, and DeQuincey that: "I have, however, found writers superior to their books." Hitler proves Emerson's point. I have often had people tell me: "You should write like you speak." In pondering that statement and thinking of it in the context of Emerson's observation, I conclude that what is most often wanting in writing are the obvious person-to-person communications that are only viable in such contact.

There is simply no way for the written words to convey what is only possible by force of personality and "body language." It is in this context that we understand that even God's Word, The Bible, is given "Life" and reality by God's Holy Spirit. Apart from God's Spirit it remains simply a book. In this same vein, Jonathan Edwards' great sermon, "Sinners In The Hands Of An Angry God," lacks any of the discernible force that, when preached by Edwards, had the listeners hanging onto the pillars of the church to keep from falling posthaste into hell. And so it is that, as history evidences, that "Leader" which will, inevitably, come on the scene, will be just such a charismatic individual, who will, like Hitler, be able to persuade people to believe "glorious lies."

Thinking of Magic Johnson and the tremendous effect his HIV has had on society I am reminded of the Banning High school principal not allowing the school's football team to compete against Dorsey, an "inner city" school because of the danger. Folks, it isn't a "game" any longer. I can't help wondering what Johnson finds, looking back, that will make dying easier, that will make "It" all worthwhile?

Often, just the strain of a melody sets events in motion that have far-reaching impact. It is written of Moses that he disdained the pleasure of sin for "a season" for the greater joy of obeying God. And that folks is the ultimate, bottom line. Will a person, because of his belief and faith in God, do what is right no matter the consequences or will he bow to the idols of expediency, greed, lust, envy, selfishness and egotism?

I will anticipate some of you: "Why Magic Johnson and not Jimmy Swaggart?" Don't expect a satisfactory answer apart from God's Word; there isn't one. You will find part of the answer in pursuing the death of Mary Jo Kopechne to its logical conclusion and comparing that with God's choice of Pharaoh at the time of the Exodus. It is a chilling conclusion. But, at the risk of being repetitious, it is unlikely many will make the connection and I cite Thoreau and the example of a couple of young men I know very well who exemplify the problem.

Much as people credit the maxim of "Experience is the best teacher," it is the purview of youth to exult in the folly of "Presumed Knowledge." Not that age is the sole arbiter of wisdom, but true wisdom dictates its chances are better. Silly as it appears, these young men, having never married, presume to "know" all those things that can, one would think obviously, only be learned by the experience of taking on the responsibility of wife and children. Yet these silly "youngsters" actually pontificate on their presumed "expertise" in the matters of family.

Thoreau was a Harvard graduate. He excelled in the disciplines of classical languages and literature. His was a university trained and disciplined mind. Contrary to the ignorant thinking of such young men as I am writing about, Thoreau did not simply get up one morning and decide: "I think I will move to Walden, kick back and become a subject of ridicule to my fellow Concordites!" On the contrary, Walden was a calculated and expertly planned "Experience" and "Experiment."

As with his great treatise on Civil Disobedience and his decision to go to jail rather than pay an unjust tax, these things are the result of disciplined and calculated thought resulting in action. And, to his credit, he never presumed to "pontificate" on wife and children since he never married. Having never submitted to the rigors of university training, having never taken on the responsibility of wife and children, imagine, if you will, how very ridiculous these young men I mention appear when they presume to "instruct" others in these matters.

I have often pointed out the fact that real education should give one a sense of humility. Only real education gives one the sense of their own ignorance. Only a genuine "student" will bend every effort in an on-going effort to dispel more and more of that ignorance. Further, real education should lead to tolerance and understanding. But it also gives one an abhorrence of the kind of "presumed knowledge" of the truly ignorant. Even worse is the kind of presumed knowledge that is willfully ignorant. Its not only ignorant, it makes an open spectacle of foolish pride in its ignorance! It says, wrongly and loudly to a truly educated person, "I'm not only ignorant, I'm proud of it!"

Such people will make much of the fact that they are "well-read," deluding themselves with thinking that reading alone can compensate for their abysmal ignorance. These two young men are further handicapped by the fact that they are intelligent. I call it a handicap in their case because of the fact that their intelligence betrays them into thinking that just because they are capable of subtle thought; it makes up for their lack of experience and their lack of disciplined minds. Nothing could be further from the truth and their odiousness to others fails to get the message across to them. Their undisciplined egos are their downfall- obvious to others but never to themselves. Such are the characteristics of fools. I love these young fellows but I grieve for them in their dark ignorance and fleshly pride.

Why am I on such a "tear" about these two, foolish young men? Because they represent the followers of the "Himmler's, Goebbels' and Goering's" of Nazi Germany! Lacking real education, they are easy prey for those like I have named. The Nazi leaders, being educated and ruthless themselves, know how to "stroke" the egos of young men like these two. The appeal is to their outrageous egos. Lacking formal education, they presume to "know it all." They will follow any leader who appeals to their ignorant vanity.

Just how dangerous do such young men become? Hold a mirror to the years between 1928 through 1939 in Germany and examine the reflection in a contemporary context! And just how presumptuous is their ignorance? They will tell a mother they "know just how she felt" when she was pregnant or had the baby! I have a Ph. D. in Human Behavior but these two, lacking even a rudimentary bachelor's degree will wax eloquent in telling me all about the subject.

They are so busy trying to impress others with their presumed importance, they become the butt of their own ignorance; a cruel trick they play on themselves to the embarrassment of any who meet them. I'm sure some of you know such people. Much as I hate the system that penalizes men in a marriage, there is no other way for us to learn some of the most necessary lessons of life than to have a family. It's a tragedy that the times of the "Waltons" and "Little House" have been stolen from us.

Of course, there are many today who wish their children had never been born, who have found their children to be a curse rather than a blessing. And, if they have loved their children and earnestly tried to do a good job of parenting, flagellate themselves, as the father of a recent Ann Landers column, asking: "Where did we go wrong?" And they penalize couples in China for having more than one offspring.

I think there are obvious reasons to be concerned on this subject. After all, to good men and women "Family" is the only thing that makes sense of sacrifice, and that without a sense of sacrifice if made in love. As we watch the rise of Nazism in Germany, as we witness the vicious attacks of racial extremists in this country, I repeat, yes, it can happen here! It is happening here! And I don't mean the simple, overt actions of a Tom Metzger burning a cross. The more ominous is the billboards of Edwin Edwards saying in letters four feet tall: NO DUKE, followed by a Swastika. If I were a resident of Louisiana, I think I would vote for Duke on the basis of that kind of tactic alone! The people of Louisiana are certainly not going to forget how politicians from other states have tried to smear, shame and blackmail them into voting for Edwards, a man certainly proven to know how the game is played and much more suited to the good old boy "morality" and "mentality" of Congress.

At no time since Al Smith has a politician so captured the fears, garnered so much media attention and engendered such calumny as Duke; called everything from a Nazi and "Kluxer" to the Anti-Christ. And look at the men doing the name-calling? As with the vote in Pennsylvania, the entrenched pols have every right to be running scared. But can you imagine what is stirring such fear from one man that would cause them all to crawl into bed together? Folks, there is more here than meets the eye! And you know it certainly is not "moral indignation!" It is far more sinister than that!

Consider President Bush burning the midnight oil, studying the Hoover/ Roosevelt years. Will he decide to save his political skin by borrowing from F.D.R. and convince himself that government can, in fact, repeat history and spend us out of the present, dismal economic circumstances? I suspect he will; I can't see any other option for him.

And, further, what better way to further swell the ranks of the "serfs" than new programs of government "employment" such as revised WPA's, CCC's, NIRA's, PWA's, NRA's, TVA's, etc., with new FERA's going on the books. If Bush is as smart as I believe him to be, he will stop talking about a "New World Order" and start talking about a "New, New Deal!" What better way to enslave a nation than to take away their guns and make the majority "employees" (read "serfs") of the State through a multitude of "welfare programs?"

But can people trust the man who expects us to "buy" his statements that neither he nor Reagan cut a deal with the Iranians? No, but he has every reason to believe people are ready for him to "spend" us out of the present repression! And if the choice is between that course of action or more "David Dukes," guess what he is going to do?

"All men recognize the right of revolution; that is, the right to refuse allegiance to, and to resist, the government, when its tyranny or its inefficiency are great and unendurable... All machines have their friction; and possibly this does enough good to counterbalance the evil... But when the friction comes to have its machine, and oppression and robbery are organized, I say, let us not have such a machine any longer... I think it is not too soon for honest men to rebel and revolutionize... Unjust laws exist: shall we be content to obey them, or shall we endeavor to amend them, and obey them until we have succeeded, or shall we transgress them at once? Men generally, under such a government as this, think that they ought to wait until they have persuaded the majority to alter them. They think that, if they should resist, the remedy would be worse than the evil. But it is the fault of the government itself that the remedy is worse than the evil. It makes it worse. Why is it not more apt to anticipate and provide for reform? Why does it not encourage its citizens to be on the alert to point out its faults, and do better than it would have them? Why does it always crucify Christ, and excommunicate Copernicus and Luther, and pronounce Washington and Franklin rebels? If the injustice has a spring, or a pulley, or a rope, or a crank, exclusively for itself, then perhaps you may consider whether the remedy may be worse than the evil: but if it is of such a nature that it requires you to be the agent of injustice to another, then, I say, break the law. Let your life be a counter-friction to stop the machine. What I have to do is to see, at any rate, that I do not lend myself to the wrong which I condemn." H. D. Thoreau on Civil Disobedience, February 1848.

CHAPTER EIGHTEEN

The Weedpatcher

December, 1991

II Corinthians 9:15

Merry Christmas; what if I should run for President of The United States, would you vote for me?

This should confirm what most of my friends already suspect, that I have lost my mind and should now be committed to some institution and kept away from sharp objects and children. While it is to be freely admitted that for any citizen who is not a lawyer, who lacks the millions of dollars from special interest groups, who belongs to no organization, who's name is not exactly a household word, to presume to even entertain such a notion obviously qualifies him for a stint in a "secure environment" where he can't do himself or others serious injury. So, now that I have brightened your holiday season with a good laugh, I turn to the serious "insanity" of my proclamation.

Now I confess that I have enough control of my faculties that such an idea was to me, at first (and second and third) insane. But, once I had recovered my composure, which required a long walk among the pines and rocks, I had to admit it might not be quite as insane as it appeared. I hope you will bear with me while I attempt to work through the process that I had to go through to arrive at such an "insane" decision.

Somewhere along the way, we have given up any hope of honesty in government leadership. We don't expect to see men who will speak their minds and let us know what they really think. It is as though the whole election procedure has gone through some sort of "sanitizing" process where no person running for office dares express the fact that they, like us, are only human. It is a "media event" if a politician dares give an opinion of a personal nature, an opinion that will give us a glimpse of his humanity, without paying a price exacted by a "liberal" media that demands strict conformity to some kind of "code" of which they alone approve. As a consequence, we never see "natural" and "human" men running for, or holding, office. As to what the candidates or incumbents really think, what kind of men they really are, we can only determine by the way they vote. And, they consistently vote for more and more government spending.

It is this "philosophy" of tax and spend that is dooming our nation. But, if the media control who is or is not elected, what does that tell us about the media's agenda? There are some good, conservative writers in the print media but they seem voices in the wilderness. There are virtually none in TV.

Like all of you who have given up any hope that our "leadership" will be anything but worse, I had to confront the role I have played in allowing such a bunch of crooks to ruin our nation. It isn't pleasant to accept one's own contribution to the dismal state of affairs. But, in all honesty, I could have done more to help change things for the better. I could look back on the times I have said my vote didn't count, I could think of all the times I have cursed the politicians and didn't write that letter I should have written. In short, without belaboring it further, I found myself guilty of not taking an active part in helping to change things. I allowed myself to fall into the "Let George do it" syndrome and, essentially "copped-out" of any personal responsibility. After all, "What could I do?" Like you, I found I had defeated myself by not doing even the little I could do.

It has been bitter to me to discover that so many of my friends are actually afraid to get involved! This has been somewhat startling as many of them are not even aware, or will admit, of the fact. Yet, it is true. At first I simply discounted their lack of "political" interest as due to frustration or apathy. But that wasn't true at all. They are scared! They are actually afraid that if they become politically active, something "bad" will happen to them or their families. Part of this fear is grounded in the way the "system" treats those that rebel against it; a system that has become so evil that unless you learn to "play the game" according to the Devil's rules, you are going to get stomped! If this is actually true, and we give in to such evil, we don't deserve anything better. We are already slaves and might as well wear our chains without either complaint or hope; we have already put our children in bitter bondage by our very fearfulness.

It is also a bitter thing to realize that so many people are so woefully ignorant of our own history. How many young people, especially, really know the truth of the founding of our nation, the circumstances and the heroes that brought about the greatest nation in the history of the world? That should be a constant source of pride in our heritage. But unscrupulous men and women who would turn the truth into a lie and twist and distort our proud beginnings into a source of shame have betrayed our heritage. Who, you might well ask, has gained from the distortions of the truth, who have defamed the men and women who paid the price of our freedom and liberty?

I know that slavery is a reproach to our history as a nation. But no other nation would have waged a bloody civil war, brother against brother, in order to right such a wrong. No other nation would have even made an attempt to redress the evils done to Native Americans, no matter the dismal record. We can look history in the face, admitting our greatest crimes, and still be proud Americans. No other nation in history has produced the good this nation has. No other nation owes such a debt to so many, through a Revolution, a Civil War and two world wars, Korea and Vietnam, than this nation. The debt is one of honor to those that paid the price even when, as with Vietnam, the action of despicable "leaders" was dishonorable. And now, at last, we are a nation that stands at the threshold of the greatest evil the world has ever seen if we do not return to the "ancient landmarks!"

It is that time of year and it might be appropriate to ask: Where are the "Bailey's" that are good enough men to confront the "Potter's," the "David's" who will do battle against the "Goliath" of a system that has damned our children and grand-children and condemned them to a hopeless future? I ask this especially of those that dare call themselves "Christian" and slink into the woodwork and into their comfortable "prisons" and dare to say: "Politics is a dirty business, I must keep my hands clean" and by their very words condemn themselves by supporting the very evil Jesus said we were to resist, to fight against. It didn't used to be such a problem to tell who was on The Lord's side. The "warfare" was real to those saints of the past and they were willing to pay the price of obedience to all The Lord's commands, not just the ones that were "convenient" or "socially acceptable."

How dare anyone, Christian or non-Christian, tell me they care about the future of this nation or their children who is too "busy" too "frightened" too "frustrated" too "young" too "old" to confront such evil! A pox on those who give the lie to their "concern" when common sense alone dictates that their lack of involvement, their apathy, their ignorance of the vital issues that are condemning our children and our nation are meaningless to them! And especially those of you that think God cares nothing about this nation or whether you are actively resisting and confronting the evil threatening to destroy it, that He will not call you into judgment for your giving it all, including your own children, to the Devil on a silver platter!

Over the years I have tried to serve in various capacities of "Church Work," I have never been so badly treated as I have by those that claim to be "good Christians." The problem is not with The Lord, it is with those, as it has ever been, that twist and distort His Word to their own selfish, prejudiced, egotistical purposes. Therefore, it is not surprising that of all the issues I address in my "platform," the one that the religious community has damned me for is that of the "free ride" religious organizations have been getting on the backs of taxpayers.

The people that genuinely believe in God, who really believe His Word, agree that the tax-exempt status of religion is a shame to God and allows every unscrupulous charlatan like Baker, Swaggart, Roberts, et al. to make a mockery of true religion. All it has done is deny the intent of our founding fathers, shamed God and permit people like Jim Jones to ply their trade. Since a man is known by his enemies as well as his friends, I ask you to take a careful look at those that would curse me for my stand on this particular issue. If I am to be horse-whipped like Jim Lefferts, it will be by the supporters of the Elmer Gantry's of this world system, those that would kill me and say: "We do God a service!" and thereby join their true, spiritual counterparts already in league with Satan.

As to my qualifications, I am better equipped than David Duke and while he is younger the "liberals" can't smear me with a Swastika or white sheet. And any man who has been through divorce knows what those lawyer-coached statements are worth. I had to admit that, having worked hard all my life, government seemed bent on taking all I have tried to provide for my children and grand-children and I'm mad as hell about it. I know how the "system" operates. I have long careers in industry and education. I am not only well educated, I know how to "punch a clock" and earn a living with my sweat and back. I still have, intact, all those "Old World" values of "If any not work, neither should he eat, Honesty is the best policy, an honest day's work for an honest day's pay, Crime does not pay," etc. I still believe men are to lead and provide for their wives and children. I still believe men like Washington were "Heroes" and that perversion and pornography are destructive and a shame to any nation.

I have also been "through the mill" by court systems that can't seem to distinguish or identify the word "Justice!" A system that seems to delight in idiocy and caring more for so-called "rights" of criminals than what they have done to their victims, that frustrates the best of our police officers as they try to do an impossible job of law enforcement, being forced to second-guess what a judge or D. A. will do.

The so-called "Juvenile Justice System" that allows young criminals to loot, kill and rape with no more than a slap on the wrist is a travesty. If that young thug can commit an adult crime, why shouldn't he be held accountable for full restitution and suffer the same consequences of his actions as he made his victim suffer? It is insane to try to make the parents of such criminals responsible when they don't even have the right to discipline, when they are told they cannot, legally, even keep their own children from coming and going at will. The "system" teaches these young people they do not have to obey parents; that they do not have to be responsible for their actions. Small wonder so many parents have given up in frustration and lash out in anger.

If you have lost out on a job opportunity because the employer had to conform to a "quota" based on race or gender rather than the best-qualified person, you and the employer, and our nation, were cheated. I, like you, am sick to death of watching the "leadership" doing more for foreign interests than for our own, a leadership that has betrayed the working people in this nation and our very heritage by leading us to bankruptcy and denying any hope to us, our children and our grandchildren.

I am a mature adult. I am sick to death of government telling me I don't know what is best for me, "Big Brother" telling me I don't have enough sense to be outraged over the likes of Bush, Cranston, Willie Brown, Rangel, et al.; telling me I should not be outraged over rising property taxes that support the leeches and bums and the crooks in Congress and the legislatures that are taxing people out of their homes, out of hope for a future, out of existence.

A recent computer study by The National Taxpayer's Union Foundation showed that members of the House and Senate, just this year, have proposed $43 in new government spending to every one dollar in spending reduction. That is right, a ratio of forty-three to one! To quote: "This is dramatic evidence of a dynamic that is propelling Congress toward ever higher levels of federal spending. If every bill introduced in the House in the first eight and one-half months of this year alone had passed, federal spending would increase nearly half a trillion dollars. The Senate's total would be nearly $430 billion!"

While Democrats and Republicans are guilty, Democrats like Rep. Charles Rangel of New York were the worst and he, the worst of all. I simply can't say enough bad about this bigoted, racist "Tax Pig!" But of the whole lot, Senators and Representatives, Democrats and Republicans, only one, single Representative, Republican Herb Bateman of Virginia, sponsored bills that would result in a net decrease in government spending. Not one single Senator did that. But think of it! Only one man out of the entire Congress!

While Senate Democrats sponsored spending bills at the rate of 65 to one of tax reduction to the Republican's 23 to one, we lose either way. Neither party knows how to do anything but tax and spend. Neither has any intention of reducing government spending. With this philosophy of "government" spending the future of our children and grandchildren, this nation is doomed! There is an absolute necessity of a complete change in government leadership and the philosophy of government. Grace was right: "The only hope is to get rid of the whole bunch and start over!" My recommendation is a return to the fundamentals of government established by our Constitution.

Folks, no one believes the solutions to our national plight are going to be easy or simple to fix. But we all agree they need "fixing." Beware of anyone, especially politicians, whose "fixes" can be summed up in three or four "platform" statements. It might make for good campaign slogans and rhetoric but I believe people are too smart to be taken in by such simplistic statements as though the speaker had an answer just because he identifies a problem.

"We must have Welfare reform!" You bet; but how? I believe that ghetto or barrio mom and dad want the same things for their children that I do. I suggest that effectively closing our borders to further immigration and deporting the illegals will provide jobs to the young people that will take them out of the drug and crime infested areas and put them in the fields and orchards earning an honest wage, teaching them a "work ethic," in an environment that will remove them from the hopeless neighborhoods where they risk death on a daily basis and no "career opportunities" but dealing drugs, holding up liquor stores and gas stations, pimping and prostitution. Given those options, I would far rather have my son or daughter tilling the soil, being "field-hands" or taking care of livestock than risk getting shot as a gang member, dying of AIDS or a drug overdose, becoming a pimp or prostitute, or going to prison. At least there is some hope of a future in honest work.

Another thing, why can't welfare mothers cooperate in taking care of the children so some of them can take job training or do useful work in return for welfare benefits? Why should taxpayers have to subsidize day care? Why can't we have reform in welfare and divorce laws that will give men an incentive to work for, be responsible for, and stay with, their families? Why can't we restore authority to parents to discipline their children and require them to obey sensible, parental rules and values?

For those that cry "racism" I say, if you mean that my suggestions will impinge mostly on Negroes and Hispanics, you are absolutely right because that is where most of the problems exist and where the help is most needed. But I will also be ruthlessly honest with you by pointing out the fact that America cannot endure the corruption synonymous with the African and Mexican cultures.

Nowhere but in America, with its European, Christian heritage, can such opportunities be found for such an ethnic mix as we have. For you to call me "racist" for telling the truth puts the onus of proof on you! Honestly, if you are so "proud" of your Mexican or African culture that you would try to force it on me or use it as an example, why don't you move to Mexico or Africa? I'll tell you why, because you know you wouldn't have the proverbial snowball's chance of your "culture" and those governments giving you any where near the freedom and opportunities you find in America, an America with a European, Christian founding and heritage! You Hispanics, for example, would you like to vote to give California back to Mexico? I think not! Otherwise, you wouldn't be doing all in your power, largely illegally, to get all of your relatives out of there!

All those that cry and howl at my calling a spade a spade, calling me the "Mencken" or "Joyce" of the Nineties (at least those men were literate and erudite) will have to face the truth of what I am saying. I would ask all of you to consider who is doing the howling and hand wringing. What is their "justification" for crying for "special privilege," what do they say they are contributing of practical substance to our society that gives us hope for our children and their future? And don't try to hand me or any other American your "multi-cultural" crap. The European nations have enough sense to recognize the danger of this and are working hard to close their own borders. A very sensible step if they are to salvage their own identities and be of any use to the third world nations.

Ask yourself what the so-called "Reverend" Jesse Jackson, the man who consistently stabs this nation in the back by shaking hands with terrorists like Khadafy and Jackson's equally bigoted cohort, Charles Rangel are attempting to do by calling anyone "racist" that does not agree with their peculiar and prejudiced views? Just how is their rhetoric, their "campaign promises," going to promote "better citizenship" among those who they are trying to rally? And rally to what purpose? To "demand" their "rights;" their part of "the action?" Such demands will always come back on the heads of those who believe they can demand without the concomitant "sweat equity," without observance of the historical imperatives that made this nation great.

I would ask the so-called "Reverend" Jackson and his idiotic political tools, Charles Rangel and Willie Brown: "What, exactly, is your "program" for making better American citizens of those you claim to represent?" You "Latino" would-be "leaders:" What do you propose to your "constituency" that promises to make them better American citizens? Or is your "platform" exhausted by demands for money, special privilege and status you have not earned, by attempts to extort, by threat, innuendo, guilt-tripping, leading young people, especially, to think that "The Man, Charlie, Whitey," somehow "owes" them and they need the likes of you in order to "collect?"

All of you "politicians" have good grounds for your "Doomsday Government" scenario. You are all, I'm sure, interested in a "hole in the ground" somewhere when "all hell breaks loose" by an aroused citizenry. But don't believe for an instant that there is a hole anywhere that will be deep enough for you to escape, that you are going to be able to conduct your "business" to save your selfish and egotistical hides from the men and women from whom you have stolen any hope of a future for them and their children. You foolish, foolish bunch of bureaucratic idiots, there is no "safe-house" or "hole" that removes you from the crosshairs of a man who cannot take care of his own family, from a mother and father who has to listen to the cries of a cold and hungry child.

Where there is no accountability, there is no responsibility. The schools are in such deplorable condition because of this lack of accountability; just doing a "job for a paycheck." All of society is to blame for this. And the greater guilt, the greatest blame attaches to the whining bellyachers who don't even vote or know the name of their local representative.

The nation's economy is the worst it has been since WWII! Ask the landlords who cannot collect rent why? When the deadbeats can "legally" rob a property owner of up to nine month's rent who wants to be a landlord? When you can be forced, legally, to wait a year to recover property through the foreclosure process, why carry a note or mortgage just to make it easier for the "thieves" to live payment-free for a year? Property rights? We have legalized theft and wonder why people don't feel they have to be responsible.

I think our California governor, Pete Wilson, is a good man. I have supported him for several years as he has pounded his head against the brick walls of a "liberal" legislature. The fact that he wants Californians to face the grim realities of our state budget crisis is meeting with the anticipated howling and hand wringing of the racist mob, those that decry the obvious need for slaughtering a few sacred cows. The suggestions for a modest decrease in welfare, the need for an extended residency requirement, the outcry of the perverts, the need for state-fattened employees to take a modest cut in salary, all these have the bigots and their legislative cohorts crying to heaven.

Certainly I do not agree with the governor in all things. I'm sure he takes exception to more than a few things I advocate in government. But he exemplifies the problem of a good man trying to do the job in spite of the army of media distortionists and left-wingers lined up against him. Unless things change and the left-wing racists and bigots like Willie Brown let the governor do his job, California faces a dismal future.

State Senator Don Rogers is also trying to do the job that needs doing but notice how the media slant continues to attack Senator Rogers especially. If there is a "Letters to the editor" that bashes Mr. Rogers, count on the Californian printing it.

Are men like Pat Buchanan wrong for putting America first? I can't imagine any other nation in the world saying the interests of some other nation should take precedence over theirs. Then why is the media so intent on making "America First" sound like something to be ashamed of? I ask again, what is the "agenda" of the media in making it sound like there is something wrong for speaking out for our nation, for saying we should put the interests of our own citizens above that of other nations? There is something appallingly "dirty" going on with the slant the media is taking in this case and many others.

For example, speaking of "bashing," in Vancouver, B.C. you can be fined up to $50,000 for speaking out against homosexuality. You heard me right; up to $50,000 for simply saying the same things God says in the Bible! Vancouver has made it possible for the "saints" to do jail time and pay fines for quoting God! Some of you will recall me saying, years ago, the time would come when to obey God will mean going to jail. The time has come and if the perverts have their way, and they keep trying, it will happen here in this country as well. It will be interesting to see who is going to be on the Lord's side when this comes to pass. You can bet it won't be those who think they can pick and choose among The Lord's commands. On the upside, it will become increasingly easier to recognize true believers in God; they will, eventually, stick out like the proverbial sore thumbs. Reduced to wearing the skins of animals and living in caves? Of these, God says, the world was not worthy.

I have in mind a book entitled: "God's Cruel Jokes!" Imagine, if you will, some of the things God has said those that believe in Him are subject to? Now either what the Lord has for us in eternity is worth all the suffering of this world or it is all a cruel joke. But if God is serious about what Heaven is to be, and our entering into His kingdom requires us to take Him at His Word in this life, there are sure a whole lot of people talking about Heaven who aren't going there. It is all a sham and a cheat or it is worth all we have to give to it and there is no middle ground.

Sam Clemens, in his travels in Germany, came to the conclusion that the wealth of Black Forest inhabitants was measured by the size of their manure piles. I'm not so sure but what dear, old Sam was taking the measure of his own countrymen in his satire. The older I get, the more it seems to me that men's wealth consists, largely, of how high they have been able to stack what amounts to no more than manure. And, if they can bury someone else in their pile, they seem the happier for it; kind of like the little Caesars called "building inspectors" whose whole goal is to make life miserable for some poor soul who has had the effrontery to put up a patio cover without the "blessing" and permit of the city or county. These little weasels, tax-bloated bureaucrats, take a hideous delight in being able to, like the I.R.S., make life miserable for the unwary citizen who hasn't kissed their big toes before doing something our founding fathers took for granted as the rights of men, created in God's image, with dignity and the ability to do for themselves without Big Brother's "blessing."

So it is that I am coming to the conclusion that most of what passes for "wealth" in the lives of these petty tyrants is only an attempt to see who has the largest pile of manure. At least manure exemplifies the end and the meanness of their own souls and is what they will carry with them into eternity where the "worm never dies and the fire is not quenched."

Perhaps conditions in Russia reflect what happens when petty, small-minded tyrants gain control of a nation. As we watch the dreadful situation unravel and the people suffer, we should be soberly reminded and warned; it can happen here! As ethnic rivalries, some rooted in centuries, cause upheaval and riot; it should be a solemn admonition to all of us that where ethnicity is stressed there is bound to be conflict. It does no good at all to cry out for "liberal" understanding when cultures are in conflict. The hyphenated "American" is no American.

"Where there is no vision, the people perish!" What, I ask you, is the possibility of "vision" where there is no hope? "Future" and "Vision" are a synergism. The two cannot exist apart if there is to be any hope. Hope is contingent on a better future; hope cooperates with vision and builds for a better future. And where are the "builders" to come from? Our posterity? Not if we continue to jerk the rug from under them and rob them blind of any future! Here is a most sobering exercise: ask young people who their heroes are? Ask them whom they know that they wish to emulate? Invariably, if you get an answer at all, it will be some sports or entertainment personality. What you will not get for an answer is George Washington or Thomas Jefferson.

I have two sons and a daughter. I would cheerfully give my own life for them if it would help. I have three grandchildren I would also die for if I could, by doing so, offer them hope of the future, if I could spare them suffering a future without hope. But I can't do them any good by dying. But I can live for them! I can try with all my might to cry out against injustice, against the "special privilege" crowd, against the evil men and women who would doom any chances of my children realizing the dreams that should be their birthright as citizens of the most amazing and freest nation in history.

And, I am meeting with some degree of success. I have become a target of the enemy, an enemy who knows nothing of love, who cannot hear the wind in the pines or see hope in the stars, who recognizes no creed except, ego, lust and greed. The harder that enemy inveighs against me, the stiffer my backbone gets. This enemy knows the battle is to the death and no quarter given. Was it any different at Lexington, Concord, and Valley Forge? Folks, the times portend much worse than our forefathers faced. Is there any chance the same steel that forged the backbones of those great men and women will be found in this generation, the inheritors of such promise, bought at such a price? It won't be found in America's pulpits. It isn't seen in our Congress, Oval Office or High Court. Then where are we to look for her champions of liberty? Where shall we seek her latter-day Washington's, Jefferson's, Franklin's, Hale's, Revere's, Adams', Hancock's, her "Minutemen" and "Patriots?" It is June 17,

1775 once more and Bunker Hill looms ahead with its potential for liberty or death. Who will lead this charge?

I watch as people buy their Christmas trees and decorate their homes and I envy them in family circumstances. If I had a family I would be doing the same thing. But, if I still had a family I doubt I would be taking on the "Establishment" in the manner I have been doing. I would be fearful of the consequences to them. As it is, I have nothing to lose by doing all I can for the hope of a future for my children and grandchildren. Adulterous women and an evil system that rewards infidelity on their part brought about the destruction of my own family. Therefore, I have a vested motive in attacking that part of the system in my "campaign platform."

As I consider the things that made this nation great, it took a good deal more than a Declaration of Independence, a Constitution and Bill of Rights; it took good men and women, who stood together, side by side, to see this nation through its birth pangs. It took commitment to family, truth and justice. It is the lack of family, more than any other factor that is dooming this nation. When women are given carte blanche to murder the innocent through abortion as contraception, when women can divorce at the drop of a hat and make the man responsible for the economic fall-out, when men are so emasculated by an evil judicial system that their only recourse is often to run away, something must change or all is lost.

It is Christmas and I, like so many others, no longer have a "home." An adulterous woman who knew she had everything on her side when she crawled into bed with another man wiped it out. There was no thought of what the consequences of her actions would have on our children. And all she could say in her defense was that she wanted her "freedom!" To hell with family, children and husband, the woman wanted her "freedom!" But it was her children and her husband that paid the price for her "freedom!"

The only purpose for opening such a sore wound is to underline the fact that as long as people, men or women, think they can ever be "free" by causing the innocent to suffer they are badly mistaken. Such utter selfishness exacts payment in the Devil's coin. No abuser of children, including ex-wives, will ever find a more implacable enemy than me. It is always the children who are made to pay the price of divorce. The man may get stuck with the bills and lawyers will always take the woman's case without "front money" telling her the man will be made to pay, not her, but it is the children who pay the greatest price in emotional devastation and psychological scars.

Ultimately, we must face the fact that the family alone makes anything in life worthwhile, that gives any meaning to sacrifice and a reason for being. God says He hates divorce. Infidelity or death are the only Scriptural grounds on which a marriage is terminated in God's eyes. But evil men and women have created a system that makes divorce as easy as buying a pair of shoes and marriage, consequently, has about the same value in many cases. No society can long survive such a cavalier approach to "family."

I will never be a good enough "politician" to forsake the ancient landmarks of God's Word. He says that when a man and woman join together, they become one in His sight and no one may sunder that relationship by their puny and selfish "laws." AIDS is only one of the things that underscore The Lord's attitude toward the destruction wrought by the fleshly selfishness of those that think they can get away with mocking Him. "Fools make a mock of sin" but they will face "payday someday!"

As I try to make my way through the "homeless" condition that so many face because of this evil system, it is worth all I can give to it to try to make men and women face the fact that, politics notwithstanding, there are basic truths of eternal significance for which they will be held accountable. As I read those "hoary" documents of our founding fathers, I realize that our present system of government bears little resemblance to the hopes, dreams and aspirations of those worthy men.

Unless there is a "revival" of those values that led men and women to undertake the sacrifices that resulted in this unique nation with its vaunted liberties, the envy of all other nations in the world, we are doomed. The only alternative will be anarchy and the corresponding "police" authority that will destroy any vestige of freedom.

Is my "campaign" to be taken seriously? I know that one man can sometimes make a difference; history, including the Biblical record, is an account of such men. But even these men, in order to succeed, had to rally others to the cause, whether for evil or good. I know I speak for many who are too afraid to take up the battle themselves. There are many who have given up but there are far more who haven't even tried to do anything, preferring to be the "bitchers" and "bellyachers" who don't even read a paper, don't even know the name of their local congressman, who think God has some kind of "magic wand" that He will wave and make everything alright even if they don't lift a finger to help. The most charitable name I can think of for such people is "Fool!"

It is my unfortunate experience to know too many who are "good church people" that think their "Sunday offerings" go for the "Lord's Work" and haven't the haziest conception of what the real work is. "One Nation Under God!" Who is kidding whom here? If you think for one minute that church attendance is going to save our nation you have another think coming. The enemy is laughing his head off at such a foolish thing. The only thing the churches agree on is that they are in disagreement. There is no hope for our nation to be found in its pulpits no matter how loudly or piously the congregants sing their hymns or say their "Amens!" It is all a fraud when the selfsame people think they owe nothing to either our founders or our posterity. One thing is certain; pious frauds and fools are not fooling God! For those that know more about the history of ancient Israel than about their own nation's history I have nothing but contempt. I scorn all those that can quote a dozen verses of Scripture but cannot even recite the Preamble to our Constitution, which is so thoroughly rooted in God's Word.

Duty and honor, commitment and fidelity in marriage; what noble words but let them apply to some "fool" that doesn't know the "real score!" But if I'm to have a "campaign" it will be rooted in such "foolishness!" It will be on the basis of God and His Word. This means a return to those values that made this nation great. Not the values of a "Jewish, African, Hindu," or "Moslem deity." I mean values rooted in the integrity of the Bible and the historic values of those that held to those truths. I see no hope for our nation in following any other course. By "accident of birth" I am what I am, an American. I count that my unfathomably good fortune. But as an American, I am "color blind," not "culture blind." I have a huge debt to my children and to those that paid the price for my being a "Free American."

If you agree, help me get the information out to as many people as possible that we don't have to cave in to unscrupulous scoundrels that are robbing us of any hope of a future for our children. Help me to encourage others that we don't have to play the Devil's game by his rules, that there are many who want to do something if only they have honorable leaders who will do what is right. Somehow, with God's help and blessing, it can be done; but only if people get involved and accept their own responsibility for changing things. Patriotism is not a dirty word, especially not the kind of patriotism this nation used to stand for. Help me to make this the kind of nation that used to inspire the other nations of the world, that used to give hope to others that evil does not always have to triumph, that the Devil's game is not the only one in town.

This is what else I want you to do: Write your local congressman, Governor Pete Wilson, your state senators and representatives and President Bush and share with them your own concerns. Let them hear your voice! You are responsible to do that much if you claim to be an American! Also, come November I want you to go the polls and vote! If you will do at least that much we have a chance of fighting a real battle and winning- we can hope, and, reasonably expect, God to help us in the war.

Nathan Hale could, at only 21 years of age, just before the English hanged him, in all sincerity and good conscience say: "I only regret that I have but one life to lose for my country." Patrick Henry could cry: "Give me liberty or give me death!" Can you imagine any of our "leaders" cast in the mold of such sacrifice in the name of liberty? Just where will such men be found?

And how bad does it have to get before such men will heed the call? Our great leaders of the past believed they had delivered us a nation conceived in liberty, a Great Republic that has shined as a beacon of freedom to all other nations. But the solemn admonition of those great men, that the price of liberty is eternal vigilance, sounds hollow and empty to the ears of those that think it not worth fighting for, or worse, that someone else is to do their fighting for them.

I can guarantee one thing; if you do nothing, if you think the battle is not yours, if you procrastinate and let others do your fighting for you, you deserve everything you get from an evil system you have helped by your refusal to do what is right. If you think there is no hope, you better consider, carefully, what you have contributed to make a difference. I am only one man but I live in hope that I, as one man can make a difference. You should believe that of yourself.

About the Author

Samuel D. G. Heath, Ph. D.

Other books in print by the author:
BIRDS WITH BROKEN WINGS
DONNIE AND JEAN, an angel's story
TO KILL A MOCKINGBIRD, a critique on behalf of children
HEY, GOD! What went wrong and when are You going to fix it?
THE LORD AND THE WEEDPATCHER
THE AMERICAN POET WEEDPATCH GAZETTE for 2008
THE AMERICAN POET WEEDPATCH GAZETTE for 2007
THE AMERICAN POET WEEDPATCH GAZETTE for 2006
THE AMERICAN POET WEEDPATCH GAZETTE for 2005
THE AMERICAN POET WEEDPATCH GAZETTE for 2004
THE AMERICAN POET WEEDPATCH GAZETTE for 2003
THE AMERICAN POET WEEDPATCH GAZETTE for 2002
THE AMERICAN POET WEEDPATCH GAZETTE for 2001
THE AMERICAN POET WEEDPATCH GAZETTE for 2000
THE AMERICAN POET WEEDPATCH GAZETTE for 1999
THE AMERICAN POET WEEDPATCH GAZETTE for 1998
THE AMERICAN POET WEEDPATCH GAZETTE for 1997
THE AMERICAN POET WEEDPATCH GAZETTE for 1995-1996
THE AMERICAN POET WEEDPATCH GAZETTE for 1993/1994
THE AMERICAN POET WEEDPATCH GAZETTE for 1992

Presently out of print:
IT SHOULDN'T HURT TO BE A CHILD!
WOMEN, BACHELORS, IGUANA RANCHING, AND RELIGION
THE MISSING HALF OF HUMANKIND: WOMEN!
THE MISSING HALF OF PHILOSOPHY: WOMEN!
CONFESSIONS AND REFLECTIONS OF AN OKIE INTELLECTUAL
or Where the heck is Weedpatch?
MORE CONFESSIONS AND REFLECTIONS OF AN OKIE
INTELLECTUAL

Dr. Heath was born in Weedpatch, California. He has worked as a manual laborer, mechanic, machinist, peace officer, engineer, pastor, builder and developer, educator, social services practitioner (CPS), professional musician and singer. He is also a private pilot and a columnist.

Awarded American Legion Scholarship and is an award winning author.

He has two surviving children: Daniel and Michael. His daughters Diana and Karen have passed away.

Academic Degrees:

Ph. D. – U.S.I.U., San Diego, CA.

M. A. – Chapman University, Orange, CA.

M. S. (Eqv.) — U.C. Extension at UCLA. Los Angeles, CA.

B. V. E. – C.S. University. Long Beach, CA.

A. A. – Cerritos College. Cerritos, CA.

Other Colleges and Universities attended:

Santa Monica Technical College, Biola University, and C.S. University, Northridge.

Dr. Heath holds life credentials in the following areas:

Psychology, Professional Education, Library Science, English, German, History, Administration (K-12), Administration and Supervision of Vocational Education and Vocational Education-Trade and Industry.

In addition to his work in public education, Dr. Heath started three private schools, K-12, two in California and one in Colorado. His teaching and administrative experience covers every grade level and graduate school.

Your writing is very important. You are having an impact on lives! Never lose your precious gift of humor. V. T.

You raise a number of issues in your material ... The Church has languished at times under leaders whose theology was more historically systematic than Biblical ... (But) The questions you raise serve as very dangerous doctrines. John MacArthur, a contemporary of the author at Biola/Talbot and pastor of Grace Community Church in Sun Valley.

You have my eternal gratitude for relieving me from the tyranny of religion. D. R.

Before reading your wonderful writings, I had given up hope. Now I believe and anticipate that just maybe things can change for the better. J. D.

I started reading your book, The Lord and the Weedpatcher, and found I couldn't put it down. Uproariously funny, I laughed the whole way through. Thank you so much for lighting up my life! M.G.

Doctor Heath, every man with daughters owes you a debt of gratitude! I have had all three of my girls read your Birds With Broken Wings book. D. W.

I am truly moved by your art! While reading your writing I found a true treasure: Clarity! I felt as if I was truly on fire with the inspiration you invoked! L. B.

You really love women! Thank you for the most precious gift of all, the gift of love. Keep on being you! D. B.

Your writing complements coffee-cup-and-music. I've gotten a sense of your values, as well as a provocativeness that suggests a man both distinguished and truly sensual. Do keep up such vibrant work! E. R.

Some men are merely handsome. You are a beautiful man! One of these days some wise, discerning, smart woman is going to snag you. Make sure she is truly worthy of you. Desirable men like you (very rare indeed) who write so sensitively, compellingly and beautifully are sitting ducks for every designing woman! M. G.

Now, poet, musician, teacher, philosopher, friend, counselor and whatever else you have done in your life, I am finally realizing all the things you say people don't understand about a poet. They see, feel, write and talk differently than the rest of the world. Their glasses seem to be rose colored at times and other times they are blue. There seems to be no black or white in the things they see only soft pastel hues. Others see things as darker colors, but these are not the romantic poets you speak of. C. M.

You are the only man I have ever met who truly understands women! B. J.

Dr. Heath;
You are one of the best writers I've had the privilege to run across. You have been specially gifted for putting your thoughts, ideas, and inspirations to paper (or keyboard), no matter the topic.
Even when in dire straits, your words are strong and true. I look forward to reading many more of your unique writings. T. S.